SALINITY AND WATER USE

SALINITY AND WATER USE

*A National Symposium on Hydrology,
Sponsored by the Australian Academy of Science,
2–4 November 1971*

Edited by

T. TALSMA AND J. R. PHILIP

*Division of Environmental Mechanics, CSIRO,
Canberra, ACT, Australia*

MACMILLAN

First published 1971

Published by THE MACMILLAN PRESS
London and Basingstoke
Associated companies in
New York Toronto Dublin
Melbourne Johannesburg Madras

SBN 333 13309 9

Printed in Great Britain by Adlard & Son Ltd,
Bartholomew Press, Dorking

71' 15709

CONTENTS

page

PART IV Biology and Salinity

PART V Social Considerations

PART VI Perspectives

FOREWORD

For some time the Australian Academy of Science has organized symposia on subjects at the forefront of science, especially on topics of particular importance to Australia.

Few problems with scientific and technological content are more acute or are increasing more rapidly than problems of water supply. The first symposium on hydrology was organized by the Academy's National Committee on Hydrology in 1963, under the title of 'Water Resources, Use and Management'. But not only do we face problems of quantity of water, we also face problems of quality; problems of salinity, for example, although Australia-wide are also widely spread internationally. This, the second symposium on hydrology, aims at providing an up-to-date review of the scientific and, to some extent, the social problems which arise from natural and man-made salinity.

The subject is wide; the papers vary from detailed consideration of the effects of salinity on plant and animal cells to administrative and legal aspects of saline water, use and management. Altogether these authoritative papers by specialists in the different fields constitute an important volume for Australia and for other countries with similar problems.

The Academy is grateful to the Organizing Committee for arranging the symposium and particularly to the chairman, Dr J. R. Philip. Special thanks are due to Dr T. Talsma who was responsible for most of the secretarial and editorial work.

MARCH 1971, CANBERRA   *R. N. Robertson*

PREFACE

The Academy of Science's National Committee on Hydrology conceived this second National Symposium on Hydrology as an opportunity for an exchange of expertise and views between various natural and (some) social sciences involved in the problems arising from natural and man-made salinity. Such an exchange must expedite the incorporation of scientific knowledge into technical management.

We hoped to enlist authoritative speakers, each of whom would provide an up-to-date review of his field. We emphasized to all prospective contributors our hope that they would go to some trouble to make their material understandable not only to their fellow specialists, but also to members of other scientific disciplines and professions taking part in the Symposium who were concerned with salinity. That we have succeeded in getting authoritative contributors there is no doubt and, we are pleased to say, most have managed to cast aside the jargon of their speciality.

The result is, we feel, a collection of basic material which offers an invaluable scientific background to the practical hydrologic problems of salinity in the Australian continent and throughout the world.

One experimental aspect of these proceedings is that they have been published before the Symposium itself. We have aimed to avoid the all-too-common and deplorable long delay between the event and the publication, which so often reduces the immediacy and the value of symposium proceedings.

May I take this opportunity to thank the following people: my colleague Dr T. Talsma, who has carried by far the greater share of the editorial burden and has relieved me of much work on the Symposium Organizing Committee; Mr A. I. McCutchan for his work on that committee; Mr H. N. England and Dr A. E. Martin, for agreeing to undertake their onerous contributions against unreasonable deadlines; Professor E. S. Hills, chairman of the Academy's National Committee on Hydrology, for help and advice; and Professor R. N. Robertson, C.M.G., F.R.S. and president of the Australian Academy of Science, for his interest, help and participation in this Symposium.

MARCH 1971, CANBERRA   *J. R. Philip*

PART I   Nature and Origin of Salinity

The Geochemistry of Underground Water

D. J. SWAINE and J. L. SCHNEIDER

*Respectively Division of Mineralogy, CSIRO, Chatswood, N.S.W.
and B.R.G.M.-Australia, Sydney, N.S.W.*

SUMMARY

This paper discusses various geochemical aspects of underground waters, starting with the origin of the waters and effects occurring during diagenesis and compaction. Other important factors, dealt with in detail, are the composition of water and the nature of the aquifer, the modification of composition by membrane filtration effects, evaporation, sulphate reduction and ion exchange. The means of studying changes in chemical composition are also outlined.

The results of investigations in Chad, Cap Vert Peninsula, North Cameroon and the Gironde Estuary are discussed.

The importance of correct use of data is stressed. In particular, hydrogeochemical maps are most helpful in the assessment of water use and in the monitoring of pollution. Reference is made to the relevance of hydrogeochemical investigations to other fields, such as ore genesis.

1. INTRODUCTION

There is a wealth of information on the habitat, composition and resources of various underground waters, viewed mainly as possible sources of drinking water for humans and animals, or as water for industry or irrigation. Much less is known about the processes determining the major-element and trace-element contents of such waters, although these are largely dictated by the geological situation as well as the pattern and rate of circulation. The geochemistry of natural waters is concerned with their origin, composition and distribution, and consequently with the causative physical and chemical processes.

The salinity of groundwater should be considered in terms of the total dissolved solids and the nature of the constituent ions. No attempt will be made to cover all aspects of the subject, but attention will be given to the

factors determining the composition of deeper and near-surface underground waters. Details of some recent hydrogeochemical investigations will
be cited. Angino and Billings (1969), referring to brines, stated that 'relatively
few detailed modern studies have been made of the origin, chemistry and
diagenesis of these waters'—these remarks probably apply to groundwaters
generally. Geochemistry can be regarded as fundamental to the proper
study of environmental science, hence its relevance to the subjects of this
Symposium covering many aspects of water use.

2. ORIGIN OF SALTS IN GROUNDWATER

(a) During Sedimentation

Groundwaters are essentially seven component aqueous systems of Na^+,
K^+, Ca^{++}, Mg^{++}, Cl^-, $SO_4^=$, HCO_3^-, hence most of the geochemical
discussion will concern these ions. The data in Table 1 show clearly that
groundwaters are only about 0·6% of the total volume of water in the
hydrosphere, while the terrestrial surface waters constitute less than 0·02%.
However, these figures indicate the potential importance of groundwater.
Most water is in the oceans and it has been calculated that 'a molecule of
ocean water has a statistical chance of getting up into the atmosphere once
in 3500 years and even less chance of being carried over land to be precipitated' (Thomas 1970). The role of the atmosphere in the supply of major
ions to water has been treated thoroughly by Gorham (1961).

TABLE 1

Volume of water in the hydrosphere (based on U.S.
Geological Survey data—modified from Skinner, 1969)

Oceans	1300×10^{18} l	that is 97·2%
Icecaps and glaciers	29 ,,	2·15%
Surface waters	0·2 ,,	0·017%
Groundwater:		
in upper 0·8 km	4·2 ,,	0·31%
below 0·8 km depth	4·2 ,,	0·31%

What are the processes that connate waters could have undergone?
White (1965) has summarized these as follows:

1. diagenetic changes associated with the action of bacteria and the
   decomposition of organic matter during the early stages of sedimentation;

2. reactions between constituent minerals and interstitial water at various stages of diagenesis and metamorphism;
3. compaction during sedimentation;
4. membrane filtration;
5. other effects, such as contact with evaporites.

The above processes are discussed in relation to groundwater in sedimentary basins:

1. The wet porous sediments initially deposited gradually decrease in water content and porosity as diagenesis sets in. Decrease in available oxygen allows sulphate-reducing bacteria to act, forming sulphide and carbon dioxide. At the same time, some of the organic matter in the sediment is decomposed. These changes at low Eh can produce pyrite, often as framboids, with or without associated organic matter and calcite, leaving some dissolved sulphide and bicarbonate in the interstitial water. The concentration of Mg^{++} decreases with depth in the sediment, the change being related to the removal of Mg^{++} by the formation of chlorite, dolomite or mixed-layer micas. However, this decrease is not as marked as with Ca^{++}, the removal of which is controlled by carbonate formation. There is an increase in silicon with depth, probably caused by selective solution of diatoms and radiolaria.

2. Reactions between constituent minerals and interstitial water are probably controlled to a large extent by pH during the early stages of diagenesis, but during metamorphism temperature and pressure become increasingly important. While the water content of minerals is decreasing, the expelled water, together with some CO_2 and other gases is released preferentially along grain boundaries. At the same time there will be some associated movement of cations. For example, Na^+ and K^+ will migrate, but K^+ will be partly removed by the formation of potassium-rich mica and potassium feldspar, the latter by replacement of Ca^{++} in plagioclase. Ca^{++} and Mg^{++} are much less mobile, although they are involved in changes such as the formation of chlorite and epidote. At temperatures around 200°C potassium feldspar reacts with Mg^{++} in aqueous solution to give chlorite, K^+ and a decrease in pH (Ellis 1970).

Laboratory experiments under controlled conditions provide useful information for the interpretation of effects caused by increases in temperature and pressure. For example, Kissin and Pakhomov (1967) found that at high temperatures (150–200°C) the composition of the leaching solution markedly influenced cation removal from rocks. Investigations by Ellis and co-workers (e.g. Ellis and Mahon 1967) give basic information on stability conditions for various minerals at different temperatures, the dependence of water pH on mineral equilibria, and the factors controlling ion solubilities under hydrothermal conditions. Many of these effects, proven for high temperatures, are certainly possible at ordinary temperatures, albeit with diminished rates.

3. Compaction during sedimentation causes a gradual reduction in water content of the sediments. At the same time, some interstitial water of varying composition will be released, its composition depending on the stage of release from the sediment. Reactions between sodium chloride-rich and similar waters and sediments will remove traces of various elements, the fate of which depends on the ensuing history of the water.

4. One of the key questions in hydrogeochemistry is the cause of the wide variations of salinity of groundwaters. In this connexion, membrane filtration has been consistently suggested for the past two or three decades as an important factor controlling the concentrations of ions in water-rock systems (White 1965). Basic studies on the adsorption, flocculation, exchange and colloidal properties of clays led to the suggestion that shales could behave as semi-permeable membranes, allowing the passage of water with reduced salinity and simultaneously altering the concentrations of certain ions in the source solution by exchange. It is supposed that at a certain stage of compaction, clay-rich sediments have the necessary properties to act as semi-permeable membranes. After reviewing the situation, Berry (1969) suggested that 'the membrane properties of shales result from the fixed electrical charge properties of the clay minerals and minor organic material that comprise shales'. Although further investigation of the exact role of organic matter is needed, it is likely that cations would exchange for hydroxyl groups and anions for amino acid groups of the humic acid-like organic matter. One must also consider the possibility that the organic matter is present, at least partly, as a clay-organic matter complex having enhanced or reduced exchange properties. In a sedimentary environment there is likely to be preferential removal of divalent ions, e.g. Ca^{++} more than Na^+. The theory of osmosis and membrane action may be applied to certain relatively simple controlled systems, but it is inadequate for complex mineral-water systems, characteristic of sediments and the groundwater environment. Relevant factors such as clay type, the nature of organic matter, pH, Eh, temperature, and relative concentrations of major ions may change rapidly over a short distance, thereby adding to the difficulty of predicting membrane filtration effects. Limitations to the above concepts have been put forward by Mangelsdorf *et al.* (1970), who stress the importance of density and temperature gradients. In contrast with the forces required for a reverse osmosis effect necessary for membrane filtration, they postulate ion transport through 'the most permeable pathways for migration', thereby obviating the need for a confined sediment. Clearly then, further 'experimental and controlled field investigations are needed to resolve many of the aspects of membrane behaviour in shales' (Berry 1969).

(b) Surface Phenomena

Near-surface waters, in general, derive some of their constituents from the atmosphere (Gorham 1961) and from the mineral and bacterial reactions in soils. Aerated water has an Eh of about $+0.4$ V and this favours the oxidation of pyrite, often present, albeit in low concentrations, in sedimentary rocks. This in turn yields some soluble iron which is readily deposited as oxide under various conditions. Broadly, the Eh of shallow groundwaters is about $+0.2$ to 0.4 V, while connate waters are mostly in the range -0.2 to $+0.1$ V, the pH being 6–8 (Baas Becking *et al.* 1960), so that mixing will affect the status of iron and other ions. The general chemistry of iron and sulphur in groundwaters has been interpreted in detail in terms of the Eh and the pH of the system (Hem 1960; Barnes and Clarke 1964).

The overall picture for groundwaters is movement in the hydrologic cycle, the main factors being the hydraulic potential, the porosity and permeability characteristics of the strata. During this time the groundwaters either gain or lose inorganic constituents depending on several complex chemical reactions and physico-chemical effects, for example, the formation of minerals and the selective removal and changes in concentration associated with membrane filtration. Changes in chemical composition of groundwater may affect permeability, a matter of possible economic importance in some areas where there is mixing of waters from different hydrologic environments (Back and Hanshaw 1965). In the near-surface zone, biological factors exert important influences, especially on trace elements. Also, hydrous iron and manganese oxides, commonly present in sediments, may control, at least partly, the concentrations of several trace elements. These oxides are often present as surface coatings on other minerals and hence their adsorption activity is greater than their concentration may indicate (Jenne 1968).

3. COMPOSITION OF WATER AND THE NATURE OF THE AQUIFER

The chemical composition of water tends to reflect the chemical composition of host rocks, independently of climatic and hydrogeological conditions.

In sedimentary rocks, the freshest waters are located in siliceous sands and sandstones, essentially formed by quartz. Their ionic composition is: $Ca > Na > Mg$ and CO_3 combined* $> Cl > SO_4$†, but Na may exceed Ca. The HCO_3 content gives aggressive CO_2 due to low values of Ca and Mg resulting in an acid pH. The most mineralized waters are those in contact

* CO_3 combined $= CO_3 + HCO_3$; this will be written as CO_3 comb.
† Unless stated otherwise, the values are expressed in milli-equivalents per litre (meq l^{-1}).

with deposits of evaporites, with very high contents of SO_4, Cl, Ca–Mg or Na, according to the minerals present; the total saline matter may reach 200,000 ppm. Limestones contain carbonate waters, low in Cl, SO_4 and total saline matter; at more intensive fracturing, the amount of saline matter tends to increase due to the development of contact surfaces. Clays have a high porosity (sometimes $> 50\%$), the contact surface between water and rock is large. In the presence of salts retained by adsorption on colloidal particles at the time of sedimentation, the water is rather high in total saline matter (several thousand ppm) with SO_4 and $Cl > HCO_3$. Commonly, high values of SO_4 correspond with high contents of Ca and Mg, while the values of Cl and Na show a parallel development.

In eruptive rocks, such as granites, or in metamorphic rocks, like gneisses, the water is slightly mineralized with Na contents generally higher than those of Ca and Mg; it is carbonated with $Na > Cl$. In volcanic rocks, such as basalts, the contents are rather similar, although the Na values are often lower than those for Ca and Mg. White *et al.* (1963) have discussed the analyses of various waters associated with common rocks.

4. MODIFICATION OF CHEMICAL COMPOSITION

The chemical composition of groundwater often changes during circulation due to concentration, dilution, ion exchange and reduction phenomena. Water may be concentrated by two different processes—dissolution or evaporation—or by both of these together. Dissolution depends mainly on the surface and the duration of the contact, as well as on pressure and temperature. Favourable factors for an increase in water concentration are high temperature, depth of aquifer, small grain size, lack of open fractures, slow circulation, small hydraulic gradient, and long distance of flow.

Water flowing through evaporite beds could become enriched in ions characteristic of saline waters. Indeed, this is often regarded as the means of concentrating ions to produce brines. However, the relative abundance of evaporites compared with sedimentary rocks is clays: sands: carbonates: evaporites as 52 : 25 : 22 : 1 (Ronov 1968). Hence, the general influence of the main sedimentary rock on groundwater composition is surely greater than that of evaporites.

The water concentration reaches a maximum when there is physical and chemical equilibrium with the aquifer rock. This depends on the nature of the salts in the rock; the main dissolved salts are $CaCO_3$, $CaSO_4$, $MgCO_3$ and NaCl. Water is quickly nearly saturated in $CaCO_3$ and $Ca(HCO_3)_2$; depending on the amount of ions other than Ca, CO_3 and HCO_3, the CO_3 combined contents are commonly between 25 and 80 meq l^{-1}. For a total concentration level lower than 400 ppm, the water type is often calcium bicarbonate. The supply of Ca by dissolution of gypsum decreases the CO_3 combined content. The limit of solubility of $CaSO_4$ may be easily reached (about 2500 ppm in pure water), but it can be surpassed by dissolution of salts containing ions other than Ca and SO_4 (e.g. NaCl). On the other hand this limit may decrease later by SO_4 supply from the dissolution of Na_2SO_4 or $MgSO_4$ which causes $CaSO_4$ precipitation. $MgSO_4$ and $MgCl_2$ dissolve more readily than $CaSO_4$ and cause a more marked increase in the Mg content than in that of Ca. NaCl, the most common salt, has a high solubility, so that saturation with NaCl is exceptional. Theoretically, Cl must increase quicker than SO_4.

In certain situations, e.g. a flat water table near the surface in arid areas, evaporation will concentrate water considerably, and the water composition will depend mainly on factors such as the hydrolysis of silicates, carbon dioxide uptake and the addition of sulphate from the oxidation of sulphide, as happens in most inland basins (Jones 1966). Concentration by evaporation gives effects similar to dissolution, but here precipitation can be much more widespread, e.g. $CaCO_3$ in the form of concretions in soil, later $CaSO_4$ and finally different Na salts (carbonates and sulphates) according to the CO_3 and SO_4 contents. Hence, the water-concentrating process occurs in successive stages, namely

Ca (or then Na)	CO_3 combined
Ca then Na	SO_4

to reach a final composition Na > Mg > Ca and Cl > SO_4 > CO_3 combined, whatever the concentration type may be and always for a total amount of at least 300 meq l^{-1}; this composition is that of sea water.

Water dilution phenomena may be produced when an unconfined aquifer is recharged in particular areas with fresh water, either by natural action (rain, water course) or by artificial means (irrigation, artificial recharge) which causes leaching of the aquifer.

The composition of water is often modified during concentration, mainly by ion exchange effects. For the exchange of Na–K (water) against Ca–Mg (minerals), the effects are studied by the ratio $(Cl-(Na+K))/Cl$. In the case of inverse exchange, this ratio is negative and another one is used, namely, $(Cl-(Na+K))/(SO_4+HCO_3+NO_3)$. Reduction, especially of sulphates in the presence of organic matter and specific bacteria, may increase the sulphide and carbonate-bicarbonate concentrations.

5. GENERAL FACTORS INFLUENCING CHEMICAL COMPOSITION

The phenomena described above depend largely on geological and climatic conditions. The chemical composition of water tends to reflect the chemical composition of the rocks, and, therefore, the climatic influences during deposition, other deposit conditions and subsequent modifications (transgression or regression periods, salt or evaporite deposits, connate waters . . .). Thus, geological formations of the same age and similar origin give rise to identical types of water, e.g., fresh and bicarbonate waters of the Quaternary dune systems, concentrated and sulphate-chloride waters in the Alpine Triassic, concentrated and chloride waters of the New South Wales Permian. In addition, there are climatic effects, especially during the upper Quaternary, which have produced a zonal latitude differentiation. In temperate zones, the abundant rainfall causes leaching and transport of soluble salts. In arid areas, however, evaporation, due to the high temperature and low air humidity, and low rainfall, result in water concentration.

Schoeller (1962) showed an increase in water concentration from Europe to sub-tropical areas, then a decrease towards equatorial regions, due to high rainfall. The evaporation in sub-tropical zones results in high contents of SO_4 and/or Cl and cations; when the water table is shallow, supersaturation occurs and capillary rise causes precipitation on the ground surface—calcareous, then gypseous, and, finally, saline crusts. In equatorial areas, however, high rainfall produces marked leaching of the sediments and waters are less concentrated than in Europe. Thus, the recent processes of evaporation in arid countries may have caused high concentrations in the upper aquifers. However, deep aquifers (e.g. Sahara Albian) are often less mineralized because, on the one hand, only the border areas with unconfined water have been influenced by arid periods, whereas on the other hand there were important recharges with fresh water during the Quaternary rainy phase. This is an exception to the general rule in temperate countries, where commonly, for lithologically similar aquifers, the deeper the aquifer the more concentrated the water, due to much longer distances of water flow.

6. MEANS OF STUDYING CHANGES IN CHEMICAL COMPOSITION

Hydrogeochemical studies complement hydrogeological data and permit comparisons of waters in relation to problems of origin, recharge, drainage and flow (Clarke 1924; Girard 1967). Some methods of presenting results will be discussed.

Graphic representation of analytical results defines the type and makes it easier to understand the phenomena involved (Anderson 1940; Langelier and Ludwig 1942). On the rhomb diagram of Piper (1944), ionic values are given in percentages. The inconvenience of this diagram is that it does not present the water concentrations, necessary for interpretation of the results. The logarithmic diagram of Schoeller–Berkaloff is more satisfactory as the actual values are plotted, and useful indications are given, especially if the solubility products for $CaSO_4$ and $CaCO_3$ are reached. This diagram will therefore be used for the examples cited in this paper.

Maps can be prepared from the results of various measurements, e.g. conductivity (or resistivity or total saline matter), cations, anions, ratios of cations and anions (SO_4/Cl, Mg/Ca, Na/Ca, $(Cl-(Na+K))/Cl$), pH, and also for water type. It should be noted that for a valid interpretation the concentration of each principal ion should exceed 1 meq l^{-1}, if routine analytical methods are used.

Composition changes have to be studied with regard to the aquifer lithology and the flow directions given by the piezometric surface. Geochemical data add greatly to the knowledge of aquifer lithology, sedimentation conditions, and also paleogeography and sometimes regional tectonic structure. As long as there is no dilution by infiltration of fresh water or by membrane filtration effects, water will be concentrated during flow. Regional decreases may be explained only by recent tectonic movements, as in north Chad (Schneider, 1970). Natural chemical evolution of waters may be affected either by artificial recharge (including irrigation) or by pumping, which may cause pollution by more mineralized waters from other aquifers or from the sea.

Study of natural radionuclides often makes an important contribution to the hydrogeological study of an aquifer. The most widely used nuclides are ^{14}C (half-life—5568 years) for large hydraulic systems and tritium, ^3H (half-life—12·26 years) for recent recharge of unconfined water. Stable isotopes are also used, e.g., ^{18}O and ^2H for studying climatic conditions during infiltration.

The processes of present recharge by rain may also be studied by variations in Cl content by a method of Schoeller (1955). It permits determination of the hydrologic balance of an aquifer system and is based on the fact that only Cl is unmodified during the chemical evolution of the water. This applies only to formations with a very low natural content of Cl, like aeolian sands or certain limestones (particularly karsts). The recharge coefficient is calculated as follows:

If the Cl content in rain water $\quad = Cl_R$
      Cl content in groundwater $\quad = Cl_G$
      Cl dissolved by infiltration water $= Cl_I$
      Volume of infiltrated water $\quad = I$
      Run-off coefficient $\quad = r$
      Volume of rain water $\quad = R$

then
$$I\,Cl_G = Cl_I + (1-r)R\,Cl_R$$

and the recharge coefficient $A \quad = I/R = (1-r)Cl_R/Cl_G + Cl_I/R\,Cl_G$

In formations with low salt contents and without run-off, $A = Cl_R/Cl_G$. This method has been used in several aquifers, like the sands of Landes, France and of the Cap Vert Peninsula, Senegal (Anon 1967).

Electrical prospecting methods (particularly resistivity methods) are also useful. In an aquifer with homogeneous lithology, they allow observation of an increase of mineralization (decrease of resistivity) of unconfined waters or the delineation of an area of saline encroachment (the resistivity of a fresh water saturated sand is 50–150 ohm m; this decreases to 0·5–1·5 ohm m after salt intrusion). In the latter case, the salt content of the water is also obtained (Mathiez and Huot 1966).

7. EXAMPLES OF MODIFICATION OF CHEMICAL COMPOSITION

It is not easy to find well-defined examples for the separate processes of concentration or modification, because the phenomena are always more or less inter-related under natural conditions. Examples are given in several treatises, e.g. by Castany (1968). The examples presented in this paper are mostly from Africa (Fig. 1).

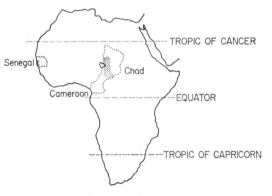

Fig. 1. Africa—location of areas

The first example shows the homogeneity of the chemical composition of underground water over very large areas, due to the homogeneity of the aquifer lithology. It concerns the water-table aquifers of Chad (Schneider 1970). Figure 2 shows the location and nature of the aquifers, all of continental origin, the groundwater flow conditions, and the concentration and type of water. Rainfall decreases notably from south to north, with a change in climate from tropical to arid. The purest waters in the south of the country, where Tertiary formations were deposited under high leaching conditions, are of type Ca CO_3 comb. (Fig. 3, line 1). They are concentrated afterwards in the Lower Quaternary formations, in which the flow velocity

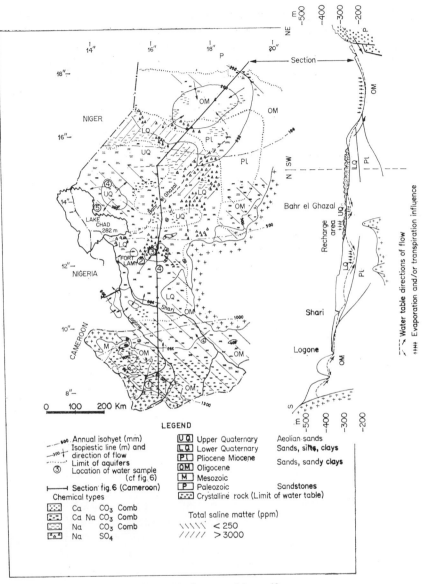

Fig. 2. Chad water-table aquifers

is very low. The Na content increases by base exchange to give a type Na CO₃ comb. (line 2). Finally, in the clayey formations east of Fort Lamy, where evapo-transpiration forms deep depressions (to 60 m below the surface), there are several areas with type Na SO₄ water corresponding to the dissolution of salts contained in clay layers (line 3).

North of Lake Chad, there is fresh water in aeolian sands of the Upper Quaternary of type Na–Ca CO_3 comb. (line 4). These sands give way to a lacustrine series of Lower Quaternary age with a water type mostly Na SO_4 and increasing concentration up to 6000 ppm. Down gradient in the Oligocene–Miocene formations, the water is less mineralized, in spite of present-day evaporation (the water table nearly reaches the surface), and the type becomes Na CO_3 comb. This means that the low area, which presently forms the lowest part of the Chad Basin, subsided after deposition of the Lower Quaternary salt series.

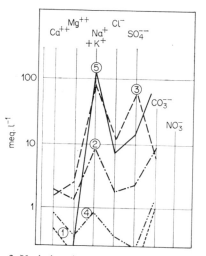

Fig. 3. Variations in composition of Chad water

The groundwater on the north slope of the depresson is replenished by fossil waters from the large reservoir of Paleozoic sandstones of type Ca–Na CO_3 comb. The waters, concentrated by evaporation in the depression, keep their type Na CO_3 comb., but the concentration may reach 2000 ppm. The same processes in the interdune areas near Lake Chad may give, due to recent evaporation, concentrations up to 300,000 ppm (Na CO_3, line 5). This shows the similarity in chemical character of aquifers and water, for fresh water (Ca CO_3 comb. in Tertiary) as well as salt water (Na SO_4 in Lower Quaternary). Some phenomena modify the composition, e.g. ion exchange (water Ca→Na during concentration by dissolution) and present-day evaporation (type remaining Na CO_3 comb.). Sulphate reduction is absent due to the lack of organic matter.

Where aquifers occupy smaller areas the chemical type of the water may change over short distances. For example, the Cap Vert Peninsula, Senegal (Anon 1967) is formed of limestones, marls and sands of different origin

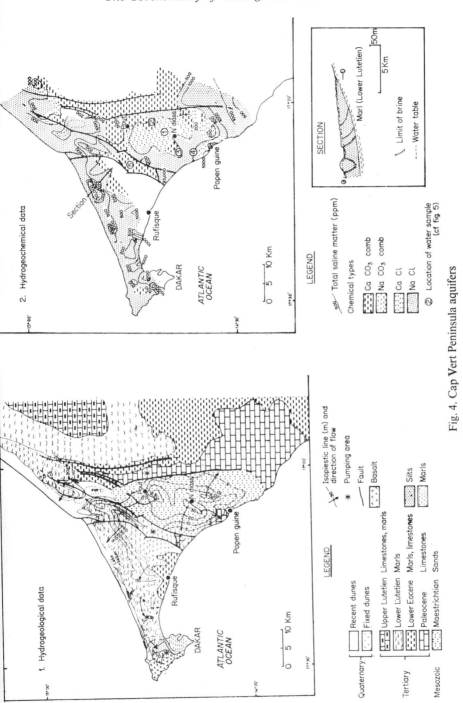

Fig. 4. Cap Vert Peninsula aquifers

which show several chemical types (Fig. 4), besides saline intrusion near the shore. The clayey sands of the Maestrichtian contain water of three different types (Table 2).

TABLE 2

Types of water in clayey sands of the
Maestrichtian, Cap Vert Peninsula

Type	Total saline matter, ppm	Line on Fig. 5	Remarks
Ca Cl$_2$	< 200	1	The Ca content is explained by base exchange $$\left(+0\cdot2 < \frac{Cl-(Na+K)}{Cl} < +0\cdot8\right)$$
Ca CO$_3$ comb. {south:	~ 200	2	
north: up to 600		3	CaCO$_3$ saturation due to flow in calcareous sandstone
Na Cl	~ 350	4	Water formed by concentration of type Ca Cl$_2$

The evolution of the groundwater during flow through the aquifer may be summarized as follows:

Up-stream   *Mid-course*   *Down-stream*
(Recharge area)

rain water
     Na Cl
     ↑↓
    infiltration
     Na Cl
      ↓

aquifer : sands,   Cl increases with flow   aquifer : sands, clays,
clays, (no Ca CO$_3$) ————————————→ Ca CO$_3$ leached
water: Ca Cl$_2$ water: Na Cl

           attack of CaCO$_3$
           ————————————→   aquifer: sands, clays,
           Cl increases with flow   CaCO$_3$ partially leached
                         water: Ca HCO$_3$ (no saturation in HCO$_3$)

           attack of CaCO$_3$
           ————————————→   aquifer: sandstones, limestones
           Cl increases with flow   water: Ca HCO$_3$

The Paleocene limestones have a high permeability, and the water type is Ca CO₃, with saturation in CaCO₃ (Fig. 5, line 5). Sulphate may be abundant, but the absence of organic matter prevents reduction. In the south of the western aquifer, the water is very salty (type Na Cl), the concentration reaching 93,000 ppm. After some years of exploitation, the north

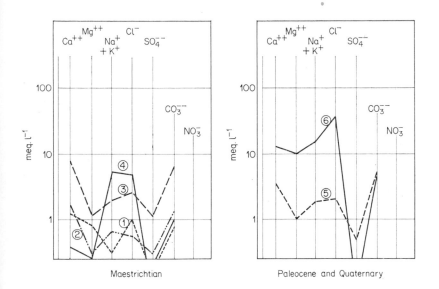

Fig. 5. Variations in composition of Cap Vert Peninsula waters

area was subject to saline pollution and the water type Ca CO₃ comb. became Na Cl. The building of a recharge dam controlled saline encroachment. There is also salt water (up to 6000 ppm) in the south of the eastern aquifer, especially at depth; the type is Na Cl.

Quaternary formations, situated in the west of the country, contain several aquifers with different types of water, namely,

1. Ca CO₃ comb. under the basalt layer in the upstream part; the concentration is <300 ppm; this type is related to the presence of calcareous formations.

2. Ca Cl₂, in the north, with concentrations of 200–600 ppm.

3. Na Cl, the most common type, as in siliceous sands the ions come from rain water. The longer the flow distance, the better defined is the water type; the concentration may reach 90,000 ppm in lakes by dissolution of fossil salts and present-day evaporation.

The general scheme is:

Up-stream	Mid-course	Down-stream
(Recharge area)		

Rain water Na Cl

　　　↑↓

Infiltration water Na Cl

| Attack on CaCO₃

↓ of substratum

Water: Ca HCO₃　Cl increases　　　　Cl increases

　　　　　　　　→　　　　　　　　　　→

　　　　　　　　with flow　　　　　with flow

　　　　　　　　water: HCO₃ Cl　　water: Na Cl

During circulation of the water, base exchange causes the ratio Na/Ca to change from < 1 to > 1, and sulphate reduction is common. These phenomena occur in natural (particularly towards lakes) or artificial (exploitation) flows, with possible salt intrusion; the high base exchange ratio corresponds then to the seawater ratio (Fig. 5, line 6).

Isotopic measurements are useful for studying the relationship between

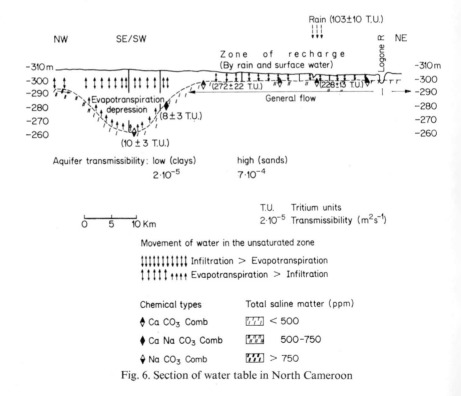

Fig. 6. Section of water table in North Cameroon

chemical composition and aquifer lithology, as shown by an investigation in the Cameroons (Biscaldi 1970). The section (Fig. 6) shows another exception to the generalization that the concentration of water increases down gradient. The change in chemical types is from Ca CO_3 comb. to Ca–Na CO_3 comb. and finally to Na CO_3 comb., which is normal in the Chad Basin. In the depression area of the water table, the water is less concentrated (< 500 ppm) than on the border (500–750 ppm). Apparently the concentration and type of water correspond to different formations at different depths; the depression is formed by evapotranspiration and vertical transfer is more important than horizontal transfer, due to the low permeability of the aquifer. This is confirmed by tritium values of 10 T.U. in the lower area, indicating that recharge, if at all, was before 1955. However, in the upper parts, tritium values of about 250 T.U., i.e. higher than present rains (about 100 T.U.), indicate recent recharge. The water table in the lower part of the depression is now located in aquifers less salty than the upper formation.

The pollution of pumped water by leakage of salt water occurs in an area near Bordeaux, France (Bourgeois 1967), where there is 12–25 m of sandy and gravelly alluvium (Quaternary), 30–35 m of detrital sandstones (Tertiary) and Eocene sands. These sands contain confined fresh water, pumped at 1 m^3 sec^{-1}, and they outcrop 3 km away in the Gironde Estuary banks.

The influence of the Gironde salt water (tidal) was tested for a year, by pumping at a rate of 103 m^3 hr^{-1} (Fig. 7, line 4). Cl was constant at 75 ppm for 3 weeks, then increased at the rate of 12 ppm per week to 330 ppm. The water types were Ca $>$ Mg $=$ Na and CO_3 comb. $>$ Cl $>$ SO_4 (Fig. 7, line 1),

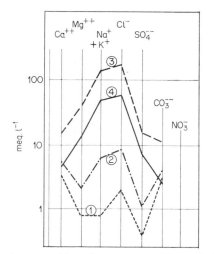

Fig. 7. Variations in composition of waters pumped near the Gironde Estuary

leading to $Na > Ca > Mg$ and $Cl > CO_3$ comb. $> SO_4$ (Fig. 7, line 2). Cl increased too rapidly for lateral flow from the estuary, hydraulic data showed recharge from Quaternary alluvium by vertical leakage (Fig. 7, line 3).

Examples of Australian investigations are those carried out by Randal (1967, 1969) on the Barkly Tableland and the Northern Wiso Basin (Northern Territory), and by Johns (1968) in the Otway Basin (Victoria). In each case the project was on a broad scale and the data were well interpreted geochemically. Hydrodynamic and geochemical results enabled certain general conclusions to be drawn. On the Barkly Tableland much of the groundwater is in aquifers in Cambrian marine rocks, mainly carbonates. In most of the Northern Wiso Basin the important source of groundwater is in Lower Cambrian basement rocks, beneath Lower Cretaceous rocks which are usually poor aquifers. In the Otway Basin the aquifers are in confined sands of Upper Cretaceous–Lower Tertiary sediments. At present, underground waters are being investigated in the Gwydir, Macquarie and Murrumbidgee valleys using modern hydrological methods.

Although discussion has been restricted to sedimentary basins, it is realized that useful aquifers also occur in other geological environments.

8. HYDROGEOCHEMICAL MAPPING

It is clear that the water type depends on various factors, e.g., the lithology and permeability of the aquifer, and the depth of the water table (for unconfined water). Hydrogeochemical investigations yield much data which has to be interpreted in relation to hydrogeological factors, such as recharge areas, drainage lines, zones of loss, hydraulic characteristics and gradient. All data may be represented diagrammatically, but the most useful compilations for the hydrogeologist, especially for concentration and type, are hydrogeochemical maps (Siline–Bektchourine 1957; Castany and Margat 1965).

Hydrogeochemical maps, which complement the hydrogeological maps, are mainly relevant to water use, as indicated below:

1. domestic use—different classes (Anon 1958; Schneider 1970), data for Ca, Mg, Cl, SO_4, concentration, toxic elements;
2. stock use—limits of concentration;
3. irrigation use—different classes (Greene 1948; Berkaloff *et al.* 1953; Wilcox 1955; Richards 1954), conductivity, per cent $Na = (Na + K)/(Ca + Mg + Na + K)\%$, SAR (sodium absorption ratio $= Na/(\sqrt{(Ca + Mg)/2})$, B, F;
4. industrial use—different data according to possible use (Anon 1950), aggressiveness and corrosivity (Ca, CO_3, HCO_3, CO_2, pH—Bremond 1966), elements relevant to pollution.

It appears that hydrogeochemical maps are seldom prepared in many countries and that chemical data are not always used to advantage. A world list of hydrogeochemical maps is given by Margat and Monition (1967). Different scales are used, ranging from small scale synthesis maps (up to 1 : 2,000,000) to large scale detailed maps (1 : 100,000 to 1 : 25,000). Detailed maps of areas under development (agriculture, industry, etc.) should be revised periodically, particularly to indicate changes caused by salt intrusion in near-shore areas and by pollution. Computers are being used increasingly to process chemical data, which can then be presented on diagrams and maps (Morgan *et al.* 1966). These are especially useful for monitoring pollution.

9. CONCLUDING REMARKS

Although water use is often the prime reason for groundwater investigations, the correct broad-based approach gives a better chance of understanding groundwater resources in terms of quality of water, recharge, sources of water (especially when mixing has occurred), and reasons for changes in major- and trace-element contents. Consequently, hydrogeochemical studies should be carried out on large areas, delineated by the local geology, and carefully planned to ensure that the necessary data will be obtained, thereby permitting valid and full interpretation. Much published chemical data for waters would be more useful geochemically, if the original sampling had been done carefully and related to the background geology.

Present theories of ore-genesis take into account the early mobilization of cations from rocks by reactions with brines, and hence knowledge of the formation and movement of such waters, as well as their effects on rocks, is important. Trace elements in groundwaters, e.g., B, Cu, F, I, Mn, Zn, should be considered in relation to the general distribution of such biologically-active elements.

The theoretical background to much of the chemistry of groundwaters is inadequate. Laboratory studies on interactions between saline waters and rocks will provide useful data, but the sensible application of the results of such studies depends on close collaboration between chemists and geologists. Indeed, all aspects of hydrogeochemistry need the interdisciplinary approach and herein lies one of the benefits of this Symposium, namely, the opportunity to assess the present situation.

Finally, there is no doubt that the proper evaluation of water pollution, whether naturally occurring in groundwaters or the result of waste disposal, depends largely on sound background hydrogeochemistry. In some areas, even in Australia, the geochemical interpretation of data for lakes and rivers may be already influenced by the effects of pollution. However, there is time to study most underground waters in their pristine state.

This Symposium will surely catalyse further basic and practical studies of the geochemistry of Australian waters.

REFERENCES

Anon (1950). *Water Quality and Treatment* 2nd Edn. Amer. Water Works Assoc., New York.

Anon (1967). Com. interafr. d'etudes hydraul. 14 vols. B.R.G.M., Paris.

Anon (1958). *Internat. Standards of Drinking Water*. WHO, Geneva.

Anderson, V. G. (1940). *Aust. chem. Inst. J. & Proc.* **7**, 187.

Angino, E. E., and Billings, G. K. (1969). *Chem. Geol.* **4** (1/2), 7.

Baas Becking, L. G. M., Kaplan, I. R., and Moore, D. (1960). *J. Geol.* **68** (3), 243.

Back, W., and Hanshaw, B. B. (1965). *Adv. Hydrosci.* **2**, 49.

Barnes, I., and Clarke, F. E. (1964). Prof. Paper U.S. Geol. Surv. No. 473–A, 1.

Berkaloff, E., Finielz, H., and Tixeront, J. (1953). *Hydraulique et Hydrologie* ser. 1, fasc. 3. Ministere des Travaux Publics, Tunis.

Berry, F. A. F. (1969). *Chem. Geol.* **4** (1/2), 295.

Biscaldi, R. (1970). Rapp, B.R.G.M. Paris. Direction des Mines et de la Geologie, Yaounde.

Bourgeois, M. (1967). Int. Assoc. Sci. Hydrol., Haifa Symp. Publ. No. 72, 365.

Bremond, R. (1966). Rapp. com. interafr. d'etudes hydraul. Paris.

Castany, G. (1968). *Prospection et Exploitation des Eaux Souterraines.* p. 212. Dunod, Paris.

Castany, G., and Margat, J. (1965). *Bull. Assoc. Int. Hydrogeol.* No. 1, 74.

Clarke, F. W. (1924). 'The Data of Geochemistry' 5th Edn. *Bull. U.S. Geol. Surv.* **770**.

Ellis, A. J. (1970). N.Z. Geochem. Group Newsletter No. 18, 11.

Ellis, A. J., and Mahon, W. A. J. (1967). *Geochim. et Cosmochim. Acta* **31**, 519.

Girard, R. (1967). *Eau*, **54**, Nos. 5 and 6.

Gorham, E. (1961). *Bull. geol. Soc. Amer.* **72**, 795.

Greene, H. (1948). 'Using Salty Land.' *FAO Agric. Stud.* No. 3.

Hem, J. D. (1960). *Water-Supply Paper U.S. Geol. Surv.* No. 1459–C, 57.

Jenne, E. A. (1968). In 'Trace Inorganics in Water', *ACS Advs. Chem. Ser.* No. 73, 337.

Johns, M. W. (1968). *J. Hydrol.* **6**, 337.

Jones, B. F. (1966). In 'Second Symp. on Salt'. (Ed. J. L. Rau.) *North Ohio Geol. Soc.* **1**, 181.

Kissin, I. G., and Pakhomov, S. I. (1967). *Geochem. Internat.* **4** (2), 295.

Langelier, W. F., and Ludwig, H. F. (1942). *J. Amer. Water Works Assoc.* **34**, 335.

Mangelsdorf, P. C., Manheim, F. T., and Gieskes, J. M. T. M. (1970). *Bull. Amer. Assoc. Petrol. Geol.* **54** (4), 617.

Margat, J., and Monition, L. (1967). Rapp. B.R.G.M., Paris.

Mathiez, J. P., and Huot, G. (1966). Rapp. com. interafr. d'etudes hydraul., Paris.

Morgan, C. O., Dingman, R. J., and McNellis, J. M. (1966). *Ground Water* **3**.

Piper, A. M. (1944). *Trans. Amer. Geophys. Union* **25**, 914.

Randal, M. A. (1967). *Bur. Min. Resour. Aust. Bull.* **91**.

Randal, M. A. (1969). *Bur. Min. Resour. Aust. Rec.* 1969/16.

Richards, L. A., (Ed.) (1954). *Diagnosis and Improvement of Saline and Alkali Soils.* USDA Handbook No. 60.

Ronov, A. B. (1968). *Sedimentology* **10**, 25.

Schneider, J. L. (1970). Mem. B.R.G.M., Paris.

Schoeller, H. (1955). *Terres et Eaux*, Suppl. Sci. No. 4, Annexe to No. 24.

Schoeller, H. (1962). *Les Eaux Souterraines.* p. 257. Masson, Paris.

Siline-Bektchourine, A. I. (1957). Abstr. 11th general assembly Int. Union Geodesy Geophys., Int. Assoc. Sci. Hydrol., p. 69. Akad. Nauk S.S.S.R., Moscow.

Skinner, B. J. (1969). *Earth Resources.* Prentice-Hall, New Jersey.

Thomas, H. E. (1970). *Circ. U.S. Geol. Surv.* No. 629, 1.

White, D. E. (1965). *Mem. Amer. Assoc. Petrol. Geol.* **4**, 342.

White, D. E., Hem, J. D., and Waring, G. A. (1963). *Prof. Paper U.S. Geol. Surv.* No. 440–F.

Wilcox, L. V. (1955). *Circ. U.S. Dept. Agric.* No. 969.

Salinity and the Hydrologic Cycle

J. W. HOLMES

School of Physical Sciences
The Flinders University of South Australia

SUMMARY

The hydrologic cycle, as a concept to allow orderly description of the ways in which precipitation on the land surface is partitioned between evaporation, run-off and other lesser consumption, usually exists in a natural steady state. If not, then at least, natural perturbations have a time scale of the order of thousands of years.

The hydrologic cycle transports salts as the solute load of the various water discharges. The salt cycle also usually exists in a steady state. Irrigation, and other less drastic changes in land utilization, which affect the components of the water budget, perturb the hydrologic and salt cycle with a time scale that may be of the order of tens of years. Deterioration of water quality in rivers and secondary salinization of soils are two major consequences of a disruption of the natural regime, initiated by the needs of civilization.

1. INTRODUCTION

Good water supply has been one of the achievements which has gained for man his present mastery of the physical environment. Urban living has always tended to release waste products which can poison water supply, whether the poison is in the form of disease transmitting organisms, or latter day radioactive debris, heavy metals and pesticides. These are the hazards countered by public health and engineering authorities.

Agrarian production, the complement of the attainment of urbanity, has sometimes wrought changes in the hydrology of whole regions. Water and salt are proving to be distressingly inseparable. What follows is an account of salinity and the hydrologic cycle, restricted in scope to the hydrology of catchments and irrigated areas that may be threatened with salinization caused by a land use and management that has disrupted the natural regime.

25

2. THE WATER BUDGET

At the land surface, the water budget is simply expressed by an equation such as

$$P = E + SD + UD + \Delta S, \qquad (1)$$

where P is the precipitation, E is evaporation, SD is surface drainage, UD is underground drainage and ΔS is the change in water storage of the system, usually the change of soil water storage. The terms in equation (1) can be observed, and the balance evaluated for some suitable interval of time. The calendar year and the water year are both used. Table 1 shows the water budget of lysimeters in grassland near Mount Gambier during the water years 1963–64, 1964–65 and 1965–66, taken from a CSIRO experiment (Holmes and Colville 1970*a*). Precipitation may vary greatly from year to year, and so therefore will the other elements of the hydrologic cycle, which depend upon the rainfall. Nevertheless, the hydrologic parameters have mean values, estimated from observations extending over many years, and are sometimes thought to be constants of a particular catchment and ecosystem. Indeed they are either constant in the steady-state situation, or change only exceedingly slowly, under natural conditions. Change does occur, but the time scale is long, in response, for example, to climatic shifts such as the onset of a more pluvial regime after the relatively dry, climatic optimum of about 6000 years B.P. Catastrophe, occasionally, may alter the water balance of a region, as when the Hwang-Ho changed course in the middle of the nineteenth century. Generally it is civilization, with its accompanying changes of land management and land use, which vitiates the assumption of steady state.

TABLE 1

The water budget of lysimeters in grassland near Mount Gambier, S.A.

	10/4/63 to 2/4/64 (mm)	2/4/64 to 18/3/65 (mm)	18/3/65 to 6/1/66 (mm)
Precipitation	493	836	580
Evaporation	453	682	514
Underground drainage	40	134	72
Soil water increment	0	20	−6

Disturbances to the hydrologic cycle cause changes of the water budget terms of equation (1). We must examine the physical nature of the symbolism of equation (1), in order to understand the consequences of a non-steady hydrological regime.

In a well-watered region, where rainfall considerably exceeds evaporation, streams are perennial and the relation of underground water flow to stream flow can be depicted by Fig. 1. The surface level of the water flowing in an effluent stream is shown to be lower than the water table in the alluvium, or rocks, through which the stream has cut its course. Beneath the water table, the flow of water through the aquifer can be described by potential theory and displayed by the flow-net of streamlines and equipotential lines. Water infiltrates nearly vertically from the soil surface through the unsaturated zone to the water table.

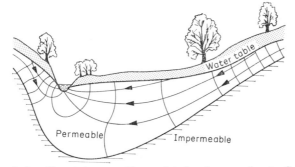

Fig. 1. An effluent stream, with associated underground water flow.

The term underground drainage, UD, in equation (1) contributes the base flow of perennial rivers and streams, the discharge of springs, and the intake of aquifers whose discharging areas may be very remote from the recharge. The principle of continuity, or conservation of mass, is often invoked in this context to enable the simple statement to be made that UD is equal to the known spring discharge and so on, averaged over a sufficiently long time. The surface drainage, SD, sometimes linked with inter-flow or shallow subsurface flow, contributes to the characteristics of the flood hydrograph of a stream. Generally water received by a stream from surface runoff is of better quality than that contributed by base flow. The evaporation, E, is the actual evaporation (transpiration) from the land surface. It is nearly always less than potential evaporation. The increment of water storage, ΔS, in soil and aquifers often becomes zero or negligible compared with the other terms for periods longer than several years. For periods less than the water year, ΔS is very important. The water yield from a catchment depends not only upon $P-E$, but also upon ΔS, which is then to be identified with the soil moisture deficit and is influenced strongly by E during periods of depressed evaporation.

The volume of water stored in a water table aquifer is usually large compared to the volume of water conducted through it annually to the stream. Consider a stream with a mean dimension of 1000 m from stream bed to groundwater divide. If the annual runoff, by all processes, is 100 mm the water yield would be 100 m³ yr⁻¹ per metre width of strip between stream and divide. But if the depth of soil and weathered parent rock is 15 m, with mean water content 0·3 cc cc⁻¹, the volume of water stored is 4500 m³ per strip 1 m wide and 1000 m long. The ratio of storage to annual flow therefore is at least 45. This ratio, which may be characteristic of a region, generally increases with increasing aridity.

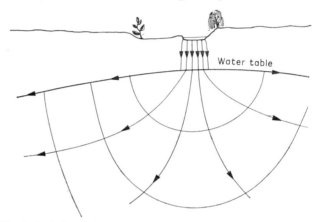

Water table

Fig. 2. An influent stream, with associated underground water flow.

In an arid region where streams are ephemeral or seasonal, the water table usually occurs at a level lower than the stream bed, and is fed by infiltration through the bed as depicted by Fig. 2. A river may be an effluent stream in its upper course, but lose water by leakage in its downstream reach, the transition being determined by sub-surface geology and proximity to the sea or some other terminus for groundwater discharge.

The discussion so far has concerned the fate of the underground drainage, UD of equation (1), whether it reaches an effluent stream by flow in an aquifer, or whether by leakage from a stream bed, water enters an aquifer to be conducted to a remote discharge region. Underground drainage is often very small in magnitude compared with precipitation or evaporation. It may be negative, which implies upward movement of water into that part of the soil profile from which it can be lost by evaporation at or near the land surface. Figure 3 shows a typical relationship between evaporation from the bare soil surface and depth to the water table, computed from the expression (Childs 1969)

$$z = - \int_{0}^{\psi_z} \frac{d\psi}{1 + E/K}. \tag{2}$$

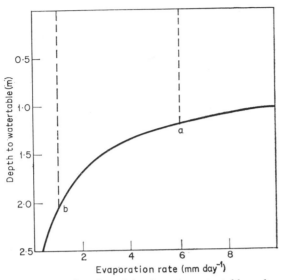

Fig. 3. Evaporation rate as a function of depth to the water table. *a, b* represent typical limiting magnitudes of potential evaporation during summer and winter in southern Australia. (Data for Yandera loam, M.I.A., after Talsma 1963.)

None of the parameters are allowed to vary with time, in this steady-state expression, and the height of the soil surface, z, above the water table, regarded as the datum level, is somehow constant. The matric potential, ψ, of the soil water at the surface has the value ψ_z. For a given function of the hydraulic conductivity of the soil, $K(\psi)$, the evaporation rate, E, is then determined.

In arid regions rainfall generally infiltrates only a few cm below the soil surface (Jackson 1958) and the soil water is soon absorbed by plant roots or evaporates from the surface. There may be appreciable runoff to lower lying areas, at both the micro-relief and the landscape scale, so that some areas habitually receive water sufficient to penetrate deeply into the soil beyond reach of plant roots and surface evaporation. Such areas are a very small fraction of the total landscape area, but they are the recharge areas for underground water. The principal areas of this kind are the wadis, or ephemeral stream courses.

If underground water is recharged at all, and we should accept it as axiomatic that it is, then its ultimate fate must be that it discharges either by leakage to streams, by seepage to the oceans or to enclosed basins from which it evaporates, or possibly by a combination of all three processes. Water in an enclosed basin from which there is no surface or sub-surface outflow, is discharged entirely by evaporation. The playa lakes of the arid regions are the termini for sub-surface flow. It is not uncommon, if the underground flow is large enough, to observe free water on the surface of a playa lake during winter, when the evaporation rate is at a minimum, and a withdrawal of the water table beneath the dried-up surface of the lake during summer to maintain approximate equality between evaporation and inflow. The evaporation rate is then described by equation (2), rather than being determined by micrometeorological conditions. Accumulation of salt in an enclosed basin is seen to be inevitable.

Finally, in this discussion of the water balance, the special role that water in a deep aquifer under considerable pressure may play in natural salinization of the soil is worth exploring. Suppose an aquifer exists at a depth of 200 m below the land surface and at that depth the upper confining bed is 5 m thick. A common value for water pressure at the roof of the aquifer could be a piezometric head of 195 m, i.e. the water would rise to 5 m below the soil surface in a cased bore-hole, whereas at the upper side of the confining bed there could be a piezometric head of 175 m, i.e. free water occurs in a water table aquifer at a depth of about 20 m below the soil surface. Assuming a realistic value of hydraulic conductivity of the confining bed, of 0·1 mm day^{-1}, leakage through the confining bed into the overlying sediments would be $\sim$0·3 mm day^{-1}. If the total dissolved solids (TDS) of the water occurring in the aquifer are 1 g l^{-1}, the deposit of this salt in the uppermost 30 m of the water table aquifer, assuming a porosity of $\frac{1}{3}$, would increase the salinity of the pore fluids at the rate of about 0·01 g l^{-1} yr^{-1}. Salinity does not go on increasing forever, however. Just as there is a water balance, so there is a salt balance, which will be described in the next section.

3. THE SALT BUDGET

If each term of equation (1) be multiplied by the salt content of the water it represents, we have equation (3),

$$C_p.P = C_E.E + C_S.SD + C_u.UD, \tag{3}$$

which with equation (1) allows the salt budget to be expressed quantitatively. It is however, not useful to go much further in this generalized, formal manner. Taking up again the particular example, given above, of leakage of water, through an upper confining bed, from an artesian aquifer, a more complete expression for the salt balance could be represented by Table 2. The salt remaining in the water table aquifer by the evaporative dissipation of the water which has leaked upwards from the pressure aquifer, itself is then dissipated by the lateral flow in the upper aquifer.

It appears that salt does not continue to accumulate forever in salt lakes. Rather there is a cyclic transport of salt borne aloft by the winds as salt crystals, or attached to dust particles, which may approximately maintain a steady state. Bonython (1956) stated that there appeared to be a balance

TABLE 2

An example of the salt budget of water contained in a water table aquifer replenished by upward leakage

Rate of upward (leakage) flow	0·10 m yr^{-1}
Salt content of leakage water	1 g l^{-1}
Evaporative dissipation of leakage water	0·09 m yr^{-1}
Dissipation of leakage water by lateral flow in the water table aquifer	0·01 m yr^{-1}
Salt content of water in the water table aquifer	10 g l^{-1}

The input and output of salt is equal

between salt input to Lake Eyre, South Australia, and salt loss, the mechanism of which presumably is transport by the wind. It is of interest to remember that the theory of the evolution of the oceans considers that the sea is not becoming more saline. Rather, its salinity now is much the same as it was at least as long ago as the close of the Cambrian Period, although the relative abundance of sodium to the other cations has increased several-fold.

4. SOURCES OF SALT

Figure 4 shows the concentration of chloride ion in rainwater as a function of distance of the sample collecting station from the ocean. This relationship, taken from the survey of southern Australian rainwater undertaken by Hutton and Leslie (1958), illustrates the significance of the oceans as a

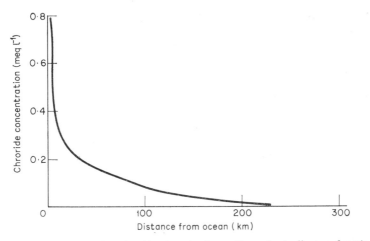

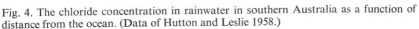

Fig. 4. The chloride concentration in rainwater in southern Australia as a function of distance from the ocean. (Data of Hutton and Leslie 1958.)

source of salt to the land within about 50 km of the shore line. At distances larger than 50–100 km from the coast, not only is the salt content, as evidenced by chloride concentration, much less than in rainfall of coastal stations, but also the relative abundances of the different ionic species are much altered from those of sea water. Figure 5 shows how the relative abundance of sodium diminishes with distance from the coast at rainfall stations sampling a transect across western Victoria. It appears that the proportion of solutes derived from terrestrial dust predominates at inland stations.

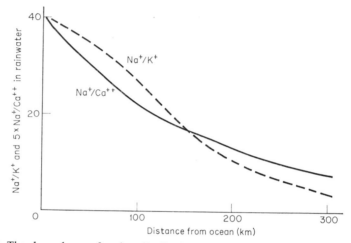

Fig. 5. The dependence of cation distribution in rainwater in southern Australia on oceanic and terrestrial sources of salt. (Data of Hutton and Leslie 1958.)

Weathering of the mineral constituents of soil and rock produces soluble salts which are carried in groundwater. In regions of high rainfall, the amount of dissolved matter in stream and river water is usually small, though it does depend upon the local lithology. Table 3 shows the ionic composition of water in the Mitta Mitta River at Tallandoon (Anon 1970), and the composition of rainwater multiplied by 4, collected near Tallandoon (data of Hutton and Leslie, 1958). The mean annual runoff from the Mitta catchment above Tallandoon is about 300 mm and the mean rainfall about 1200 mm. Therefore, assuming that actual evapotranspiration is 900 mm and that no salts are removed by this process, the dissolved material of the rainfall is concentrated four times in the underground drainage. Further more, if the net gain in HCO_3^- in the river water (0·25 meq l^{-1}) is considered to be conferred by soil microbiological processes and to bring into solution an equivalent cation content, then it is seen that the cations in rainwater make up about half the cations in the river water not brought into solution by pedologic carbonic acid. This is also in agreement with the chloride ratios.

TABLE 3

Analyses of water from the Mitta Mitta River at Tallandoon and of rainwater × 4 collected near Tallandoon (Data from Anon 1970; and Hutton and Leslie 1958)

	River water (meq l^{-1})	Rainwater × 4 (meq l^{-1})
Na	0·17	0·04
Mg	0·16	0·04
Ca	0·15	0·04
Cl	0·10	> 0·04
SO_4	0·02	—
HCO_3	0·29	> 0·04

In arid regions, salt dissolved in the groundwater is not much leached by the very sluggish groundwater flow. Salt may accumulate and be concentrated by evaporation. It may also be connate salt, remaining from a former geological time when the sediments were laid down in a marine environment and would have included sea water in the pore space. Table 4 shows water analyses of groundwater taken from two locations in South Australia. The aquifer in each case is a bryozoal limestone deposited in a marine environment. The annual recharge of the groundwater in the Hd.* of Gambier is approximately 100 mm, by direct infiltration of soil water through the soil profile during the months June to November. In the Hd. of Bakara, recharge has not been measured but it is probably zero or even negative, the source of the water in the Morgan–Mannum limestone

TABLE 4

Analyses of groundwater taken from water table aquifers in humid and arid South Australia (Data from O'Driscoll, 1960)

	Hd. of Gambier, Co. Gray	Hd. of Bakara, Co. Albert
Na	1·5 meq l^{-1}	79 meq l^{-1}
Ca	6·3	4·7
Mg	1·6	14
Annual rainfall	750 mm	250 mm
Depth to static water level from the soil surface	2 m	50 m
Aquifer lithology	Gambier limestone (lower Miocene)	Morgan–Mannum limestone (lower Miocene)

* Hd. = Hundred (Lands Dept. subdivision unit).

aquifer being further to the south-east as indicated by the equipotential map (O'Driscoll 1960). In the former case connate seawater has been entirely leached; in the latter case the dissolved salts must be attributed in part to connate salt, though the relative abundances of the ions have been much altered since the initial occlusion.

During the planning phase of reclamation projects, salt budgets are sometimes estimated for the purpose of enabling water requirements to be projected. Dieleman et al. (1963) state that the total area of land in the central and southern parts of Iraq suitable for irrigation (1.5×10^7 ha) contain 10^9 metric tons of salt in the 0–5 m depth of the soil profile. There is a more intense salinization in parts of Soviet Central Asia. According to the statement of Borovskiy (1968), the ancient delta of the Syr-Darya River possesses soils which range from 80 to 800 t ha^{-1} salt content in the 0–2 m depth. Northcote and Skene (in press) have evaluated the areas of salt-affected soils for the Australian continent according to more than 20 criteria for saline, sodic and alkaline soil profiles. Only in a few areas, however, could a reliable salt budget be estimated, because little has been done in a survey of salt distribution with depth.

5. DISTURBANCES TO THE HYDROLOGIC CYCLE

(a) Under Natural Rainfall

An examination of the data of Table 1 reveals that evaporation so closely approaches the total rainfall for the year, even in a relatively humid environment, that any disturbance to the prevailing pattern of evaporation must alter the underground drainage and surface drainage components quite profoundly. It has proved unexpectedly difficult to demonstrate experimentally that there are significant differences in the evaporation from different plant communities. However, precision of measurement is now improving and numerous comparative studies have been published recently. CSIRO work has shown that evaporation from Pinus radiata forest on the Gambier Plain is so much more than it is from pasture land (Holmes and Colville 1970b) that groundwater reserves are not recharged under forest, whereas there is an annual recharge of 85 mm or more under grass. Clear-cut logging of an evergreen conifer forest in the Pacific Northwest of the U.S.A. resulted in stream-runoff increasing from 1450 mm to 1950 mm in a region of very high rainfall (Rothacher 1970).

Observable effects of a change in the elements of the hydrologic cycle caused by change in land use, usually develop slowly. The best attested examples in Australia come from Western Australia (Burvill 1950; Bettenay et al. 1964). Catchment salting there confronts wheatland farmers with major economic losses as the area of saline soils along the valley floors inexorably enlarges. Replacement of the perennial eucalypt and heath communities by cereal cropping with pasture leys has caused an increase in underground flow to the drainage ways. Naturally choked with saline groundwater even under the virgin land cover, the valleys have experienced a rise in the water table over quite extensive areas with consequent salinization of the soils wherever the winter rainfall is not sufficient for adequate leaching, that is, in the less than 500 mm zones. Similar, though less spectacular examples of catchment salting may be cited from many regions of temperate southern Australia (Cope 1958).

The time scale for the development of soil salinity of this kind appears to be ∼10's of years. The following order of magnitude calculation may illustrate the physical factors that are involved. Consider again a natural drainage network with a characteristic dimension of 1000 m from groundwater divide to the drainage line. According to Darcy's law, the quantity of water transported in an aquifer, Q, is related to the gradient of the water table, dh/dx, and the transmissivity, T, by

$$Q = T \frac{dh}{dx} \tag{4}$$

where Q is in $m^3 \, m^{-1} \, yr^{-1}$ if T is in $m^2 \, yr^{-1}$. The natural gradient of the water table accommodates itself to the flux of water that has to be transported. So for values of $UD = 5 \, mm \, yr^{-1}$, and $T = 1000 \, m^2 \, yr^{-1}$, the gradient of the slope of the water table near the drainage line would be about 1/200. If a change of land use were to increase the mean underground drainage to 10 mm yr^{-1}, i.e. a doubling of the water yield which, nevertheless, is beyond our ability to observe directly, the gradient would steepen to 1/100. We could say approximately that the water table at 200 m from the drainage datum would rise from 1 m to 2 m above datum. The gain in water storage of the aquifer and overlying soil, ΔS, is related to the increment of water table height, Δh, and the specific yield, ϵ, by the relation,

$$\Delta S = \epsilon . \Delta h. \tag{5}$$

Using a realistic value $\epsilon = 0.2$, we would find that $\Delta S = 0.2$ m for a water table rise of 1 m. This gain in storage is made up by absorption of the increase in the underground drainage, that is, at 5 mm yr^{-1} increase, the time needed to raise the water table 1 m would be 40 years. This sort of treatment is clumsy and inexact but it does illustrate the time scale involved in natural perturbations of the hydrologic cycle.

A more exact treatment involves solutions of the equation

$$\nabla^2 h = \frac{\epsilon}{T} \frac{\partial h}{\partial t}, \tag{6}$$

for the appropriate boundary conditions. An example is shown in Fig. 6,

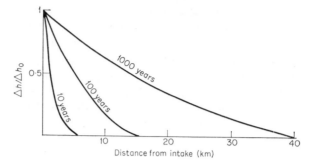

Fig. 6. The approach to a new equilibrium water table configuration after a step-wise change in water head at the recharge boundary. (Data for sand aquifer near Coorong, S.A. after Luthin and Holmes 1959.)

which demonstrates the time scale of change in water table configuration, following upon a step-wise rise in level of water at the inflow boundary.

Enhanced underground drainage and consequent rise in the water table promotes salinization of soils if the content of soluble salts in the soil solution is sufficiently large. The quality of base flow to rivers and streams may deteriorate after land clearing. Wood (1924) quotes analyses of water taken from the Blackwood River at Bridgetown, W.A. (see Table 5) and states that an alternative supply for locomotive watering had to be procured after 1912. He ascribed the increase in river water salinity, to agricultural development of the catchment of the Arthur River, which is tributary to the Blackwood.

TABLE 5

Increase in salinity of the Blackwood River, W.A., at Bridgetown caused
by clearing of native vegetation
(Data from W. E. Wood 1924)

Date	TDS (ppm)	Remarks
26/1/1904	270	First test of supply
28/12/1910	660	
23/12/1912	1290	Water no longer used for locomotive supply
Feb. 1915	1650	

(b) Under Irrigation

Irrigation of arid zone soils profoundly alters the water budget. Soils and natural drainage systems that developed under a climate with 200 mm annual rainfall, let us say, receive 500–1000 mm additional water per year when irrigated, and in addition there are the inevitable accessions to deep groundwater from channel leakage and inadvertent overwatering. The result usually is that the water table begins to rise soon after the construction of a new irrigation area. Unless artificial drainage is provided to protect the irrigated fields, water logging and salinization ensue.

TABLE 6

The mean salinity of the Murray River along its length, for the years 1966–67 and 1967–68
(Table 5.3 of Anon 1970)

Station	River mileage	Total dissolved solids in ppm	
		1966–67	1967–68
Below Hume Dam	1385	37	37
Cobram	1197	35	39
Torrumbarry Weir	1020	65	60
Barham	945	122	75
Pental Island	903	116	161
Swan Hill	875	224	211
Tooleybuc	818	185	189
Boundary Bend	761	138	178
Euston Weir	692	139	176
Red Cliffs	564	151	225
Lock 9	479	199	328
Lake Victoria	—	254	342
Lock 6	388	260	400
Chowilla Homestead	381	299	na
Berri	327	324	498
Lock 3	268	335	560
Waikerie	238	381	690
Morgan	199	375	738
Blanchetown	171	414	744
Walker's Flat	129	397	753
Mannum	93	383	756
Murray Bridge	70	399	822
Tailem Bend	55	391	776
Goolwa	8	759	2993

An irrigated area is so heterogeneous with respect to water distribution, drainage and water application that water budget estimations must be restricted to elements of the land use pattern. However, saline water flows in drains and the deterioration in quality of water in distribution systems caused by return seepage, can serve as indicators of the salt status of extensive areas. Table 6 shows the salinity of the Murray River during the years 1966–67 (July to June) and 1967–68, after Anon (1970). It is seen that the salinity for the drought year 1967–68, when river discharge was minimal, was much greater than salinity during a normal discharge year represented by 1966–67. The increase in salinity between Torrumbarry Weir and Swan Hill should be ascribed largely to saline drainage flows from irrigation areas.

The improvement in water quality between Swan Hill and Boundary Bend is caused by dilution flow from tributaries, particularly the fresh Murrumbidgee water. In the South Australian section, from Lock 9 downstream, there are three mechanisms of saline flow into the river, viz. escape of saline drainage water from irrigation areas, artificial groundwater flows caused by head differences of the river levels at weirs and control structures, and natural groundwater seepage into the river.

Nearly all rivers used for supply of irrigation water show the feature of increasing salinity both along the river length, and with time from the first development of irrigation districts. An extreme example of deteriorating water quality is afforded by the Rio Grande River in the western U.S.A. Table 7 implies that the operating regimen for irrigation no longer uses the river bed below American Dam as a distributary for supply.

TABLE 7

Salinity (in ppm TDS) and discharge (in m^3 sec^{-1}) of the Rio Grande River, U.S.A.
(Data from U.S. Geol. Survey Water-Supply Papers)

Station	Lobatos, Colo.	Otowi Bridge, N. Mex.	El Paso,* Tex.	Old Fort Quitman†, Tex.
1959–60 Discharge (mean)	8·2	32·0	14·6	1·2
TDS (weighted mean)	238	211	856	2124
1963–64 Discharge	2·0	15·0	3·0	0·5
TDS	213	242	1140	3769
1964–65 Discharge	16·4	46·1	7·8	‡
TDS	213	205	555	—

* 2 river miles above American Dam
† 80 river miles below American Dam
‡ No flow at gauging station for 8 months of the water year

Because water quality depends so markedly upon discharge it has proved difficult to demonstrate unambiguously a deterioration of water quality over a time scale of 10's of years. The salinity (TDS) of Murray River water at Red Cliffs increased on the average by 3–5 ppm per year during 1948–67 (Anon 1970).

Finally, in this section, it should not be out of place to draw attention to the inevitable deterioration in quality of water as it goes through the urban cycle of use in domestic and industrial processes. The data of Table 8 demonstrate that water from sewerage treatment works may need partial desalination or dilution with purer water.

TABLE 8

Quality of water supply and sewerage effluent, South Australia in
ppm (TDS)
(Data furnished by Engineering and Water Supply Department,
South Australia)

		Sewerage effluent	
Mains water supply		Bolivar works	Glenelg works
April 1967	360–400 mean	1280	1300
September 1967	up to 800	1390	1470
June 1968	360–400 mean	1400	1870
June 1969	mean	1370	1570
September 1970	mean	1450	1650

6. HYDROLOGY IN HISTORY

Brevity permits only a bare mention of the effects of salinity and changed hydrology in the historical context. The civilization of the Mesopotamian Plain, which cradled man's emergence from savagery, suffered what proved to be an irreversible decline in the eleventh and twelfth centuries A.D. Siltation of the plain by sediment in the irrigation water caused such changes in levels that, progressively, water could not command formerly irrigated regions. Possibly a subdued tectonic tilting of the plain was also involved, but the chief factor undoubtedly was salinization of the soil profile. According to Jacobsen and Adams (1958) the Mongol invaders of the thirteenth century have been unjustly blamed for the destruction of Islamic Mesopotamia. The region had suffered hydrologic devastation, canals were ineffective and the salt desert had turned hostile a century before the arrival of Hulagu Khan.

On the other hand, irrigated land in Egypt has sometimes ceased production for political reasons during the period of the historical record, but has never been abandoned as unworkable due to salinity. Nor has the vast alluvium of China-in-the-east, watered by the rivers from the mountainous west, ever suffered irreparable damage by secondary salinization.

The relatively modern development of irrigation in the Punjab has brought in its train widespread salinization of the soils of West Pakistan and Indian Punjab. The salt problem there was recorded about 1850 for the first time. Jain (1961) states that, in this region of the Five Rivers, the salt that causes salinization is inherent in the soil profile. Very little is brought by the irrigation water. The same is true of the irrigation areas of northern Victoria now threatened by salinization.

Leaching combined with drainage can prevent secondary salinization. Under suitable environmental conditions reclamation can be swift. The new Zuiderzee polders of The Netherlands are leached sufficiently free of sea-water to enable a first crop of millet to be grown in about three years, under natural rainfall, with adequate subsoil drainage. The technology may be equal to the task (Luthin 1957; Hagan *et al.* 1967) but social investment demands a favourable cost/benefit ratio and possibly some contemporary sacrifices for the future good, neither of which may be attainable.

REFERENCES

Anon (1970). *Murray Valley Salinity Investigation.* Report for the River Murray Commission by Gutteridge, Haskins and Davey.

Bettenay, E., Blackmore, A. V., and Hingston, F. J. (1964). *Aust. J. Soil Res.* **2**, 187.

Bonython, C. W. (1956). *Trans. Roy. Soc. S. Aust.* **79**, 66.

Borovskiy, V. M. (1968). *Trans. 9th Int. Congr. Soil Sci.* **1**, 473.

Burvill, G. H. (1950). *J. agric. W. Aust.* **27**, 174.

Childs, E. C. (1969) *The Physical Basis of Soil Water Phenomena.* John Wiley and Sons, London.

Cope, F. (1958). *Catchment Salting in Victoria.* Soil Cons. Authority, Vic.

Dieleman, P. J. (Ed.), Boumans, J. H., Hulsbos, W. C., Lindenberg, H. L. J., and van der Sluis, P. M. (1963). Int. Inst. Land Reclamation and Improvement, Publ. No. 11.

Hagan, R. M., Haise, H. R., Edminster, T. W. and Dinauer, R. C. (Eds.) (1967). *Irrigation of Agricultural Lands.* Am. Soc. Agronomy, Madison, Wisconsin.

Holmes, J. W., and Colville, J. S. (1970*a* and *b*). *J. Hydrology* **10**, 38 and 59.

Hutton, J. T., and Leslie, T. I. (1958) *Aust. J. agric. Res.* **9**, 492.

Jackson, E. A. (1958) *CSIRO Soil and Land Use Series* No. 24.

Jacobsen, T., and Adams, R. M. (1958) *Science* **128**, 1251.

Jain, J. K. (1961) *UNESCO Arid Zone Res.* **14**, 111.

Luthin, J. N. (Ed.) (1957). *Drainage of Agricultural Lands* Am. Soc. Agronomy, Madison, Wisconsin.

Luthin, J. N., and Holmes, J. W. (1959). *J. geophys. Res.* **65**, 1573.

Northcote, K. H., and Skene, J. K. M. (in press). Australian Soils with Saline and Sodic Properties. CSIRO Soils Publ.

O'Driscoll, E. P. D. (1960). *Geol. Survey of South Australia, Bull.* **35**.

Rothacher, J. (1970) *Water Resources Res.* **6**, 653.

Talsma, T. (1963) *Meded. Landb. Hoogesch. Wageningen* **63** (10), 1.

Wood, W. E. (1924) *J. Roy. Soc. W.A.* **10**, 35.

PART II   Chemistry and Chemical Processes

Thermodynamics of Saline Water

J. E. LANE and W. W. MANSFIELD

Division of Applied Chemistry, CSIRO, Fishermen's Bend, Victoria

SUMMARY

The thermodynamic state of a saline solution is completely specified by the temperature, pressure and chemical potentials of the components that are present. The chemical potential can be defined rigorously in mathematical terms but in this form often provides difficulty in conception. In order to overcome this difficulty for solutions, it is useful to relate the chemical potential to some ideal reference solution; the deviation between real and ideal solution is formalized in terms of an activity coefficient, and sometimes in the case of a solvent by an osmotic coefficient. The activity coefficients can be obtained from experiment, and are well tabulated.

Changes in the chemical potentials of the components of a saline solution due to variations in temperature, pressure, environment or the external field can be obtained by the use of very simple expressions; any additional information required is measurable. These relationships are applied to desalination by distillation, by freezing and by reverse osmosis, to Donnan membrane equilibria, to the resting potential of a nerve fibre, and to surface effects in a porous solid.

1. INTRODUCTION

Solutions moving through soils, plants and animals encounter surrounds of differing chemical composition, temperature and pressure. Apart from more-or-less obvious changes in temperature and pressure, a change in environment of a salt solution may lead to considerable changes in its physical and chemical nature. For instance, there may result distillation or freezing of water, precipitation of some salts and adsorption of others.

Clearly a systematic way of describing, and predicting generally, the direction and possible extent of such changes is desirable. In this review we summarize some thermodynamic concepts and relations useful for this purpose.

We begin with a few definitions. Generally saline solutions are able to exchange both mass and energy with their environment; so that we are

43

discussing *open systems*. Sometimes mass interchange is insignificant, giving a *closed system*. Within a system a number of physically and chemically distinct regions may be discerned; a salt/water complex may contain solid salt, ice, aqueous solution and water vapour. These distinctive regions are called *phases*. The properties of each phase may be divided into two groups— *extensive properties* and *intensive properties*. Extensive properties vary directly with the quantity of a phase and are additive for a number of phases. Energy, entropy and volume are examples. Intensive properties, like temperature and pressure, are independent of the amount of a phase.

Thermodynamic analysis follows from the observation that *natural processes* involve the flow of extensive properties along gradients of intensive properties. In a simple system containing only a temperature gradient, thermal energy flows from regions of high to regions of low temperature. Natural processes proceed in the direction promoting *equilibrium*. The equilibrium of a system is always specific to some property or properties, and involves a zero net flux of the property in any direction. Thus heat flow moves towards thermal equilibrium (constant temperature), and volume flow towards hydrostatic equilibrium (constant pressure), in elementary systems.

Accordingly we may expect the existence of an intensive property, the *chemical potential*, controlling the movement of the *chemical content* of each substance present, towards states of chemical equilibrium. The next section is devoted to examining these properties.

Before proceeding, however, we feel that two points need emphasis. In any one phase for given conditions, there may exist a clear relation between the chemical potential and the concentration of a substance. Nevertheless, chemical potential and concentration are separate entities, and must not be confused. At $20°C$ water vapour of concentration $17 \cdot 1$ mg l^{-1} and pure liquid water of concentration $998 \cdot 2$ g l^{-1} have the same chemical potential. The second matter is that any net flow of a property is inconsistent with equilibrium in that property. Time-independence of an intensive property is not enough to indicate equilibrium, since such independence also characterizes a steady state.

2. THERMODYNAMIC RELATIONS

Only an outline of the development of the thermodynamic relations can be given, but more detailed accounts are readily available (Guggenheim 1957; Robinson and Stokes 1959; Harned and Owen 1958; Denbigh 1957; Prigogine and Defay 1954). We use an approach based on the principles enunciated by Gibbs (1961) and extended by Lewis and Randall (1961), de Donder (in Prigogine and Defay 1954) and Guggenheim (1957).

The zeroth law of thermodynamics can be stated as follows (Guggenheim 1957, p. 9). If two systems are both in thermal equilibrium with a third system, then they are in equilibrium with each other, and they each have the same temperature, an intensive variable denoted by T.

For a system closed to the flow of matter, the first law of thermodynamics can be written in a differential form by

$$dU = dq - dw \quad \text{closed system} \tag{1}$$

where U is the internal energy, q the flow of heat into the system, and w the work done by the system.

For the second law of thermodynamics, it is postulated that there exists an extensive variable S, called entropy, which is a function of the thermodynamic state of the system. Any change in the entropy of the system can be divided into two parts such that

$$dS = d_e S + d_i S \tag{2}$$

where $d_e S$ is the entropy exchanged with the surroundings and is given by

$$d_e S = dq/T \tag{3}$$

and $d_i S$ is the entropy produced within the system. A natural, or irreversible process is one in which the system changes spontaneously from a non-equilibrium to an equilibrium state and is characterized by

$$d_i S > 0 \quad \text{natural process} \tag{4}$$

A reversible change is one in which the system passes through a sequence of internal equilibrium states, and it is possible for the change to be reversed by an infinitesimal change in the constraints applied to the system. Such a change is described by

$$d_i S = 0$$
$$\quad \text{reversible change} \tag{5}$$
$$dS = d_e S = dq/T$$

If the only work that can be done on the surroundings by a closed system is the result of a change in volume of the system then

$$dw = PdV \tag{6}$$

where P is the pressure. If heat is also exchanged with the surroundings, then combination of equations (1), (5) and (6) gives

$$dU = TdS - PdV \quad \text{closed system, reversible change} \tag{7}$$

For a natural process the system can be divided into a number of sub-systems, each of which is sufficiently small so that it is sensibly homogeneous at any stage of the process and therefore separately undergoes an essentially reversible change. Equation (7) can be applied separately to each sub-system, and the change in internal energy for the whole system is obtained by summing over the change for every sub-system. Gibbs (1961, p. 63) generalized equation (7) to allow transfer of matter between sub-systems, or with the surroundings by writing

$$dU = TdS - PdV + \sum_i \mu_i dn_i \tag{8}$$

where μ_i and n_i are respectively the chemical potentials and the numbers of moles of the ith species. From equation (8) it can be seen that for any sub-system T, $-P$ and μ_i are respectively the partial derivatives of the internal energy with respect to the variables S, V and n_i.

An isolated system is defined as one in which there is no exchange of heat, work or matter with the surroundings and hence by equations (2) and (3) $dS = d_i S$. If the system is not in equilibrium then according to equations (4) and (5) $dS \geqslant 0$ and thus equilibrium is established when the entropy reaches its maximum value, i.e.

$$dS = 0, \quad d_2 S \leqslant 0 \qquad \text{equilibrium, isolated system} \tag{9}$$

For a closed system, that in addition cannot exchange work with the surroundings, and in which the entropy is held constant throughout any change occurring within the system (but dq need not be zero), Gibbs (1961, pp. 56–62) showed that equation (9) is equivalent to

$$dU = 0, \quad d_2 U \geqslant 0 \qquad \text{equilibrium, closed system,}$$
$$dS = 0, \quad dw = 0 \tag{10}$$

If an equilibrium system is divided into a large number α of sensibly homogeneous sub-systems (the intensive variables of the kth sub-system being T_k, P_k, $\mu_{1, k}$ etc.) application of equation (8) to each sub-system and equation (10) to the system as a whole gives

$$T_1 = T_2 = \ldots = T_\alpha = T \quad \text{thermal equilibrium}$$

$$P_1 = P_2 = \ldots = P_\alpha = P \quad \text{mechanical equilibrium} \tag{11}$$

$$\mu_{i, 1} = \ldots = \mu_{i, \alpha} = \mu_i \quad \text{mass or chemical equilibrium}$$

provided there are no external fields, the effect of surfaces can be neglected and the sub-systems are open to the flow of all components.

The mathematical properties (Callen 1960, pp. 47–48) of the extensive variables U, S, V and n_i when used in conjunction with equation (11) allow equation (8) to be integrated as

$$U = TS - PV + \sum_i \mu_i n_i \tag{12}$$

Differentiation of equation (12) and combination with equation (8) gives the Gibbs–Duhem relation

$$0 = -SdT + VdP - \sum_i n_i \, d\mu_i \tag{13}$$

The result (12) allows us to define a number of other useful energy functions including the enthalpy, H and Gibbs function, G by

$$H = U + PV = TS + \sum_i n_i \mu_i$$

$$G = U - TS + PV = H - TS = \sum_i n_i \mu_i \tag{14}$$

These functions can be differentiated and combined with equation (8) giving

$$dH = TdS + VdP + \sum_i \mu_i \, dn_i$$

$$dG = -SdT + VdP + \sum_i \mu_i \, dn_i \tag{15}$$

G and H have the property of having minimum values at equilibrium under the constraints of constant T, P, n_i and S, P, n_i respectively.

The partial derivative, at constant T and P, of any extensive quantity with respect to n_i, all other n_j, n_k ... being kept constant, is known as a partial molal quantity and is often distinguished by a superior bar, with a subscript to identify the species being varied. Common examples are

$$(\partial G/\partial n_i)_{T, P, n_j} = \bar{G}_i = \mu_i$$

$$(\partial H/\partial n_i)_{T, P, n_j} = \bar{H}_i = \bar{G}_i + T\bar{S}_i \tag{16}$$

$$(\partial S/\partial n_i)_{T, P, n_j} = \bar{S}_i$$

$$(\partial V/\partial n_i)_{T, P, n_j} = \bar{V}_i$$

The Maxwell relations, and other similar results, can be obtained as second partial derivatives of any energy functions that are dependent only on the state of the system. If X is an energy function, and Y and Z are two independent variables

$$\frac{\partial^2 X}{\partial Y \, \partial Z} = \frac{\partial^2 X}{\partial Z \, \partial Y}$$

As examples, using equation (15)

$$\frac{\partial^2 G}{\partial n_i \, \partial P} = \left(\frac{\partial \mu_i}{\partial P}\right)_{T, n_i} = \left(\frac{\partial V}{\partial n_i}\right)_{T, P, n_j} = \bar{V}_i$$

$$\frac{\partial^2 G}{\partial n_i \, \partial T} = \left(\frac{\partial \mu_i}{\partial T}\right)_{P, n_i} = -\left(\frac{\partial S}{\partial n_i}\right)_{T, P, n_j} = -\bar{S}_i \tag{17}$$

Bridgman (1914) has listed a large number of relations of this type. They can be modified to yield many other useful results, e.g.

$$\frac{\partial(\mu_i/T)}{\partial T} = \frac{-(\mu_i + T\bar{S}_i)}{T^2} = \frac{-\bar{H}_i}{T^2} \tag{18}$$

The relations (11) were derived from the Gibbs equation (8) in which the energy lost to the system through working on the surroundings is restricted to changes in the volume of the system. If the system is subjected to external fields, or the effect of surfaces between phases cannot be neglected, additional work terms must be added to equation (8) and the new equilibrium conditions are derived in a manner similar to those used to derive the conditions (11). The derivation of these other conditions have been given in detail by Gibbs (1961), and we quote the desired results.

For an equilibrium system in a gravitational field, the conditions (11) are modified thus

$$T_1 = T_2 =, \ldots T_\alpha = T, \text{all phases}$$

$$P = P^o + g \int_o^h \rho_\beta(h) \, dh, \text{ each phase } \beta \tag{19}$$

$$\mu_i + gh = \text{constant}, \qquad \text{all phases}$$

where P^o is the pressure at some arbitrarily chosen horizontal reference plane, h is the height of the point considered above this plane, g is the gravitational constant and $\rho_\beta(h)$ is the density of phase β at the height h.

Anticipating that electrolytes in aqueous solution dissociate into ionic species $k, l, \ldots$, with electronic charge per ion of $z_k, z_l \ldots$ (including the sign of the charge) we can consider the effect of an electric field. An electric potential difference can only be defined in thermodynamic terms for two phases α and β of identical composition (Guggenheim 1929). The potential difference $\psi_\alpha - \psi_\beta$ between the phases α and β is then given by

$$\mu_{i,\alpha} - \mu_{i,\beta} = z_i F(\psi_\alpha - \psi_\beta) \tag{20}$$

where F is the Faraday. The terms $\mu_{i,\alpha}$ and $\mu_{i,\beta}$ are often called the electrochemical potentials of ionic species i in phases α and β.

If the surfaces between phases α, β, $\ldots$ in a heterogeneous system cannot be ignored, additional terms of the form $\sigma_{\alpha\beta} \, dA_{\alpha\beta}$ must be added to equation (8), where $\sigma_{\alpha\beta}$ and $A_{\alpha\beta}$ are respectively the surface tension and surface area of the interface between phases α and β. If the interface is curved at any point with principal radii of curvature R_1 and R_2, then the condition of mechanical equilibrium in (11) must be modified to

$$P_\alpha - P_\beta = \sigma_{\alpha\beta}(1/r_1 + 1/r_2) \tag{21}$$

if the centres of curvature be in phase α.

The Gibbs–Duhem relation (13) must also be modified to

$$0 = -S\,dT + \sum_\alpha V_\alpha\,dP_\alpha - \sum_{\alpha\beta} A_{\alpha\beta}\,d\sigma_{\alpha\beta} - \sum_i n_i\,d\mu_i \qquad (22)$$

Equation (22) will be simplified in a later section.

If there are any chemical reactions between the species in which reactant species k are converted to product species l, i.e.

$$\sum_k \nu_k k = \sum_l \nu_l l \qquad (23)$$

where the ν_k and ν_l are stoichiometric coefficients then by using equations (8) and (10) it is readily shown that at equilibrium

$$\sum_k \nu_k \mu_k - \sum_l \nu_l \mu_l = 0 \qquad (24)$$

We now have all of the necessary relationships involving the chemical potential, but in an impractical form. It is convenient for experimental situations to relate the chemical potential to a concentration scale such as the mole fraction or molality scales. The mole fraction x_k and molality m_k of component k in a phase β are defined by

$$x_k = n_{k,\,\beta} / \sum_i n_{i,\,\beta}$$

$$m_k = 1000\,n_{k,\,\beta} / (n_{j,\,\beta} M_j) \qquad (25)$$

where M_j is the molecular weight of component j, this component having been arbitrarily chosen as solvent for the molality scale.

For ideal (Raoult's law) mixtures in a condensed phase the chemical potential of component k is given by

$$\mu_k = \mu_k^o + RT \ln x_k \qquad (26)$$

where μ_k^o is the chemical potential of pure k at the same temperature and pressure, R is the gas constant and ln is the natural logarithm.

For non-ideal solutions, Lewis (in Noyes and Bray 1911) introduced the activity coefficient f_k by

$$\mu_k = \mu_k^o + RT \ln f_k x_k$$

$$\lim_{x_k \to 1} f_k = 1 \qquad (27)$$

Another activity coefficient γ_k is defined by

$$\mu_k = \mu_k^o + RT \ln \gamma_k m_k$$

$$\lim_{m_k \to 0} \gamma_k = 1 \qquad (28)$$

The μ_k^o of equation (28) does not have the same value as the μ_k^o of equation

(27). This is unimportant as we are only ever concerned with changes in the μ_k, and it is never necessary to know the value of μ_k^o, it being sufficient that μ_k^o is independent of concentration. It is legitimate to use both equation (27) and (28) for different components in a single mixture. Generally equation (27) is used for the solvent and (28) for the solutes.

For an ionizing solute, the definition (28) can be applied to every ionic species. However, it is never possible to obtain experimentally the activity coefficient of an ionic species, but it is possible to obtain the activity coefficient for a salt. If a neutral salt A dissociates into ionic species 1, 2, ..., with ionic charge z_1, z_2, ..., then by equation (24)

$$\mu_A = \nu_1\mu_1 + \nu_2\mu_2 + \ldots \tag{29}$$

and in order that A be neutral

$$\sum_i \nu_i z_i = 0 \tag{30}$$

Combining (28) and (29)

$$\mu_A = \sum_i \{\nu_i\mu_i^o + RT \ln (\gamma_i m_i)^{\nu_i}\} \tag{31}$$

We now define some useful terms by

$$\mu_A^o = \sum_i \nu_i\mu_i^o$$

$$\nu = \sum_i \nu_i \tag{32}$$

$$(\gamma\pm)^\nu = \gamma_1^{\nu_1} . \gamma_2^{\nu_2} \ldots$$

$$(m\pm)^\nu = m^\nu(\nu_1^{\nu_1} . \nu_2^{\nu_2} \ldots)$$

where $\gamma\pm$ and $m\pm$ are known as the mean ionic activity coefficient and mean ionic molality respectively. Using the definitions of (32), equation (31) can be rearranged as

$$\mu_A = \mu_A^o + \nu\, RT \ln \gamma\pm m\pm \tag{33}$$

The activity coefficients $\gamma\pm$ are directly accessible to experimental measurement and excellent summaries are available (Robinson and Stokes 1959; Harned and Owen 1958). Fortunately, experimental values of activity coefficients at 25°C over an extensive range of concentration for many electrolytes are tabulated by Robinson and Stokes (1959, App. 8), together with the data for NaCl and KCl over a range of temperature. Figure 1 shows activity coefficients at 25°C as a function of concentration for the salts NaCl, KCl, K_2SO_4, $CH_3.COO$ Na and $CaCl_2$. Robinson and Stokes also give the activity coefficients of water in these solutions in the form of the molal osmotic coefficient ϕ defined by

$$\ln f_w x_w = -\phi\nu n_s/n_w \tag{34}$$

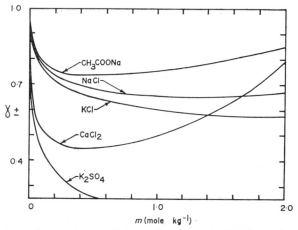

Fig. 1. Experimental mean ionic activity coefficients $\gamma\pm$ at 25°C as a function of concentration m for aqueous solutions of NaCl, CH$_3$.COO Na, KCl, K$_2$SO$_4$ and CaCl$_2$.

where n_s and n_w are the numbers of moles of undissociated salt and water respectively.

The Debye–Hückel (1923) theory can be used to calculate activity coefficients of completely ionized salts up to concentrations of 0·001 molar. Robinson and Stokes (1959, pp. 238–251), and later Gluekauf (in Prigogine and Defay 1954) have attempted to extend the Debye–Hückel model to higher concentrations by considering the hydration of ions. However, these models only provide a method of curve fitting experimental data and have limited predictive value.

Davies (1962, p. 41) has shown that for completely dissociated electrolytes at 25°C and concentrations <0·1 molar, the activity coefficients can be estimated (within 2% of the experimental values) using the empirical relation

$$-\log_{10} \gamma \pm \;=0\cdot5\; z_1 z_2 \{I^{1/2}/(1+I^{1/2})-0\cdot3I\}$$

where $I=\frac{1}{2}\sum_i m_i z_i^2$ is the ionic strength.

3. APPLICATIONS

(a) Separation of Water from Saline Solutions

The mixing of components to form a solution is a spontaneous process and hence by equation (4) $d_i S > 0$. Obviously, the un-mixing or separation process is not spontaneous, and can only be achieved if coupled with another process such that $d_i S \geqslant 0$ for the overall process. It is sometimes stated that the separation requires a certain minimum energy to be achieved. This is not strictly correct as the coupled process could be the mixing of two other components to form a different solution. However, if the separation is achieved by supplying energy there is either a minimum requirement of energy in the form of work that can only be recovered as heat, or heat supplied at a temperature higher than the temperature at which it is recovered and hence could have been used to produce work. In both cases the minimum requirement corresponds to an overall process that is reversible, and hence $d_i S = 0$. These comments are analogous to statements about the perfect heat engine or perfect refrigerator. In the perfect heat engine an amount of heat q_A is taken from a reservoir at temperatures T_A and an amount of heat q_B is given to a reservoir at temperature $T_B < T_A$. The maximum work w_M obtained is given by Lewis and Randall (1923).

$$w_M = q_A - q_B = q_A(T_A - T_B)/T_A \qquad \text{heat engine} \quad (35)$$

Similarly, for the perfect refrigerator an amount of work w_M allows heat q_B to be taken from a reservoir at T_B, and heat q_A given to a reservoir at $T_A > T_B$, and

$$w_M = q_A - q_B = q_B(T_A - T_B)/T_B \qquad \text{refrigerator} \quad (36)$$

(b) Separation by Freezing

The freezing temperature $T_{F,\,s}$ of a salt solution is lower than the freezing point $T_{F,\,w}$ of pure water at the same pressure. To a good approximation the ice formed is pure and hence by equations (11) and (27)

$$\mu_{\text{ice}} = \mu_w = \mu_w^o + RT_{F,\,s} \ln f_w x_w \qquad (37)$$

where the subscript w indicates water in solution. This equation may be re-arranged as

$$-R \ln f_w x_w = \mu_w^o/T_{F,\,s} - \mu_{\text{ice}}/T_{F,\,s} \qquad (38)$$

At the freezing point of pure water, because ice and pure water have the same chemical potential,

$$\mu_w{}^o/T_{F,\,w} - \mu_{\text{ice}}/T_{F,\,w} = 0 \qquad (39)$$

Combination of equations (38), (39) and (18) gives

$$-R \ln f_w x_w = - \int_{T_{F,\,w}}^{T_{F,\,s}} L/T^2 \, dT \qquad (40)$$

where $L = \bar{H}_{\text{ice}} - \bar{H}_w{}^o$ is the change in enthalpy (or heat removed) at constant pressure on freezing one mole of pure water to form one mole of ice at the temperature under consideration. To a first approximation L is independent of temperature and (40) may be written

$$-RT_{F,\,w} \ln f_w x_w \approx L(T_{F,\,s} - T_{F,\,w})/T_{F,\,s} \qquad (41)$$

The separation process consists of cooling the salt solution from the ambient temperature T_{AM} to the freezing temperature of the solution $T_{F, s}$, removing heat L at this temperature to form one mole of ice (the solution must be in large excess so that there is no significant change of concentration), separating the ice and solution, returning the solution to ambient temperature T_{AM}, and warming the ice to $T_{F, w}$ and melting it by the addition of heat L, and returning the resulting pure water to the ambient temperature. The assumption of constant L implies that the specific heats of the ice and of the water in solution are equal. Therefore, the cooling and warming process can be carried out with a perfect heat exchanger and no energy need be introduced. However, the latent heat L is removed at temperature $T_{F, s}$ and returned at temperature $T_{F, w} > T_{F, s}$ and hence by equations (36) and (41) work w_F given by

$$w_F = L(T_{F, s} - T_{F, w})/T_{F, s} = -RT_{F, w} \ln f_w x_w \tag{42}$$

is required. However, an amount of heat $q_E = w_F$ in excess of the heat L is supplied at the melting point for pure ice $T_{F, w}$ and must be returned to the ambient temperature T_{AM}, our only heat reservoir, requiring the further introduction of work w_E given by equations (36) and (4) as

$$w_E = q_E(T_{AM} - T_{F, w})/T_{F, w} = -R \ln f_w x_w (T_{AM} - T_{F, w}) \tag{43}$$

The total work w_S required for separation is then given by equations (42) and (43) as

$$w_S = w_F + w_E = -RT_{AM} \ln f_w x_w \qquad \text{freezing} \quad (44)$$

(c) Separation by Distillation

The separation of water from a salt solution by distillation relies on the fact that the vapour in equilibrium with the solution consists essentially of pure water, and as a result the boiling point of a solution is higher than that of pure water at the same pressure. The separation can be achieved by supplying heat at the boiling point of the solution, and recovering the heat at the boiling point of the pure water, and the analysis is similar to that given above for freezing. We shall consider a different process.

At any temperature T_D the vapour pressure P_s of water above a salt solution is less than that for pure water. The chemical potential μ_v of the vapour is equal to that of the water in the solution, and using equation (27),

$$\mu_v = \mu_w = \mu_w^o + RT_D \ln f_w x_w \tag{45}$$

If some of the vapour is separated from the remainder of the system, and compressed to the vapour pressure P_w of pure water at the same temperature, the chemical potential of the vapour equals that for pure water, and water can be condensed. According to equations (45) and (17) the pressure and volume $\bar{V}_v$ of one mole of vapour satisfy

$$\int_{P_s}^{P_w} \bar{V}_v \, dP = -RT_D \ln f_w x_w \qquad (46)$$

The work done w_V on the vapour is given by integrating equation (46) and on carrying out the integration by parts,

$$w_V = -\int_{\bar{V}_{v,\,s}}^{\bar{V}_{v,\,w}} P \, dV = P_s \bar{V}_{v,\,s} - P_w \bar{V}_{v,\,w} + \int_{P_s}^{P_w} \bar{V}_v \, dP \qquad (47)$$

where $\bar{V}_{v,\,s}$ and $\bar{V}_{v,\,w}$ are the molar volumes of vapour at the pressures P_s and P_w respectively. If the water vapour is considered ideal $(P\bar{V}_v = RT)$ then $P_s \bar{V}_{v,\,s} = P_w \bar{V}_{v,\,w}$ and using (46), equation (47) becomes

$$w_V = -RT_D \ln f_w x_w \qquad (48)$$

The ideal gas has the property that the molar internal energy is dependent on temperature, but not on pressure or volume, and hence to conserve internal energy an amount of heat $q_V = w_V$ must leave the system at the temperature T_D. This heat can be coupled with the heat reservoir at the ambient temperature T_A and thus can do an amount of work w_E given by equations (35) and (48) as

$$w_E = -R \ln f_w x_w (T_D - T_{AM}) \qquad (49)$$

Assuming that the solution is warmed from the temperature T_{AM} and cooled back together with the pure water to this temperature via a perfect heat exchanger, the work w_S required for separation of the water from solution via distillation is given by equations (48) and (49) as

$$w_S = w_V - w_E = -RT_{AM} \ln f_w x_w \qquad \text{distillation} \quad (50)$$

(d) Separation by Reverse Osmosis

Reverse osmosis is a process in which water is forced from a solution through a semi-permeable membrane by applying a pressure to the solution. The process can be carried out at the ambient temperature and is most efficient if the membrane is ideal, i.e. impermeable to all solutes. Denoting the pressure of pure water and solution by P_w and P_s, at equilibrium with respect to the transport of water, the chemial potential of water in solution μ_w must equal that of pure water μ_w^o and by equations (27) and (17)

$$\mu_w = \mu_w^o + RT_{AM} \ln f_w x_w + \int_{P_w}^{P_s} \bar{V}_w \, dP = \mu_w^o \qquad (51)$$

The pressure difference $P_s - P_w$ satisfying this condition is called the osmotic pressure π. If the pressure difference exceeds π by an infinitesimal amount, pure water will flow from the solution through the ideal membrane.

If $\bar{V}_{w,\,s}$ and $\bar{V}_{w,\,w}$ are the partial molal volumes of water at the pressures P_s and P_w, the work of separation (per mole of water) w_S is given by combining the integration of equation (6) for both the solution and pure water as

$$w_S = P_s \bar{V}_{w,\,s} - P_w \bar{V}_{w,\,w} \tag{52}$$

If the osmotic pressure is not large, then $\bar{V}_{w,\,s} \approx \bar{V}_{w,\,w}$ and equations (51) and (52) give

$$w_S = -RT_{AM} \ln f_w x_w \qquad \text{reverse osmosis} \tag{53}$$

(e) Discussion of separation processes

It is no accident that w_S as given by equations (44), (50) and (53) is the same for freezing, distillation and reverse osmosis. In all of these separations the system was changed from a common initial state to a common final state by a reversible process, and hence the work required must be the same. Although we made several approximations, an exact treatment would have produced the same result. Figure 2 shows the work requirement in joules mole^{-1}, with $T_{AM} = 25°C$, as a function of concentration for aqueous solutions of NaCl and CaCl$_2$. It should be remembered that these values of the work of separation are minimum values. The real processes are unlikely to be reversible, and in practice one of the three processes discussed may be more efficient than the others.

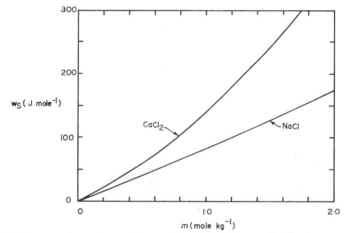

Fig. 2. Minimum work requirement (or work equivalent) w_S needed for the separation of 1 mole of water from a large excess of solution at 25°C as a function of concentration m for aqueous solutions of NaCl and CaCl$_2$.

4. ELECTROCHEMICAL EFFECTS

Potentials of many types are observed experimentally with saline solutions in different environments. A simple arithmetical example explains the ubiquity of these electrochemical effects. If a sphere of water of weight 1 g acquires an excess of only 10^{-16} gram-ion of some ion like H^+, Na^+ etc., its electric potential increases by about 14 volt. Few of these observed potentials, however, are related simply to the thermodynamic electric potential. Some are obviously non-equilibrium potentials, while others contain complex components. We give here a brief account of the thermodynamic approach.

The electric potential ψ of relation (20) controls the flow of electrons. In chemical systems electronic and ionic flows are interdependent, so that ψ influences ionic equilibria. This means that, for ions, equations (20) and (28) should be combined formally to give a controlling electrochemial potential

$$\mu_i = z_i F \psi + \mu_i^* + RT \ln \gamma_i m_i \qquad (54)$$

where μ_i^* is independent of the electric state of the phase. For two solutions in a common solvent separated by a non-osmotic membrane permeable only to an ion i,

$$0 = z_i F (\psi_\alpha - \psi_\beta) + RT \ln \frac{(\gamma_i m_i)_\alpha}{(\gamma_i m_i)_\beta} \qquad (55)$$

In this instance $(\psi_\alpha - \psi_\beta)$ may be computed after analysing the solutions, provided the activity coefficients are known. When the solvents differ, however, equation (55) retains an additional term in μ_i^* inseparable from the term in ψ. Thus electric potential differences between solutions in different solvents cannot be defined thermodynamically.

Further, even with a common solvent the potential difference must be computed from equation (55) or a similar relation. Electrodes reversible to the ion i placed in each of the phases α and β show no difference in potential, since the relative potential of each is determined by the electrochemical potential μ_i.

The separation of two solutions by an osmotic membrane introduces the additional feature of an osmotic pressure difference to equilibrium. For a membrane permeable to an ion i and to solvent, at the Donnan equilibrium

$$0 = \frac{z_i F}{RT} (\psi_\alpha - \psi_\beta) + \ln \frac{(\gamma_i m_i)_\alpha}{(\gamma_i m_i)_\beta} + \frac{\bar{V}_i}{RT} (P_\alpha - P_\beta) \qquad (56)$$

provided that we may ignore the compressibility of the solutions. The pressure difference may be determined from the equilibrium for solvent as

$$P_\alpha - P_\beta = \frac{RT M_1}{\bar{V}_1} \left\{ \phi_\alpha \left(\sum_i m_i \right)_\alpha - \phi_\beta \left(\sum_i m_i \right)_\beta \right\} \qquad (57)$$

where ϕ is the osmotic coefficient of equation (34). In this instance, also, the electric potential difference is defined and may be computed after measuring equilibrium concentrations and activities.

In summary, electric potential differences are defined distinctively only for solutions in the same solvent. They may be computed from concentration measurements, to an accuracy dependent upon the perfection of the membrane separating the solutions.

(a) Resting Potential in a Nerve Fibre

A nerve fibre consists of a cylindrical membrane of selective permeability containing a mixed electrolyte system of different composition to the external solution (Hodgkin 1967, pp. 30–32). In the resting state (no signal is being transmitted) the membrane is permeable only to K^+ ions. In the squid axon, the internal solution (axoplasm) has $m_{K^+, a} \approx 0.4$, and the external squid blood solution has $m_{K^+, b} \approx 0.002$. The total cation concentration in both solutions is approximately equal but whereas the Cl^- ion is predominant in the external solution, the axoplasm contains a large proportion of organic anions. In spite of this, indirect evidence (Hinke 1961) suggests the ionic activity coefficient of the K^+ to be similar in the two solutions, and hence $(\gamma_{K^+, b} m_{K^+, b} / \gamma_{K^+, a} m_{K^+, a}) \approx 20$. Substituting this result into (55) with $T = 298$ K (25°C) gives the potential of axoplasm as 75 mV below that of the blood solution. Experimental measurement using similar electrodes in the two solutions, that are not reversible to the K^+ ion, gives a potential difference of approximately 70 mV.

5. SURFACE PHENOMENA

In any system, surface phenomena become more important as the surface/volume ratio increases. For a given ratio, however, their significance depends upon surface curvature and upon the extent of adsorption.

From equation (21), for mechanical equilibrium the hydrostatic pressure is greater on the convex side of a curved interface between two fluid phases (e.g. between a saline solution and air). This difference influences markedly the flow of liquids in capillary spaces, but it also leads to changes in chemical potential. Thus, equations (17) and (21) give

$$\left(\frac{\partial \mu_i}{\partial r}\right)_{T, \, n_i} = -\frac{2\sigma \bar{V}_i}{r^2} \tag{58}$$

for the simplification of $r_1 = r_2 = r$.

Changes in the chemical potential of water in saline solutions give corresponding changes in the equilibrium vapour pressure p. With water vapour taken to behave as a perfect gas, and σ and $\bar{V}$ taken as constant, equations (27) and (58) give

$$d \ln p = d \ln f_1 x_1 - \frac{2\sigma \bar{V}_1}{RTr^2} \, dr \tag{59}$$

5

For a pure solvent ($x_1 = 1$), equation (59) reduces to the Kelvin relation (Adam 1941, p. 13) describing the relative vapour pressure of droplets and capillary condensates. We also note from equation (59) that a droplet of a saline solution may have the same vapour pressure as a pool of pure water; for example, a droplet of radius about 0·3 μm of a 0·1 mol kg^{-1} solution of NaCl is isopiestic to water. Equilibria of this type often define the stability of mists and clouds (Defay *et al.* 1966, p. 262). They do not involve equilibria between solutes like NaCl etc., since these are involatile. For this reason relations like equation (59) should not be used to describe the equilibria between segments of solutions in capillary structures unless it is certain that surface flow of solutes (Adam 1941, p. 215) is unimportant.

We now consider adsorption, which may be either positive or negative. At equilibrium a positively adsorbed substance has a greater mean concentration near an interface than in the bulk of the solution. There is no abrupt change in concentration along the path between surface and bulk, so that any separation into surface and bulk regions is arbitrary.

In a two phase system, one arbitrary division of the system into two phases may lead to volumes V_α and V_β of the bulk phases α and β, with an interfacial area $A_{\alpha\beta}$. If there are n_i moles of component i in the system, and the bulk phase concentrations of this component in moles/unit volume are $c_{i, \alpha}$ and $c_{i, \beta}$, the surface excess Γ_i of this component is defined by

$$\Gamma_i = (n_i - V_\alpha c_{i, \alpha} - V_\beta c_{i, \beta})/A_{\alpha\beta} \tag{60}$$

and is dependent upon the choice of arbitrary division. For any such arbitrary division, there is equilibrium between the regions created, and we may equate the chemical potentials of each component in different regions. We use equation (22) for the interface with surface tension σ and equation (13) for the residual bulk regions. At constant temperature and pressure this gives

$$-\mathrm{d}\,\sigma = \sum_i \Gamma_{i, 1}\, \mathrm{d}\mu_i \tag{61}$$

$$\Gamma_{i, 1} = \Gamma_i - \Gamma_1(c_{i, \alpha} - c_{i, \beta})/(c_{1, \alpha} - c_{1, \beta}) \tag{62}$$

The quantity $\Gamma_{i, 1}$ is known as the 'relative adsorption' of component i and is independent of the arbitrary division of the system. For component 1, $\Gamma_{1, 1} = 0$. For all thermodynamic work either the relative adsorption, or a good approximation to it, should be used.

If phase α consists only of component 1 and is a porous solid with pore volume V_P and pore surface area A_P, and phase β is a solution containing components 2, 3, . . . , then by equation (62) the average concentration $\bar{c}_{2, P}$ in the pores is

$$\bar{c}_{2, P} = c_{2, \beta} + \Gamma_{2, 1}\, A_P/V_P \tag{63}$$

When $\Gamma_{2, 1}$ is non-zero, the average concentration in the pores is dependent upon the ratio (surface area/volume) of the pores. A modified form of equation (63) is used as the basis of the measurements of adsorption at a solid-liquid interface.

With saline solutions, equations (61) and (62) are used together with expressions of electroneutrality and ionic equilibria. For instance, with an exactly neutral solution of NaCl we have

$$m_{Na^+} = m_{Cl^-} \quad \text{and} \quad m_{H^+} = m_{OH^-}.$$

For the surface region, however, we cannot advance beyond

$$\Gamma_{Na^+} + \Gamma_{H^+} = \Gamma_{Cl^-} + \Gamma_{OH^-}$$

without further information about the relation between H^+ and OH^- ions in the surface region. Obviously this information is vital for adsorption on clays, ion-exchangers and the like.

Finally, we sound a caveat. The surface tension of a $1\cdot0$ mole kg^{-1} solution of NaCl at 20°C exceeds that of water by $1\cdot6$ mN m^{-1}. Virtually undetectable concentrations of substances like some waxes and proteins may lower the tension by up to 40 mN m^{-1}. In many instances the surface behaviour of saline solutions is decided by trace contamination.

REFERENCES

Adam, N. K. (1941). *The Physics and Chemistry of Surfaces* 3rd Edn. Oxford University Press.

Bridgman, P. W. (1914) *Phys. Rev.* **3**, 273.

Callen, H. B. (1960). *Thermodynamics*. John Wiley and Sons, New York.

Davies, C. W. (1962). *Ion Association*. Butterworths, London.

Debye, P., and Hückel, E. (1923). *Phys. Z.* **24**, 185.

Defay, R., Prigogine, I., Bellemans, A., and Everett, D. H. (1966). *Surface Tension and Adsorption*. Longmans, Green, London.

Denbigh, K. G. (1957). *The Principles of Chemical Equilibrium*. Cambridge University Press.

Gibbs, J. W. (1961). *The Scientific Papers of J. Willard Gibbs*, vol. 1, *Thermodynamics*. Dover Publications, New York.

Guggenheim, E. A. (1929). *J. Phys. Chem.* **33**, 842.

Guggenheim, E. A. (1957) *Thermodynamics* 3rd Edn. North-Holland Publishing Co., Amsterdam.

Harned, H. S., and Owen, B. B. (1958). *The Physical Chemistry of Electrolytic Solutions* 3rd Edn. Reinhold Publishing Corp., New York.

Hinke, J. A. M. (1961). *J. Physiol.* **156**, 314.

Hodgkin, A. L. (1967). *The Conduction of the Nervous Impulse*. Liverpool University Press.

Lewis, G. N., and Randall, M. (1923). *Thermodynamics and the Free Energy of Chemical Substances.* McGraw-Hill, New York.

Lewis, G. N., and Randall, M. (1961). *Thermodynamics* 2nd Edn. Revised by K. S. Pitzer and L. Brewer. McGraw-Hill, New York.

Noyes, A. A., and Bray, W. C. (1911). *J. Amer. chem. Soc.* **33**, 1646.

Prigogine, I., and Defay, R. (1954). *Chemical Thermodynamics.* Translated by D. H. Everett. Longmans, Green, London.

Robinson, R. A., and Stokes, R. H. (1959). *Electrolyte Solutions* 2nd Edn. revised. Butterworth, London.

A Survey of the Principles of Metallic Corrosion and its Control in Saline Waters

W. T. DENHOLM and E. C. POTTER

*Division of Mineral Chemistry, CSIRO, at Garden City, Victoria
and Chatswood, N.S.W., respectively*

SUMMARY

An outline of the theory of corrosion processes is presented, using pH-potential diagrams to summarize theoretical and experimental data relating to corrosion; the pitting corrosion of iron in chloride-containing waters is treated in some detail.

The complicating effects of the many factors which influence corrosion behaviour in practical cases are discussed and the more common methods of corrosion control explained. It is emphasized that catalogued information relating to corrosion behaviour must be interpreted with caution, and if possible should be supplemented with the accumulated experience and judgment of specialists in the field.

1. INTRODUCTION

Metallic corrosion occurs when a metal reacts with its environment, whether this be solid, gaseous, or aqueous liquid. All metals and alloys, even the most noble, are capable of being corroded, and the everyday metals (such as iron, copper, zinc, brass, lead, and aluminium) are attacked by a wide variety of moist atmospheres and aqueous solutions. As a rule the corrosive constituents of natural and artificial waters are acidity, alkalinity, salinity, and dissolved oxygen, but, as will emerge later, the course and severity of a corrosive situation are normally easier to observe than to predict and quantitative generalizations about corrosion behaviour are seldom precise even for a selected metal. However, the electrical conductivities of saline waters are sufficient to support electrolytic corrosion processes and there is little impediment due to resistivity. On the other hand, the nature of the salts can be dominant in determining the speed and distribution of metal attack, and the pitting influence of chloride ions is discussed in detail later.

The electrochemical nature of metallic corrosion is readily appreciated by recalling that a base metal (zinc) is being sacrificed whenever a current is drawn from the familiar Leclanché (or dry) cell. By a comparable process stray electric currents in soil can be intercepted by a buried steel pipeline, causing local destruction of the steel where the current elects to leave the pipeline for the surrounding environment. In the absence of a perfect coating over the buried steel, this particular corrosion problem is overcome (in principle and in practice) by making the pipeline the cathode of a rival electrolytic cell. The protective effect is greater the stronger the cathodic action (determined by the size of the negative potential difference between the pipeline and the soil). This method of corrosion control and other important tenets of electrolytic corrosion science are conveniently summarized by the potential-pH diagram derived from the appropriate thermodynamic data for the metal-solution system of interest.

2. PRINCIPLES OF CORROSION THEORY

(a) Potential-pH (or Electrochemical Equilibrium) Diagrams

Pourbaix and co-workers have published such diagrams for many systems (Pourbaix 1966) and Shrier (1963, p. I. 1) has given a simplified description of their construction and use. The lines on the diagrams show the electrode potentials for reactions which occur on the surface of a metal in a pure solution* of given pH. The lines divide the diagrams into areas showing the theoretical conditions for formation of the different types of corrosion products. In an area marked 'immunity', corrosion is thermodynamically unfavourable (see below). In an area marked 'corrosion', the products of corrosion are soluble, while in an area marked 'passivation', the products are insoluble.

(b) Anodic Processes

In Fig. 1a, which is the 'corrosion, immunity, and passivation diagram' for iron in pure* aqueous solution at ordinary temperature, line (1) separates the zone of immunity from the zone of corrosion. This line represents the theoretical dissolution potential (E_h in volts on the hydrogen scale) for iron by the anodic reaction:

$$Fe - 2e^- = Fe^{2+} \qquad (1)$$

At more negative potentials, there is no thermodynamic driving force for the dissolution process and the metal is in the state of 'immunity'. Above line (1)

---

* 'Pure' in this context means that the solution does not contain either complexing agents or surface-active substances that block metal sites or interfere with nucleation of solid corrosion products.

in the (shaded) corrosion zone, dissolution proceeds faster with increasingly positive potential. An increase in either pH or potential at the metal surface may bring about precipitation of insoluble oxides, e.g. Fe_2O_3. This anodic reaction,

$$2Fe^{2+} + 6OH^- - 2e^- = Fe_2O_3 + 3H_2O \qquad (2)$$

is represented in Fig. 1a by the sloping line (2), which forms the boundary between the zones of corrosion and passivation.

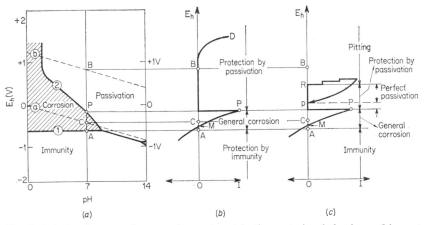

Fig. 1. Relation between theory and experiment in the corrosion behaviour of iron at pH=7.

(a) Theoretical prediction of corrosion, immunity, and passivation.
(b) Experimental potential-sweep curve for conditions favouring stable passivation.
(c) Experimental potential-sweep curve for conditions conducive to pitting (after Pourbaix 1965).

Actually, the zone of passivation defines only the conditions under which insoluble corrosion products are formed, and it does not always follow that these products build a reliably-passivating film. However, Hoar (1963) has stated that a film-covered metal will enjoy the most complete passivation when the film substance has low ionic conductivity; appreciable electronic conductivity; low chemical solubility and dissolution rate; a large range of electrode potential in which it is thermodynamically stable; and high compressional strength and good adhesion to the metal.

The corrosion, immunity and passivation diagram for any metal can thus assist in predicting whether the anodic oxidation of the metal will lead to active corrosion with formation of soluble products or to passivation by insoluble products. In either case, the anodic reaction can only take place in association with a suitable cathodic reaction which will consume the electrons liberated.

(c) Cathodic Processes

pH-potential diagrams such as Fig. 1*a* usually include lines for the oxygen and hydrogen electrodes, showing the theoretical or reversible potentials of the two main cathodic processes in aqueous metallic corrosion:

Line (*a*), Hydrogen electrode (hydrogen evolution reaction),

$$2H^+ + 2e^- = H_2, \tag{3}$$

Line (*b*), Oxygen electrode (oxygen reduction or absorption reaction),

$$O_2 + 2H_2O + 4e^- = 4OH^-. \tag{4}$$

A cathodic reaction can occur only on a surface whose electrode potential is more negative than the reversible potential. Spontaneous corrosion requires a cathodic reactant whose reduction potential is more positive than the anodic dissolution potential of the metal.

Figure 2 illustrates the differences in corrosion behaviour between iron and copper in the absence of complexing and surface-active agents. Since the dissolution potential for iron lies below the reversible potential for hydrogen evolution, iron can corrode in air-free acidic solutions with evolution of

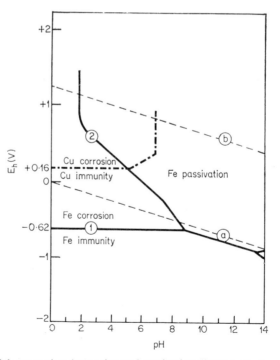

Fig. 2. Parts of the corrosion, immunity, and passivation diagrams for iron and copper at ordinary temperature. (Heavy dashed line for copper; heavy solid line for iron.)

hydrogen. It can also corrode over the whole pH range by the oxygen-reduction mechanism. On the other hand, with copper, the dissolution potential lies above the hydrogen potential but below the oxygen potential, and therefore copper may corrode by the oxygen-reduction mechanism but will not corrode in non-oxidizing acid solutions.

(d) Corrosion as a Rate Process

The foregoing discussion illustrates how published thermodynamic data give a lead to corrosion behaviour. However, corrosion is a rate process and a full understanding must take this into account. For example, the fact that a metal forms an insoluble corrosion product carries no certainty of effectiveness as a passivating film. Since aqueous corrosion involves electrochemical reactions, the techniques of electrode kinetics can be used, with the currents measuring the rates of the reactions taking place.

(e) The Behaviour of Pure Iron

Figure 1 (after Pourbaix 1965) shows how the results of kinetic studies can be related to the pH-potential diagram. The lower branch of the curve in Fig. 1b shows the changes in an externally-impressed current (I) which are required when a freshly-etched (essentially oxide-free) iron surface is placed in a pure air-free solution at pH 7 and forced to progressively more positive potentials. Point C lies at the reversible potential for the hydrogen evolution reaction, while point A denotes the reversible metal dissolution potential. The potential M with no impressed current (i.e. the so-called 'mixed' potential of the freely corroding metal) lies between points A and C. As the potential is made more positive the rate of the anodic dissolution reaction, as measured by the current, increases along the curve MP until at point P there is a sudden decrease when the potential enters the zone of passivation and the surface becomes covered with a stable, passivating oxide film. The dissolution reaction remains extremely slow throughout the range of stability of this passivating film, the iron specimen being in a condition of anodic protection. The curve BD is the potential-current relation for the evolution of oxygen, i.e. the reverse of reaction (4), taking place on an oxide-covered iron surface.

In many environments, however, passivating films are subject to breakdown and undermining, with formation of corrosion pits. Figure 1c illustrates a typical anodic behaviour in the presence of chloride ions, which particularly promote this type of corrosion, as discussed later.

(f) Simultaneous Anodic and Cathodic Processes

The curve representing the relation between potential and current density for the cathodic processes may be superimposed on the anodic curve. In

Fig. 1, point B shows the reversible potential for the reduction of oxygen. When this reaction occurs on an iron surface the potential is 'polarized', i.e. it deviates downwards from point B to an increasing extent with rising current. Figure 3a shows typical 'cathodic polarization curves' drawn with a logarithmic scale to expand the low-current region, with the line CX representing the hydrogen electrode reaction and BY representing reduction of oxygen at typical oxygen concentration in solution. BZ denotes the increase in rate of this reaction brought about by stirring, while DE represents the reduction of a strong oxidizing agent, e.g. chromate ion.

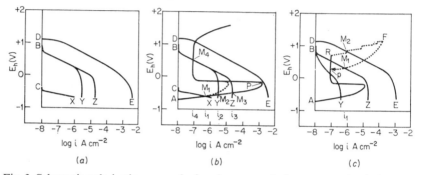

Fig. 3. Schematic polarization curves for iron in near-neutral pure aqueous solution.

  (a) Typical cathodic polarization curves.
  (b) and (c) Superimposed anodic and cathodic polarization curves for various conditions of corrosion and passivation (for details see text).

  N.B. The curves illustrate a particular set of experimental data and do not yield numerical data for general application. Lines RF and Fp in Fig. 3c are dashed to indicate two of numerous possible paths from R to F and from F to p.

When these curves are superimposed on the anodic curves, an indication of the possible types of corrosion behaviour of pure iron is obtained. The full argument is given in the standard texts, e.g. Shrier (1963, p. I. 49), where it is shown that the co-ordinates at the point of intersection of an anodic and a cathodic curve mark the potential of the metal surface and the rate at which it is corroding at the potential. Thus Fig. 3b shows that a bare iron surface, when corroding purely by the hydrogen evolution mechanism, exhibits a mixed potential M_1 and a corrosion rate i_1. The addition of oxygen to the solution will increase the rate of corrosion to i_2 and shift the potential slightly in the positive direction to M_2. Increasing the oxygen availability, by stirring, will further increase the corrosion rate to i_3 and shift the potential slightly to M_3. In the presence of a strong oxidizing agent such as nitrite or chromate having reduction behaviour illustrated by curve DE, the rate of the cathodic process may exceed the current required to reach the passivating potential P. Simply increasing the rate of oxygen supply is unlikely to bring about passivation of a bare iron surface, but corrosion usually results in the formation of a loose covering of oxide which would decrease the current required to promote passivity. The modified anodic behaviour in the presence of a relatively loose, poorly adherent covering is illustrated by the dashed line in Fig. 3b, and the cathodic current BZ due to stirring would now be sufficient to promote passivation.

Once the specimen has achieved the state of passivity, the potential shifts to the point M_4 in the passive range with the corresponding very low corrosion rate i_4. The passive condition may only be preserved by maintaining sufficiently oxidizing conditions, and it could happen that, if all the oxygen in the solution were consumed and the passivating film damaged, active corrosion (represented by the dashed anodic curve) would ensue. On recovery of the former oxygen supply, active corrosion at rate i_2 would again be observed, while passivation could be re-established by enhancing the supply of oxygen still further.

(g) Pitting Corrosion by Chlorides

Pourbaix (1969, 1970) has employed potential-pH diagrams to illustrate and interpret the pitting corrosion behaviour of copper, iron and some alloy steels in the presence of chlorides. All these systems exhibit a characteristic 'rupture potential' for their passivating films (such as point R, Fig. 1c), above which rapid pitting occurs with continual formation of new pits. If after film-rupture the current at the anodic areas falls to zero (e.g. by stagnation of previously aerated water) the potential drifts back to the more negative value marked 'p', and corrosion at the base of the pits ceases so that the specimen exhibits 'perfect passivation'. While the potential rests between 'p' and 'R' corrosion may proceed at existing pits but no new pits are able to form.

Experimentally-derived areas of 'generalized corrosion', 'pitting', 'imperfect passivation', 'perfect passivation', and 'immunity' may be plotted on pH-potential diagrams from the points on a series of curves as in Fig. 1c determined at a series of pH values. Examples are shown in Fig. 4 for commercially pure iron in chloride-free (4a) and chloride-containing (4b) environments.

The 'protection potential', p, is an important parameter in any pitting corrosion system since a specimen which suffers severe pitting corrosion probably spends a large part of its service life in the range of 'imperfect passivation'. The small black circle in each of Figs. 4a and 4b shows the experimental values for pH and potential determined by Brown et al. (1969) inside pits and stress-corrosion cracks, for a variety of steels irrespective of the pH of the bulk solution. This potential corresponds closely with the 'protection potential' which is almost independent of pH and chloride content. By contrast, the 'rupture potential' is dependent on both pH and

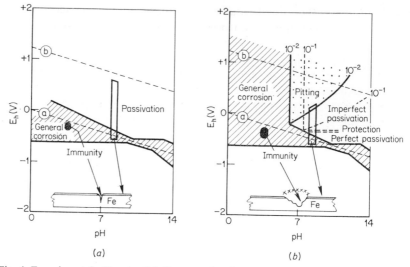

Fig. 4. Experimental pH-potential diagrams showing:
(1) Areas of immunity, general corrosion, pitting, imperfect passivation, and perfect passivation for commercially pure iron (a) in absence of chlorides; (b) in 10^{-2} molar chloride ion, indicating shift of pitting area with 10^{-1} molar chloride ion;
(2) Conditions of pH and potential inside pits and cracks (as indicated by small black circles) and on the passivated metal surface in contact with bulk solution of pH$=8$ (indicated by narrow unshaded vertical areas).

chloride content, as shown by the curves in Fig. 4*b* for chloride concentrations of 10^{-1} and 10^{-2} molar.

Acidification inside pits has been observed by many workers (Baylis 1925; Evans 1960, p. 116; Pourbaix and van Muylder 1963), and it results from secondary reactions between water and metallic cations produced by the primary corrosion process in the pit (Pourbaix 1969).

Some examples are:

$$3Fe^{++} + 4H_2O \rightarrow Fe_3O_4 + 8H^+ + 2e^-; \tag{5}$$

$$Cr^{3+} + 3H_2O \rightarrow Cr(OH)_3 + 3H^+; \tag{6}$$

$$Al^{3+} + 3H_2O \rightarrow Al(OH)_3 + 3H^+; \tag{7}$$

and

$$2CuCl + H_2O \rightarrow Cu_2O + 2H^+ + 2Cl^-. \tag{8}$$

In an active pit a steady state is reached with an invariant equilibrium existing between the metal, its hydrated ion and the oxide product, leading to a fixed pH and potential. Since the entire surface outside the pits is in the passivated state, and is free to adopt any potential imposed on it, the measured potential of the corroding specimen is dominated by the pH- and potential-determining reaction inside the pits. This in turn determines the 'protection' potential as shown by the coincidence of this potential with the small black circle in Fig. 4*b*.

Figure 3*c* illustrates simultaneous anodic and cathodic processes in the case where pitting occurs. In a well-aerated solution with cathodic reduction of oxygen represented by curve *BZ* a specimen with active pits will adopt a potential close to M_1 corresponding to rate of corrosion i_1. All corrosion will be confined to the pits while the cathodic reaction can occur on the whole surface. The rate of penetration into the existing pits can thus be quite rapid but no new pits will be formed. A faster cathodic reaction such as that represented by *DE* would raise the potential to M_2, more positive than '*R*' not only increasing the corrosion in existing pits but initiating new ones. Pitting corrosion would cease and 'perfect passivation' prevail only with a reduced cathodic rate such as *BY* permitting the potential to fall below '*p*'.

This behaviour pattern is characteristic of all metals and alloys which corrode by pitting in chloride solutions. Other cases, namely stainless steel, copper, aluminium alloys, and titanium alloys, have been discussed from the same viewpoint by Pourbaix (1969).

(*h*) Generalizations Concerning Pitting in Chloride Solutions

1.   Pitting can only be initiated in strongly oxidizing media which cause the surface potential to exceed the 'rupture potential' and it occurs more readily with higher chloride contents.

2.   Active pits may continue to corrode when the oxidizing environment in solution causes the potential to lie below the 'rupture' potential but above a 'protection' potential determined by a three-phase equilibrium between the metal, its hydrated cations and a hydroxide or oxide *inside* the pits, e.g. reaction (5).

3.   Pits will cease to be active when the environment causes the potential to lie below the 'protection' potential in a range of 'perfect passivation'.

4.   General corrosion can occur in reducing media which permit the potential to fall below the 'passivation' potential (above which the passive state is maintained). This potential is not as clearly determined in the case of iron–chromium alloys as it is with pure iron.

5.   The potential range adopted by the corroding metal under a given set of circumstances depends largely on the oxidizing potential of the bulk solution and on the catalytic activity of the passivated surface towards the cathodic reduction of oxygen. The behaviour of copper covered by a thin cracked carbon layer provides a striking illustration of this catalytic effect (Campbell 1963; Pourbaix 1969).

3. THE COMPLEXITY OF CORROSION PROCESSES

Although metallic corrosion in aqueous environments is basically electro-chemical, it requires specially-designed experiments (Evans 1960, p. 861) to prove this and, in practice, there is rarely a clear manifestation of electro-lytic events as a metal corrodes. The reason rests with the profusion of factors, mostly non-electrical, that can influence or dictate the course and kinetics of a corrosion process. Among these factors are: the composition and uniformity of the metal; the nature and concentration of dissolved gases and salts; temperature; time; intensity and fluctuation of stresses; vibra-tion; occurrence of crevices and pits; contacts with other metals; stray currents; stagnation and inconstancy of the corrosive environment; fluid movement; abrasion; differential shielding of surfaces by deposits or deteriorating coatings; bacteria; and naturally-occurring promoters or inhibitors.

There are many opportunities for these factors to interact, and two examples follow. First a deposit may shield a surface and originate a stagnant micro-environment so different from the bulk environment that anaerobic bacteria can flourish and the shielded metal is pitted; and second, a seasonal deoxygenation of a water body may interact with chloride intrusion or abrasion by sand with the result that immersed stainless steel cannot repair the oxide film on which its corrosion resistance vitally depends. Seemingly minor circumstances may trigger or accelerate a corrosion outbreak: a repair weld may not be stress-relieved, an earth terminal may become defective, copper may touch or plate out on to sus-ceptible aluminium, pitting corrosion may ensue when inhibitor concentra-tion is or becomes insufficient, or, a softer water may remove the protective chalky scale that a harder water once deposited on immersed mild steel.

Evidently, the correct interpretation of practical corrosion failures requires enlightened examination of the past and present environmental circumstances backed by a wide experience of the vagaries of corrosion phenomena. Many corrosion processes are slow to mature and are well advanced when discovered, so that the specialist faces formidable diagnostic difficulties at times, particularly when the initial stimulus to corrosive attack has passed unnoticed or has been destroyed by the corrosive events themselves. Fortunately, remedies for corrosion failure can often be sug-gested without a full case-history, and the skill comes in selecting anti-corrosive measures that are not only effective but practical and economic as well. On occasion it must be recognized that some corrosion problems may have to be tolerated rather than subdued. In illustration, it is an incon-venient fact that the incorrodible noble metals are rare and expensive, while the common metals are corrodible and have first to be extracted from ores, to which they tend to revert as corrosion later takes its toll. In practice this means that a metal immune to corrosion through its thermodynamic stability usually prices itself out of consideration, and consequently something less than intrinsic immunity must be accepted as sound technology. A variety of anticorrosion principles have thus emerged and will now be discussed.

4. PRINCIPLES OF CORROSION CONTROL

(a) Control Through Metal Selection

In forthright terms, a purposely-uncoated metal which reacts with its environment to the unacceptable detriment of either or both has been wrongly selected in the first place. Two examples may be given. First, a soft water that is rather too saline to drink can be expected to ruin common types of brass fittings because a progressive dissolution of the zinc from the alloy takes place leaving behind a weak porous mass consisting only of copper. In some cases the dissolved zinc is precipitated as basic carbonate, which forms a 'meringue' deposit capable of blocking pipes and valves. Short of a radical alteraton (Turner 1961, 1965) of the balance between bicarbonate hardness and salinity of the water (usually an impracticable step), the solution to this corrosion problem is to replace the susceptible brass by metal not prone to the attack, for instance bronze, monel, alloy steel, or an aluminium alloy. The second example is the eventual perforation of galvanized steel (say a water tank) when copper is used for an associated connection (say an inlet pipe). The action begins with a minute dissolution of copper (of no consequence to the copper or to the water quality) followed by displacement of the dissolved copper as metallic particles upon nearby galvanized surfaces. This creates small active galvanic cells that effect rapid local corrosion of the zinc coating and of the steel beneath it. The action is not avoided by making sure that the copper is electrically insulated from the galvanized steel, because the copper that triggers the attack is transferred on to the zinc by the water itself. The common solution to the problem is to avoid the use of metal more noble than either zinc or iron (especially on the inlet or upstream side of the galvanized steel). Thus the offending copper would be replaced, say by galvanized steel itself or, if preferred, by a non-metal.

(b) Control by Modifying the Environment

For various reasons there may be no question of overcoming a corrosion problem by metal-selection, but effective corrosion-control can be sought through acceptable alteration of the aqueous environment. Where large water schemes and potable supplies are concerned there are obvious public-health constraints to deliberate compositional changes and, in addition, only the cheapest of substances and processes can be contemplated on economic grounds. Thus processes that radically diminish the total dissolved solids of a saline water (such as distillation or ion exchange) are not yet attractively cheap on the scale of tens of millions of gallons treated each day, and in any case removal of salinity would not be practised for the express purpose of avoiding corrosion that the salinity may cause. While, however, salinity is excluded from adjustment for the present, the control of other corrosive factors is possible, as is now described.

In broad terms the immersed aqueous corrosion of cast iron and mild steel is encouraged by acidity (pH < 7 at 25°C) because ferrous ions (the first product of iron oxidation) are appreciably soluble under these conditions. On the other hand, sufficient alkalinity (pH > 10 at 25°C) inhibits the corrosion, because ferrous hydroxide, magnetite, and hydrated ferric oxide are all virtually insoluble under these conditions and will readily build protective films on the metal surface. These statements are compatible with Fig. 1*a*, and are valid whether the aqueous phase is air-saturated or deoxygenated. However, dissolved oxygen (usually atmospheric) has supplementary effects in that the corrosion product in mildly acid and near-neutral conditions is fully oxidized, i.e. hydrated ferric oxide (rust), and forms a non-protective incrustation. The incrustation itself is an impediment to diffusion of dissolved oxygen, but the corrosion continues unabated under the electrical driving force of the differential concentration of dissolved oxygen and a pit develops, over-filled with granular magnetite surmounted by a cap of rust (Evans 1960, p. 128). Any porous adherent deposit on iron will cause the effect provided enough oxygen is present to form and sustain a significant differential of dissolved oxygen concentration. Moreover, salinity favours the entire process by reducing the electrical resistance of the differential oxygenation cells.

Acidity in natural fresh and brackish waters is often due to free carbon dioxide. Cascading the water in air helps to reduce this acidity, and the pH may be further raised to the alkaline side of neutrality by dosing with relatively small quantities of a common alkali such as lime or soda ash. When natural waters are devoid of oxygen, it usually means that they are in an undesirable sulphidic and biological condition and as such are corrosive. Aeration remedies this situation, but introduces the potential for differential oxygenation corrosion. Full-scale deoxygenation of natural (or re-aerated) waters as a method of corrosion control in municipal or rural applications is impracticable, and pH adjustment must therefore be used if rusting is to be controlled. However, to guarantee the absence of aqueous corrosion of iron by exploiting alkaline passivity requires elevation of the pH to nearly 10, a value possibly inconvenient in water for consumption or for crops. Fortunately there is an opportunity for film protection to occur naturally at pH values nearer neutrality, as explained in the next section.

(c) Control by Protective Films (Excluding Passivity)

For practical and economic reasons neither metal-selection nor alteration of the corrosive environment can be frequently practised with brackish waters, and the principle of separating the metal from its environment by means of protective films on the metal is the most common anticorrosive measure. A water that is effectively supersaturated with respect to calcium carbonate has both the power to reject this substance from solution and the opportunity to asemble the chalky particles into a compact coating over nearby surfaces, say the internal walls of a pipeline or main. Experience shows that many a steel water main escapes tuberculation and perforation through the chalky deposit of egg-shell thickness laid down by the water. The protective quality and stability of such a coating cannot yet be controlled, and there is no guarantee of calcareous film protection in any given instance (Bell and Campbell 1965). Nevertheless, it is useful to know whether a water has the physicochemical capability of depositing calcium carbonate (Uhlig 1963), for, if it has not, then there is forewarning of cast iron and steel being at risk.

The saturation solubility of calcium carbonate in a natural water depends on its pH, which is largely controlled by its concentration of free carbon dioxide. The more acid the water, the greater is the concentration of calcium it can retain in solution (Butler and Ison 1966). If, therefore, the concentration of calcium dissolved in a naturally-carbonated underground water exceeds that corresponding to the saturation solubility of calcium carbonate as calculated for the same water decarbonated, then the water on equilibrating with air will eventually reject chalk from solution and this may deposit protectively on corrodible ferrous surfaces. This approach can also indicate if the amount of calcium available to be deposited in this way is too sparing to build up a useful calcareous film in a reasonable time. On the other hand, a water may be under-saturated with calcium carbonate at all practicable pH conditions, and then no calcareous deposition is possible and a chalky film already present on ferrous surfaces will be gradually dissolved and eventually removed. A water with these properties is conveniently detected by passage over marble chips, which will gradually lose weight by dissolution and increase the pH of the water.

Corrosion protection based on natural deposition of calcareous films is accidental and precarious, and the modern water engineer prefers the soundness of cement as a lining or as an external coating for water mains and pipelines. The technique of cement-lining pipes *in situ* is well-established and numerous cities throughout the world must have cured 'red water' and given

6

deteriorating mains a new lease of life in this way. There is, however, a wide variety of other protective coatings available to the water engineer, ranging from the traditional bituminous compositions, through externally-applied tapes impregnated with water-repellant materials, to the latest factory-applied plastics coatings based, for example, on polyvinyl chloride, poly-ethylene, or epoxy resins. On account of the enormous variety of water, soil and other conditions no general guidance on the choice of protective coating can be offered here, except that anticipated performance tends to be in rough proportion to initial cost. In the coatings business, continual development produces a changing and competitive situation, and commer-cial pressures create the position where the users' experiences are a useful supplement to the manufacturers' programmes of product-development.

(d) Control by Cathodic Protection

Figure 1a displays the domains of stability of iron in pure aqueous solutions at selected pH values at ordinary temperature. The display is of limited help if the potential taken up by the metal is unknown or indefinite, and no information is included on the rate or intensity of corrosion when it occurs. The metal potential is, of course, open to measurement, but for our present purpose we may invoke common experience to decide that the potential taken up by bare iron in pure aqueous solutions below about pH 8 rests in the shaded region designated 'corrosion'. Evidently, if this rest potential is deliberately moved downwards to more negative (more cathodic) values, then a position is eventually reached where the metal enters the area labelled 'immunity', meaning that its corrosion is thermodynamically impossible. This transition is equivalent to conferring noble-metal properties on iron, which is thus said to be cathodically protected.

Cathodic protection is now an established industry for the preservation of buried and immersed metal (especially iron and steel), and is regularly applied to buried pipelines, underground cables, jetties, ships' hulls, and tanks. Although the principle of such protection is simple, its practical and efficient implementation over the entire area of an installation at risk demands much experienced judgment following a preliminary survey and realistic field trials. For these reasons the day of do-it-yourself cathodic protection has not arrived, although enlightened users with their own technicians and a good textbook can successfully design and operate protection schemes if they so wish. Costs are rather dependent on the character and complexity of the plant or installation requiring protection, but the initial outlay may readily amount to tens of thousands of dollars for a project of industrial magnitude. The running costs are relatively small and are kept so by coating the metal beforehand, so that only those areas where the coating is missing or faulty contribute to the electric-power demand. That savings accrue from properly-applied cathodic protection is undisputed, but actual figures are elusive and the convinced user invests in cathodic protection to be free from unheralded corrosion-failure and costly repairs or replacements.

In practice cathodic protection amounts to the construction of one or more large electrolytic cells. In a typical case the cathode would be an underground steel pipeline, the electrolyte would be the soil, and the anodes would be buried about pipeline depth at intervals of less than one mile and up to about one mile distant from the pipe. Insulated wires (usually themselves buried) complete the electric circuit between the anodes and the pipeline, and the associated current is adjusted until the pipeline potential is everywhere shifted negatively to at least a value of -0.85 volts* measured against a copper/saturated copper sulphate reference cell. Electrolysis on the scale necessary for protection militates against uniform throw of current from the anodes over the pipeline surface, and substantial areas have to be made excessively cathodic (over 1 volt beyond the -0.85 V criterion) to obtain protection everywhere. A skilful compromise between wasteful over-protection and expensive multiplication of anodes is achieved if the design and survey work has been successful. With relatively small protection schemes the anodes may be magnesium or zinc alloy, which provide the protective current through their own spontaneous dissolution. Such sacrificial anodes need replacing every few years. More commonly, electric power has to be impressed on the system, in which case the anode beds can either be consumable (e.g. scrap iron) or permanent (e.g. lead alloy or platinized titanium). Elaborations of cathodic protection in terms of centralized display and control, automatic voltage monitoring and adjustment, and safety and reliability of equipment in adverse or isolated conditions are all practicable, but application of the method to the *interior* of pipelines requires regular and frequent spacing of anodes inside the pipes and is rarely attempted.

(e) Control by Inhibitors

Certain substances termed inhibitors greatly decrease the aqueous corrosion of particular metals. Inhibitors are usually effective at small concentrations and many operate by adsorption or physical attachment to the corroding surface, interrupting the electron exchange that must proceed there when the metal is attacked. It is not now usual to classify as inhibitors those additives that prevent corrosion by changing the pH of the aqueous environment to values corresponding to regions of 'immunity' or 'passivation' (refer to Fig. 1a). In this category fall the ready sources of hydroxide ion such as the caustic alkalies, lime, ammonia, and alkali metal carbonates and ortho-phosphates, which all stop rusting by pH changes at a concentration of no

* -0.95 volts if sulphate-reducing bacteria are active.

more than a few per cent. Milder sources of hydroxide ion such as the alkali metal silicates, borates, and polyphosphates are more properly described as inhibitors since they have specific surface effects at concentrations below 0·01 % in addition to raising pH to more alkaline values. Small concentrations of other inorganic salts such as alkali metal chromates, nitrites, tungstates, vanadates, and molybdates inhibit rusting of iron in near-neutral solutions and seem to operate by stabilizing and reinforcing the film of iron oxide that always seeks to passivate the iron in these solutions. Provided their concentrations are raised (possibly ten times) these inhibitors are also effective in the presence of the aggressive anions of brackish waters such as chloride and sulphate, which are recognized to destroy the protective properties of adherent iron oxide films.

As mentioned above, adsorption or filming inhibitors obstruct the electrolytic action at the corroding surface, and thus include a large number of organic compounds, both ionic and non-ionic, often containing bound nitrogen, or sulphur, or both. Such molecules may be relatively small, such as aniline, pyridine, or thiourea; or large, such as octadecylamine and certain metal soaps. Many naturally-occurring materials or their degradation products are corrosion inhibitors and this class includes substances of plant origin such as tannins, gums, and derivatives of the humic acids found in many soils. Consequently, the opportunities for varied corrosion performance among different soils are very numerous, and the balance among aggressive and inhibiting constituents can be extremely difficult to rationalize both in specific cases and in general. An illustration of the difficulties arises from the finding that copper is protected from corrosion in some fresh waters by a naturally-occurring inhibitor (Campbell 1954a and b). The substance can be detected electrochemically, but it does not appear to have been isolated and its source and chemical identity are apparently recognized only to the extent that it is possibly of plant origin and dark in colour, and contains phenolic and carboxyl groups. Apart from the analytical difficulties the incentive to characterize this inhibitor further is dimmed by the prospect of its being unacceptable even as a trace constituent of public water supplies.

This point emphasizes a frequent drawback of inhibitors, for many are toxic or otherwise unusable as additives to potable water and to soils. In any event it is usually uneconomic to add an inhibitor to a once-through water system, since the additive passes to waste (presuming a permissible dump is found) before losing any of its effectiveness. Closed circulating or cooling systems are better suited to the use of inhibitors, but care must be taken to ensure an adequate supply over all susceptible metal areas. A proportion of inhibitors act by specifically blocking the anodic (corroding) areas of the metal, and if there is insufficient inhibitor to stifle all anodes, then the remaining amount of corrosion is concentrated over a few unprotected areas and these then become pitted. The end result of inhibitor starvation may therefore be at least as serious as would have occurred in the absence of inhibitor. Paints and similar protective coatings are used as vehicles for inhibitors and most primers for ferrous metals incorporate an inhibitive pigment either by intention (for example zinc tetroxychromate or calcium plumbate) or by interaction (for example red lead forms inhibitive lead soaps).

5. CONCLUSION

We have attempted to outline the mechanisms of metallic corrosion in aqueous environments, particularly saline waters, choosing to use potential-pH diagrams for this purpose. At the same time we have indicated that corrosion processes are influenced by a multiplicity of factors and circumstances, thus explaining why metals often behave in apparently erratic and unpredictable ways in natural waters. Ideally the selection of anticorrosive measures ought to await an exhaustive diagnosis of corrosion failure, but this is seldom possible and we have therefore described the principal methods available to combat and avoid corrosive attack in saline conditions.

It is often imagined that the performance of metals in natural environments ought, by now, to have achieved quantitative description in the form of reference tables, graphs, and formulae. Compilations of such data have been published (Rabald 1968), but they are not comprehensive enough to cover all the relevant variations of aggressive and protective situations that metals encounter in natural waters. At present, therefore, it is necessary to supplement the published information with the experience and judgment accumulated by specialist companies and consultants. It is hoped that this paper contributes in these ways to the theme of the Symposium.

REFERENCES

Baylis, J. R. (1925). *Metallurgical chem. Engng.* **32**, 874.

Bell, W. A., and Campbell, H. S. (1965). *Chem. Ind. (London)* (1965). p. 305.

Brown, B. F., Fujii, C. T., and Dahlberg, E. P. (1969). *J. electrochem. Soc.* **116**, 218.

Butler, G., and Ison, H. C. K. (1966). *Corrosion and its Prevention in Waters.* p. 31. Leonard Hill, London.

Campbell, H. S. (1954a). *J. appl. Chem.* **4**, 633.

Campbell, H. S. (1954b). *Trans. Faraday Soc.* **50**, 1351.

Campbell, H. S. (1963) *Proc. 2nd Int. Congr. metallic Corros.* (Houston). p. 237.

Evans, U. R. (1960). *Corrosion and Oxidation of Metals.* Arnold, London.

Hoar, T. P. (1963). In *Corrosion.* (Ed. L. L. Shrier.) p. 149. Newnes, London.

Pourbaix, M. (1965). *Corros. Sci.* **5**, 677.

Pourbaix, M. (1966). *Atlas of Electrochemical Equilibria in Aqueous Solutions.* p. 31 and 70. Pergamon, Oxford.

Pourbaix, M. (1969). Rapport Technique CEBELCOR, RT 157.

Pourbaix, M. (1970). Rapport Technique CEBELCOR, RT 167.

Pourbaix, M., and van Muylder, J. (1963). Rapport Technique CEBELCOR, RT 93.

Rabald, E. (1968). *Corrosion Guide* 2nd Edn. Elsevier, Amsterdam.

Shrier, L. L. (1963). In *Corrosion.* (Ed. L. L. Shrier.) p. I.1 and I.49. Newnes, London.

Turner, M. E. D. (1961). *Proc. Soc. Water Treat. Exam.* **10** (2), 162.

Turner, M. E. D. (1965). *Proc. Soc. Water Treat. Exam.* **14** (2), 81.

Uhlig, H. H. (1963). *Corrosion and Corrosion Control.* p. 102 and 347. John Wiley and Sons, New York.

Chemistry of Saline Soils and Their Physical Properties

J. P. QUIRK

Department of Soil Science and Plant Nutrition, Institute of Agriculture,
University of Western Australia

SUMMARY

An outline of the forces involved in clay particle interaction (swelling and dispersion) is given as a background for the interpretation of the physical behaviour of sodic soils, especially in relation to electrolyte levels. The electrolyte concentration below which appreciable decreases in soil permeability are encountered has been termed the threshold concentration and this concentration increases with the degree of sodium saturation of the soil colloids. The application of the threshold concentration concept to the management and reclamation of sodic soil is discussed.

1. INTRODUCTION

The structure of soils is now commonly defined as the arrangement of soil particles (Baver 1940) and although very limited quantitative definition of this property exists in terms of such measurements as pore size distribution it has been customary for a long time to discuss structure in terms of macropores (i.e. drained at 100 cm suction) and micropores—the remainder of the total porosity. The principal reason for such a separation clearly derives from the fact that permeability is a function of the square of the pore radius (intrinsic permeability of a soil has the units cm^2) so that any treatment or process which eliminates or decreases the macroporosity can have dramatic effects on the permeability of the soil to water. Since the macropores are also those which drain readily after irrigation or rainfall they also play a significant role in soil aeration, and gas exchange. An additional factor is that for a porous material the coarser pores constitute points of weakness so that soils with a reasonable macroporosity are friable and do not tend to form a uniform coherent mass or surface crusts, through which germinating plants may emerge only with great difficulty. Quirk and Panabokke (1962) have demonstrated that organic matter stabilizes soil aggregates by strengthening or reinforcing the coarse pores. Thus the water stability of soil aggregates is strongly influenced by organic matter and its disposition within the soil pore space.

For convenience the whole soil structure may be thought of in terms of a 'structural'* and 'textural' porosity. Thus while the structural porosity may be affected by mechanical treatment of a soil and its cropping history, the textural porosity is considered to be an intrinsic property arising from the arrangement of the fundamental particles especially those of colloidal dimensions within the soil mass.

The nature of the interaction between clay particles within the textural porosity can profoundly affect the structural porosity. Stated alternatively, some of the swelling of clay particles in a soil is internally accommodated leading to a reduction in the macroporosity. This may become extremely pronounced when a proportion of the exchange sites on clay particles are balanced by sodium ions. When the exchangeable cations in a soil are predominantly calcium or magnesium the clay particles interact or repel each other to only a limited extent and hence the particle separations are not large. However, when the proportion of sodium ions is appreciable, considerably greater swelling is encountered and this leads to a diminition of the favourable characteristics conferred on a soil by its macroporosity.

A high level of salts in a soil can reduce the particle interaction due to sodium ions however, for satisfactory plant performance the salt concentration in the soil solution has to be controlled so that crop or pasture production is not adversely affected.

An outline of the fundamental forces involved in particle interaction will be given as a background to a consideration of the effects of sodium ions on the structure of a soil and the ways in which the effect of sodium can be diminished. It is especially germane that the effect of sodium ions on the swelling properties of clays is so pronounced that even in soils of light texture, such as a sandy loam, very marked changes in soil permeability may be involved if the soil has an appreciable exchangeable sodium percentage.

2. SALINE AND SODIC SOILS

The United States Department of Agriculture's Handbook *Diagnosis and Improvement of Saline and Alkali Soils* (Richards 1954) provides the most comprehensive review from the point of view of soil scientists of the various facets of these two groups of soils.

The predominant ions balancing the negative charge of most soils are calcium and magnesium. When the degree of saturation of the exchange

---

* Here the word structural is used in a similar way to macroporosity and implies that part of the pore space which provides favourable gas and water transfer.

sites with sodium exceeds 15% then the soil is referred to as an alkali soil. Because the term alkali has been considered possibly misleading, more recently the term sodic (sodium rich) has been adopted for this class of soils.

A saline soil is one which contains sufficient salt to impair its productivity. A quantitative definition of a saline soil is based upon the conductivity of the saturation extract. A dry soil is made up to a paste with water and the soil solution is extracted by filtration under vacuum. The conductivity is then measured and if it exceeds 4 mmhos cm^{-1} (equivalent to approx. 40 meq l^{-1}* then the soil is described as saline. When a soil is both sodic and saline the term saline-sodic is applied.

Much of the earlier research on irrigation development was done in California and, because the situation there involved many soils which were neither sodic nor saline, and the irrigation waters were such as to increase the exchangeable sodium percentage, the principal concern in assessing irrigation water quality was in relation to cation exchange relationships.

A quite different aspect of water quality becomes important in situations where the soil is already sodic and the available irrigation water has relatively low electrolyte levels. In these cases there is a clear advantage in increasing the electrolyte level in the irrigation water to maintain the soil in a flocculated and consequently permeable condition, particularly during reclamation. Such an approach to the problem of the irrigation of sodic soils with good quality waters was largely unrealized or neglected until 1955 when Quirk and Schofield provided the quantitative results relating the level of electrolyte required to maintain a flocculated and permeable state in sodic soils. It should be mentioned that Fireman and Bodman (1939), and Bodman and Fireman (1950) had shown that a satisfactory permeability could be maintained for a soil with an exchangeable sodium percentage of 30 by using a high concentration of electrolyte. They did not investigate the region between the initial high salt concentration and distilled water, the use of which resulted in a drastic reduction of the permeability.

Sodic soils can be reclaimed by the addition of an amount of gypsum or other amendments so that the sodium is displaced from the exchange complex of the soil (Richards 1954). For instance if an acre-foot is taken to be 4 million pounds then 1·7 tons of gypsum ($CaSO_2 . 2H_2O$) per acre for each milliequivalent of exchangeable sodium per 100 g of soil is required to reclaim 1 ft of soil. The usual practice is to apply the gypsum to the soil and to leach with irrigation water. Reclamation by this procedure often fails or is so slow that it is not economically feasible, mainly because of the extremely low permeability of sodic soils to the usual low-electrolyte irrigation waters (Quirk and Schofield 1955). The high-salt water dilution method of reclaiming sodic soils makes use of the flocculating effect of high-electrolyte waters to maintain a substantially higher permeability, and at the same time the

* Meq $l^{-1} \times 75 \approx$ ppm.

high-salt water may serve as a source of divalent cations for sodium replace-ment.

The basis of the technique of using a high level of electrolyte in the irriga-tion water during reclamation is germane to the topic of this Symposium and will be discussed here.

3. EXCHANGE ISOTHERMS

A number of workers have discussed the merits and limitations of the various cation exchange equations (Kruyt 1952; Helfferich 1962; Bolt 1967). One of the simplest of these equations, the Gapon equation (Gapon 1933) is used widely by soil scientists to predict the exchangeable sodium percentage (ESP) as a function of the ions, such as sodium and calcium, in the equilib-rium solution. This equation describes such reactions as:

$$\text{Clay} - \tfrac{1}{2}\text{Ca} + \text{Na}^+ \rightleftharpoons \text{Clay} - \text{Na} + \tfrac{1}{2}\text{Ca}^{2+}$$

in the following way

$$\frac{\overline{\text{Na}}}{\overline{\text{Ca}}} = K_G \frac{\text{Na}^+}{\sqrt{\text{Ca}^{2+}}} \tag{1}$$

in which the $\overline{\text{Na}}$ and $\overline{\text{Ca}}$ represent the exchangeable ions in meq g^{-1}, Na$^+$ and Ca^{2+} are concentrations of the equilibrium solution expressed in milli-equivalents per litre and K_G is the exchange constant with dimensions $1^{1/2}$ meq$^{-1/2}$. Over a wide range of soils K_G has values varying between 0·012 and 0·015 and the value 0·0125 is often taken (Richards 1954) as a basis for calculating the exchangeable sodium percentage (ESP) from the sodium adsorption ratio (SAR), that is Na$^+/\sqrt{(\text{Ca}^{2+} + \text{Mg}^{2+})/2}$. A nomogram which enables the ESP to be read off from the SAR of the saturated extract is available (Richards 1954). Since Mg^{++} does not behave very differently to Ca^{2+}, the following discussion will simply refer to Na$^+/\sqrt{\text{Ca}^{2+}}$.

The key feature of equation (1) is that to maintain a constant composition of the surface phase the ratio Na$^+/\sqrt{\text{Ca}^{2+}}$ must be kept constant. Thus, if we have a soil in equilibrium with a given solution and we want to lower the total electrolyte concentration and still maintain the same proportion of sodium to calcium ions on the surface, then if, for instance, the sodium concentration is halved, it is necessary to quarter the calcium concentration to keep Na$^+/\sqrt{\text{Ca}^{2+}}$ constant.

4. PARTICLE INTERACTION

The plate shaped clay crystals occurring in soils usually belong to one of the following groups of layer lattice alumino-silicates:

Kaolinite	$(Si_4)^{IV}(Al_4)^{VI}O_{10}(OH)_8$
Montmorillonite	$(Si_8)^{IV}(Al_{3\cdot33}Mg_{0\cdot67})^{VI}_{\uparrow} O_{20}(OH)_4$

$$M_{0\cdot67}$$

Mica	$(Si_6Al_2)^{IV}_{\uparrow} (Al_4)^{VI}O_{20}(OH)_4$

$$M_2$$

The above formulae represent unit-cell composition. The metal atoms occur within the interstices of the anionic framework which is made up of O and OH. M represents metal ions such as sodium and potassium which are too large to fit into the anionic framework in tetrahedral (IV) or octahedral (VI) co-ordination and thus are external to it. In many circumstances these metal ions are exchangeable.

The crystals of the above minerals are made up of elementary silicate sheets or lamellae stacked in the c-axis direction. For montmorillonites and micas these lamellae are about $9\cdot5$ Å thick and for kaolinite they are 7 Å thick. All the metal ions balancing the charge in montmorillonite crystals are hydrated and can be replaced by another cation by leaching with a salt solution of the cation. Thus for montmorillonite the exchange capacity corresponds to the deficiency of lattice charge due to isomorphous replacement.

By contrast, for micas the exchange capacity is considerably less than the extent of isomorphous replacement, because only those metal ions which are on the external crystal surfaces are readily exchanged. For the fine grained mica-like materials (illites) occurring in soils, the exchange capacity may be $0\cdot40$ meq g^{-1} and the isomorphous replacement revealed by chemical analysis may be in excess of 2 meq g^{-1}. Such plate shaped crystals may have an external surface area of about 150 m^2 g^{-1} and would therefore have 5 elementary silicate sheets per crystal giving an average plate thickness of 50 Å. For coarser illites the plate thickness may often be three to four times this value and the cleavage face dimensions are often within the range of $0\cdot1$–1 μ. Montmorillonites have an area of 750 m^2 g^{-1} available to water and the elementary silicate sheets are organized into units of similar thickness to those of the illite crystals.

Particle interaction may be seen as the moving apart or repulsion of two such plate-shaped crystals arising from cation hydration and the development of a diffuse space charge as a result of thermal forces acting on the cations which are concentrated near the interface by coulombic forces between the cations and the negative clay surface.

Diffuse double layer theory, as discussed originally by Gouy (see Verwey and Overbeek 1948), has been used to describe the distribution of counter ions in a solution near a charged interface. When the exchange capacity and surface area are known, then diffuse double layer theory enables us to calculate the osmotic repulsive force causing the plates to move apart.

The exchange capacity and surface area enable the surface density of charge to be obtained and, from this, the surface potential is derived. This potential (ψ_0) is expressed as the dimensionless reduced electrical potential $ve\psi_0/kT$ which combines the electrical force on an ion in the numerator and the thermal force in the denominator. v is the valency of the attracted ion, e the electronic charge, k the Boltzmann constant and T the temperature in °K.

When the electrolyte concentration and distance apart of the clay plates are known, then theoretical techniques can be used to arrive at the mid-plane potential ψ_m (Kruyt 1952). Kemper and Quirk (1970) have provided a graphic solution to obtain mid-plane potentials for a given surface density of charge, electrolyte concentration and particle separation. Using ψ_m values for different plate separations, a repulsive pressure-distance curve can be obtained for a chosen exchangeable cation and electrolyte concentration.

If the reduced electrical potential at the mid-plane $ve\psi_m/kT$ is for convenience replaced by U, then following Langmuir (1938) the excess concentration of ions at the mid-plane between the clay crystals relative to that in the external solution C_o is given by:

$$C_o[(e^U - 1) + (e^{-U} - 1)] = 2\,C_o(\cosh U - 1)$$

which leads to an osmotic repulsive pressure of

$$P = 2\,RT\,C_o\,(\cosh U - 1) \tag{2}$$

The term within the brackets indicates the extent to which the osmotic pressure at the mid-plane exceeds that of the external solution for a symmetric electrolyte. Values for plate separation as a function of suction (or confining pressure) and electrolyte concentration obtained using equation (2) are given in Table 1.

TABLE 1

Film thickness (Å) for a clay immersed in different sodium chloride concentrations at a range of hydrostatic suctions.*

Molar electrolyte concentration	Suction cm of H_2O				
	1	10	100	1000	10000
10^{-1}	60	48	36	24	12
10^{-2}	150	115	77	39	12
10^{-3}	360	240	125	44	14

* Film thickness refers to the half-separation of clay plates expressed in Å—10^{-8} cm. For calcium clays the predicted values of the film thickness are approximately half those for sodium at equal molar concentrations of calcium chloride.

The osmotic repulsive forces give rise to swelling or volume increase of soil and clay-water systems. According to the theory the repulsive forces are greater for the sodium clays which have approximately twice the film thickness of the calcium clays at equal molar concentrations. Put in another way, at a given electrolyte level, sodium systems have a greater tendency to swell however, the theory predicts that the swelling of calcium systems would also be sensitive to changes in electrolyte concentration. Nevertheless, the swelling of soils and clays which are predominantly calcium saturated is not affected by electrolyte concentration (Aylmore and Quirk 1959, 1962; Quirk 1968). Many clays when wet in a controlled fashion increase their volume by 30 to 40% and such swelling arises principally from ion hydration (Quirk 1968). By contrast such clays, when sodium saturated, are sensitive to electrolyte concentrations and in the presence of dilute solutions may increase their volume by several hundred per cent.

To appreciate these differences it is necessary to consider the arrangement of clay particles. The elementary silicate sheets of montmorillonite (≈ 10 Å thick) are arranged in a parallel fashion with ab disorder and hence the term quasi-crystal has been used (Quirk 1968). Thus the external surface area of the 'quasi-crystals' of montmorillonite as measured by low temperature nitrogen adsorption, may vary from a few $m^2 g^{-1}$ to 150 $m^2 g^{-1}$ depending on a number of factors (Aylmore and Quirk in press). These values should be compared with the total attainable area of 750 $m^2 g^{-1}$. In a similar, but less ordered, way the individual units or crystals of an illite (≈ 100 Å thick) are arranged in a parallel fashion to give what has been described as a 'domain' by Quirk and Aylmore (1960). To arrive at an estimate of the likely volume increase when diffuse double layers are developed, the appropriate surface area is multiplied by the film thickness, as given in Table 1, for a particular set of experimental conditions.

The swelling of sodium clays is described more or less quantitatively by diffuse double layer theory and it is this type of swelling which is responsible for the adverse properties of sodic soils.

A quasi-crystal of calcium montmorillonite always gives a $d(001)*$ of 19 Å whereas sodium montmorillonite passes over the potential barrier at 9 Å plate separation and gives $d(001)$ values > 43 Å, the actual value being proportional to $1/\sqrt{C}$ where C is the electrolyte concentration. The domain of an illite is similar to a quasi-crystal of montmorillonite in that when calcium saturated it behaves as an entity. However, as the percentage sodium increases the proportion of the total surface area developing diffuse double layers increases and the increased swelling reduces the size of the macropores and hence the permeability.

When swelling or particle separation proceeds to such an extent that the

---

* The $d(001)$ is the basal or c-axis spacing which includes the thickness of water between the layers and one of the layers.

attractive force between contiguous clay crystals is considerably decreased then thermal forces cause the particles to behave almost independently of one another, and the system is described as being dispersed. It is well known that many flocculated colloidal systems may be made to form dispersed suspensions by simply reducing the electrolyte concentration and that this process can be easily reversed by adding electrolyte to the suspension. While the process of flocculation/deflocculation is readily reversed in suspension, it is not so easily reversed in porous materials such as soils and the old saying that prevention is better than the cure is apposite.

In discussing the permeability of sodic soils Quirk (1957) used the term flocculation in a broad sense to cover all phenomena resulting from particle interaction. Rowell *et al.* (1969) have established correspondence between concentrations at which permeability decreases take place and the concentration at which increased swelling of oriented aggregates of the clay extracted from the soil is observed.

Further work on the nature of ion segregation in forming calcium-rich and sodium-rich surface phases within a soil mass, on pore size distribution and on particle interaction is required before the behaviour of clay particles saturated to varying degrees with sodium can be fully understood. It is of some interest to note that even when suspensions containing single elementary sheets of calcium montmorillonite are prepared the system is metastable and ultimately the particles condense into primary minima to give quasi-crystals (FitzSimmons *et al.* 1970).

Colloid chemists, clay mineralogists and soil scientists have a good appreciation of the factors involved in particle interaction, but the exact quantitative prediction of many of the phenomena in terms of basic physio-chemical forces requires further research.

5. ELECTROLYTE LEVEL AND SOIL PERMEABILITY

Quirk and Schofield (1955) measured the permeability of soils saturated to varying degrees with exchangeable sodium. For each level of exchangeable sodium they obtained a threshold concentration which was defined as that concentration of electrolyte at which the clay particle interaction (that is domain swelling and deflocculation) had an appreciable effect in decreasing the permeability. The given degree of sodium saturation of the soil colloids was attained by leaching with a relatively concentrated solution with a known $Na^+/\sqrt{Ca^{2+}}$ ratio. When equilibrium was attained, this solution was successively diluted in accordance with the Gapon equation and the permeability was measured at each dilution. Figure 1 was obtained by plotting the threshold concentrations obtained in the above manner against the exchangeable sodium percentage on the soil colloids.

The usefulness of such a relationship may be easily seen by referring to a

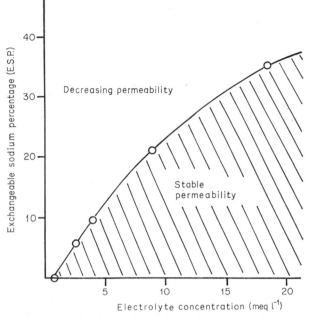

Fig. 1. Threshold concentration in relation to the exchangeable sodium percentage. Note that the ordinate is a soil property and the abscissa is a property of the irrigation water.

soil containing 20% exchangeable sodium. If the soil were to be irrigated with a water less concentrated than 10 meq l^{-1}, then structural disruption would take place and the extent of this disruption would be greater, the lower the electrolyte concentration.

The relationship shown in Fig. 2 between $Na^+/\sqrt{Ca^{2+}}$ and electrolyte concentraton may be expressed in the form

$$X = 0.56 \frac{Na^+}{\sqrt{Ca^{2+}}} + 0.6 \tag{3}$$

in which X is the electrolyte concentration required to prevent deflocculation for a particular value of $Na^+/\sqrt{Ca^{2+}}$. It should be noted that equation (3) does not contain any characteristics of the soil. Such an expression is useful in two circumstances. Firstly, when the $Na^+/\sqrt{Ca^{2+}}$ of the saturated extract of a soil is known then the electrolyte level in the irrigation water required to maintain the permeability can be predicted. Secondly, if a non-sodic soil is being irrigated with a water which is likely to increase the exchangeable sodium percentage on the soil colloids then equation (3) can be used to predict the likely effect the irrigation water will have on the soil permeability as the soil approaches equilibrium with the $Na^+/\sqrt{Ca^{2+}}$ value of the water.

McNeal *et al.* (1966), McNeal (1968) and Rowell *et al.* (1969) have attained

J. P. Quirk

some measure of success in predicting the permeability of soils to mixed salt solutions on the basis of measured permeability at high salt concentrations and swelling behaviour at a range of electrolyte concentrations for clays saturated to varying degrees with sodium.

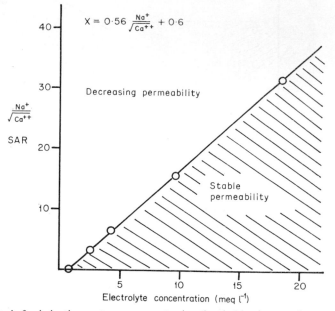

Fig. 2. Basis for irrigation water assessment using threshold concentration concept and the Gapon equation. Note that both the ordinate and abscissa could be characteristics of an irrigation water.

6. APPLICATION OF THRESHOLD CONCENTRATION CONCEPTS

The results of Quirk and Schofield (1955) just discussed indicate that it is possible to maintain the permeability of a soil irrespective of the degree of sodium saturation by using a sufficiently concentrated electrolyte solution or in practice by the addition of gypsum or another electrolyte to the irrigation water. For a sodic soil the aim is to replace sodium by calcium. This is more effectively done if the soil permeability can be maintained during the reclamation.

Quirk and Schofield (1955) used some results of McGeorge and Fuller (1950) to explain the usefulness of the threshold concentration concept. Cajon sandy loam is usually irrigated with Colorado River water, but during the years 1946 to 1948 there was little river water available, and it was necessary to pump water from an underground supply. This water contained

50 meq of sodium and 8 meq of calcium per litre and the figures given for the exchangeable sodium percentage for a number of samples of the soil after irrigation with this water for 3 years vary between 19 and 34 with 25 as the mean. The value of 25 is in good agreement with a calculation using the Gapon equation for this water. Such a soil would require 11 meq of electrolyte per litre of irrigation water to maintain flocculation. These workers report that when river water was again available in 1949 the soil froze up. The river water contained 3·9 meq of electrolyte per litre. If 8 meq of calcium ions were added to this river water for each irrigation until the majority of the sodium had been replaced satisfactory soil conditions would have been maintained and it would then have been possible to use the river water without the addition of calcium for irrigation.

Alternatively if as little as one-sixth of the well water were added to the river water this trouble could have been avoided. This proportion could subsequently have been successively decreased until it was again possible to use river water alone.

Following the above suggestion Reeve and Bower (1960) used mixtures of Salton Sea water and Colorado River water to hasten the reclamation of a saline soil from Oasis Reclamation Farm in Coachella Valley, California. Direct reclamation with Colorado River water reduced the permeability of the soil to 0·02 cm day^{-1}, and the reclamation took 120 days, whereas stepwise reclamation involving leaching successively with $1+3$, $1+15$, and $1+63$ Salton Sea water + Colorado River water (that is dilutions of the sea water of 4, 16 and 64) maintained a high permeability (0·49 cm hr^{-1}) and completed the reclamation to the use of Colorado River water in 20 days, the total addition being 6% sea water and 94% river water. In certain circumstances the growth of a crop may have to be delayed until reclamation has proceeded for some time.

Reeve and Doering (1966) have presented equations which describe the reclamation process in terms of a leaching series using successive dilutions of a divalent cation-containing high-salt water and equations are developed for calculating the amount of water required for reclaiming sodic soils based on the composition of the water, the exchangeable sodium status of the soil, and the rate at which the applied water is diluted.

The irrigation of a grey soil of heavy texture in western N.S.W. provides another example of the way in which the threshold concept can be applied (Davidson and Quirk 1961). The soil contained 23% exchangeable sodium. The irrigation water had an electrolyte concentration of 1 meq l^{-1} and when the soil was irrigated with this water it dispersed to a considerable extent (see Plates 1–3 in Davidson and Quirk 1961) and on subsequent drying formed a hard crust with the result that very poor establishment of sown subterranean clover plants resulted. The addition of 10 meq of Ca^{++} per litre as gypsum greatly enhanced establishment. Furthermore, once the

7

pasture was established the build-up in organic matter obviated the necessity for the continued use of gypsum in the irrigation water even though only a proportion of the exchangeable sodium was removed from the surface 15 cm of soil.

7. FACTORS MODIFYING THE EFFECTS OF EXCHANGEABLE SODIUM

McNeal and Coleman (1966) investigated the permeability of a number of soils saturated to varying degrees with sodium. They noted that soils high in kaolinite and sesquioxides or in amorphous materials were stable even at low electrolyte concentrations. Thus cementing agents may considerably influence the effect of exchangeable sodium. This has been demonstrated in studies which use the sodium ion and a range of electrolyte concentrations as a 'chemical hammer' to see what swelling pressures the soil aggregate can withstand without disruption. Emerson (1954) described a method of estimating the cohesion of moist soil aggregates in which he sought a limiting dilution of sodium chloride at which a bed of soil aggregates became impermeable as a result of the swelling pressure attaining a value which was sufficient to disrupt the soil aggregates. In the method the exchange complex of the soil is first saturated with sodium and then the bed of aggregates of standard size was brought into equilibrium with successively more dilute solutions of sodium chloride, the permeability being measured at each stage. By using a modified form of this method (Dettmann and Emerson 1959) Greenland *et al.* (1962) have demonstrated marked differences in permeability of red-brown earth aggregates which had supported several years of pasture as compared with the behaviour of aggregates from a wheat-fallow rotation. This work indicates the effectiveness of organic matter as a cementing agent even when the soil is sodium-saturated. In a similar study Deshpande *et al.* (1968) have concluded that the changes in physical properties brought about by dilute acid (0·05N HCl) treatment was due to the removal of 'active' oxides containing aluminium, iron and silicon.

If aggregates of soils stabilized by organic matter or active oxides are stable when sodium-saturated in dilute sodium chloride solutions then such aggregates, when only partially saturated with sodium, would also be stable. Thus the threshold concept is applicable to arid and semi-arid soils whose structure would not be appreciably affected by cementing agents.

REFERENCES

Aylmore, L. A. G., and Quirk, J. P. (1959). *Nature (Lond.)* **187**, 1046.

Aylmore, L. A. G., and Quirk, J. P. (1962). *Proc. Nat. Clay Conf. U.S.A.* **9**, 104.

Aylmore, L. A. G., and Quirk, J. P. (in press). *Proc. Soil Sci. Soc. Amer.*

Baver, L. D. (1940). *Soil Physics*. John Wiley and Sons, New York.

Bodman, G. B., and Fireman, M. (1950). *Trans. 4th Int. Congr. Soil Sci.* **1**, 397.

Bolt, G. H. (1967). *Neth. J. agric. Res.* **15**, 81.

Davidson, J. L., and Quirk, J. P. (1961). *Aust. J. agric. Res.* **12**, 100.

Deshpande, T. L., Greenland, D. J., and Quirk, J. P. (1968). *J. Soil Sci.* **19**, 108.

Dettmann, M. G., and Emerson, W. W. (1959). *J. Soil Sci.* **10**, 215.

Emerson, W. W. (1954). *J. Soil Sci.* **5**, 233.

Fireman, M., and Bodman, G. B. (1939). *Proc. Soil Sci. Soc. Amer.* **4**, 71.

FitzSimmons, R. F., Posner, A. M., and Quirk, J. P. (1970). *Israel J. Chem.* **8**, 301.

Gapon, E. N. (1933). *Zhur. Obshch. Khim.* (*Jour. Gen. Chem.*) **3**, 144.

Greenland, D. J., Lindstrom, G. R., and Quirk, J. P. (1962). *Proc. Soil Sci. Soc. Amer.* **26**, 366.

Helfferich, F. (1962). *Ion Exchange*. McGraw–Hill, New York.

Kemper, W. D., and Quirk, J. P. (1970). *Proc. Soil Sci. Soc. Amer.* **34**, 347.

Kruyt, H. R. (1952). *Colloid Science*. Elsevier, Amsterdam.

Langmuir, I. (1938). *J. Chem. Phys.* **6**, 873.

McGeorge, W. T., and Fuller, W. H. (1950). *Trans. 4th Int. Congr. Soil Sci.* **1**, 400.

McNeal, B. L. (1968). *Proc. Soil Sci. Soc. Amer.* **32**, 190.

McNeal, B. L., and Coleman, N. T. (1966). *Proc. Soil Sci. Soc. Amer.* **30**, 308.

McNeal, B. L., Norvell, W. A., and Coleman, N. T. (1966). *Proc. Soil Sci. Soc. Amer.* **30**, 313.

Quirk, J. P. (1957). *Trans. 3rd Congr. Int. Comm. Irrig. Drain.* (San Francisco). Q8, 115.

Quirk, J. P. (1968). *Israel J. Chem.* **6**, 213.

Quirk, J. P., and Aylmore, L. A. G. (1960). *Trans. 7th Int. Congr. Soil Sci.* **2**, 378.

Quirk, J. P., and Panabokke, C. R. (1962). *J. Soil Sci.* **13**, 60.

Quirk, J. P., and Schofield, R. K. (1955). *J. Soil Sci.* **6**, 423.

Reeve, R. C., and Bower, C. A. (1960). *Soil Sci.* **90**, 139.

Reeve, R. C., and Doering, E. J. (1966). *Proc. Soil Sci. Soc. Amer.* **30**, 498.

Richards, L. A. (Ed.) (1954). *Diagnosis and Improvement of Saline and Alkali Soils*. USDA Handbook No. 60.

Rowell, D. L., Payne, D., and Ahmad, N. (1969). *J. Soil Sci.* **20**, 176.

Verwey, E. J. W., and Overbeek, J. Th. G. (1948). *Theory of Stability of Lyophobic Colloids*. Elsevier, New York.

PART III   Physical Processes

Hydrology of Swelling Soils

J. R. PHILIP

Division of Environmental Mechanics, CSIRO, Canberra, A.C.T.

SUMMARY

Not all saline soils swell, and not all swelling soils are subject to salinity problems; but hydrologic difficulties often arise in connexion with the drainage and reclamation of swelling clays in flat landscapes. The paper reviews recent progress in the theory of water equilibrium and movement in swelling soils, and emphasizes that neglect of the fact of swelling may lead to serious errors of interpretation.

The point of departure is the well-established theory of water equilibrium and movement in nonswelling soils. The generalization to swelling soils is described. It is stressed that, in swelling soils, the total potential includes an additional component, *the overburden potential.* Classical concepts of groundwater hydrology, tacitly based on the behaviour of nonswelling soils, fail in many important ways for swelling ones. Aspects which differ profoundly from those of nonswelling soils include the following: equilibrium moisture profiles, the distribution of hydraulic conductivity relative to the water table, the effect of topography on moisture distribution, the variation of specific yield with water table elevation and stratum thickness, and the character of steady and unsteady vertical flows.

1. INTRODUCTION

The papers of the previous sessions have, in essence, set the geochemical and chemical scene; and the group of papers to be presented in this Session III turn now to the physical processes involved in the transport of salt in soils and in underground and surface waters.

By transport we do not, of course, mean just the uniform carriage of salt through a steady system: we are ultimately concerned, rather, with transient situations and with the consequences of disturbing more-or-less steady systems. In these transient or disturbed systems are manifested the processes which are of real interest—such processes as salt accumulation and salt leaching.

The present paper deals with the equilibrium and movement of water in *swelling* soils, and it is as well to remark at once that we use the adjective 'swelling' as shorthand for 'subject to volume-change'. Obviously such soils shrink rather than swell in appropriate circumstances.

Now it is certainly true that not all saline soils are swelling soils and that not all swelling soils are bedevilled by salinity problems: but, for all that, many of the most acute hydrologic difficulties arise in the drainage and reclamation of swelling soils of high colloid content occurring in very flat landscapes. In my opinion, the progress of hydrologic studies of such situations has been retarded by the misplaced application of notions and theories based, either tacitly or explicitly, on the behaviour of *nonswelling* soils and porous media. Until recently nonswelling theory has been applied for the want of anything better. It is my purpose here to review recent progress in the theory of water equilibrium and movement in swelling soils and porous media, and to suggest that neglect of the fact of soil swelling may lead to serious errors of interpretation and to quite misleading diagnoses.

Unfortunately, the theory is relatively complicated and involves rather more mathematics than can be decently or reasonably inflicted on this inter-disciplinary Symposium. I shall strive, therefore, to keep mathematical detail to a minimum and to develop the physical theory in as nontechnical a way as I can. This will, no doubt, irritate some of the specialists; but I shall try to placate them by referring, where possible, to more elaborate treatments elsewhere.

It will be understood that this paper falls naturally between that of Professor Quirk (1971) and that of Dr Peck (1971). Quirk has reviewed the chemistry of saline soils with special reference to their physical properties, including their volume-change characteristics ('swelling properties'). In this paper we take these swelling properties as given and to be used as part of the hydrologic characterization of the soil determining the equilibrium and movement of soil-water. In the same way Peck's review of the mechanics of salt transport in soils implicitly takes the regime of soil-water movement as given and discusses the associated salt movement. I need hardly stress that the topics treated by Quirk, myself, and Peck all overlap and interact in the applications: for example, water movement producing salt movement may induce changes in the constitution of the soil electrolyte solution which alter the swelling and hydrologic properties of the soil; and these changes, in turn, affect the course of water movement; and this influences the course of salt movement; and so on.

2. HYDROLOGY OF NONSWELLING SOILS

At the previous National Hydrology Symposium I gave a review of the theory of water movement in unsaturated nonswelling soils which pretty well covers the introductory ground on nonswelling soils we need to consider here. There (Philip 1964) I mentioned other relevant reviews and monographs; and I now refer you to the following later general treatments of the hydrology of nonswelling soils: Swartzendruber (1966), Miller and Klute (1967), Childs (1967), Philip (1969a), Childs (1969), Philip (1970a). [Not all of the cited literature contains explicit warning that the theory requires modification and extension before it applies to swelling soils.]

I limit the present discussion to the barest outline of the concepts of the nonswelling theory and to some general remarks on its practical consequences. The experts may complain that I am ignoring complications such as hysteresis and soil heterogeneity; but my purpose is to emphasize the difference between the hydrologic behaviour of non-swelling and swelling soils; and this can be brought out without going into complications which are common to both.

The basic concepts of the physical theory of water movement in unsaturated nonswelling soils are as follows:

1.   Water movement is in response to a gradient of total potential Φ made up of moisture potential Ψ and gravitational potential $-z$, so that

$$\Phi = \Psi - z. \tag{1}$$

With these potentials defined per unit weight of water*, z is the vertical coordinate, positive downward.

2.   Darcy's law holds, so that

$$\mathbf{v} = -K\nabla\Phi. \tag{2}$$

$\mathbf{v}$ is the vector flux density of water and K is the hydraulic conductivity.

3.   In appropriate circumstances Ψ and K are unique functions of the volumetric moisture content θ and so constitute a *necessary and sufficient* hydrological characterization of the soil. Combining equations (1) and (2) with the continuity requirement leads to the general partial differential equation describing unsaturated flow in a nonswelling soil. When Ψ and K depend only on θ, this is a nonlinear Fokker–Planck equation, which reduces to a nonlinear diffusion equation for horizontal systems. The 'moisture diffusivity' entering this equation is equal to $K\mathrm{d}\Psi/\mathrm{d}\theta$. Philip (1970a) gives a general review and Philip (1969a) treats, in particular, solutions of the flow equation.

The theory based on these concepts is in general agreement with the hydrostatics and hydrodynamics of nonswelling soils. Later in the paper we compare some consequences of nonswelling theory with those of the extended theory applying to swelling soils. We shall thus gain some insight into the

---

* From the viewpoint of the hydraulic engineer, Ψ and z may be regarded as pressure and gravitational components of 'total head'; from that of the chemist, they are, in appropriate units, components of the partial volumetric Gibbs free energy.

confusion possible if nonswelling theory is used to interpret the hydrology of swelling soils.

3. THE EXTENSION TO SWELLING SOILS

In nature soil volume-change tends to be *one-dimensional* in the direction normal to the soil surface. Swelling soils occur usually in flat landscapes, so the direction of volume-change can be taken as the vertical. Although individual soil aggregates may change volume three-dimensionally, the horizontal constraints on any natural mass of soil are such that only the vertical dimension of any bulk volume element in it is free to change. The plan dimensions and area of a paddock of swelling soil remain constant as the soil moisture content varies: it is only its elevation which changes. We therefore limit ourselves here to considering one-dimensional volume-change. It is fortunate that this suffices: problems involving three-dimensional bulk volume-change are much more difficult, and their analysis requires appeal to some theory of stress distribution. This aspect of soil mechanics is not in a very satisfactory state, so that it is an attractive aspect of the one-dimensional analysis that it does not rely on any particular soil-mechanical theory.

Three basic new elements enter the extension of the non-swelling theory to one-dimensional flow and volume-change in swelling soils:

1.   For systems involving self-weight and/or surface loading (including the vertical systems we consider primarily here) equation (1) must be generalized to include the *overburden potential* Ω (Philip 1969b), and is thus replaced by

$$\Phi = \Psi + \Omega - z. \qquad (3)$$

It is convenient to take Ψ as the 'unloaded' moisture potential, and Ω is then the contribution to Φ due to the normal stress P. Note that tensiometers *in situ* in the field measure $\Psi + \Omega$, not simply Ψ.

2.   In unsteady swelling systems the soil particles are, in general, in motion, so that it must be recognized (Gersevanov 1937) that Darcy's law applies to flow relative to the particles, so that equation (2) must be generalized to

$$v_r = -K \nabla \Phi, \qquad (4)$$

with v_r the vector flux density of water relative to the particles.

3.   Necessary and sufficient hydrodynamic characterization now requires in addition to K and Ψ, the void ratio function* e and particle specific gravity γ_s. In appropriate horizontal systems K, Ψ, and e may be taken as

* e is the ratio of void volume to particle volume.

functions of θ only, or, more conveniently, of the moisture ratio $\vartheta [=(1+e)\theta]$. The approximation that e is a function of ϑ only is, as we shall see, useful also in vertical systems, but it must not be overooked that, strictly, e depends on P as well as on ϑ (Youngs and Towner 1970; Philip 1970b).

Our primary concern here is with vertical systems, but we note in passing that the analysis of certain unsteady horizontal swelling systems is fairly straightforward: it involves a nonlinear diffusion equation mathematically similar to that describing comparable nonswelling systems, but with ϑ in place of θ and the ordinary space coordinate replaced by a material, or Lagrangian, coordinate (Raats 1965; Smiles and Rosenthal 1968; Philip 1968; Philip and Smiles 1969). The results of such analyses are of interest not only in connexion with the hydrology of swelling soils, but also in soil mechanics (Philip and Smiles 1969; Smiles and Poulos 1969).

4. HYDROSTATICS IN SWELLING SOILS

By a derivation due to Professor G. H. Bolt, it is readily shown (Philip 1970b) that

$$\Omega(\vartheta, P) = \int_0^P (\partial e/\partial \vartheta)_P \, dP_{\vartheta=\vartheta}$$

which is conveniently rewritten as

$$\Omega = \alpha P \text{ with } \alpha(\vartheta, P) = P^{-1} \int_0^P (\partial e/\partial \vartheta) \, dP_{\vartheta=\vartheta} \tag{5}$$

For equilibrium in a vertical soil column

$$\Phi(z) = \text{constant} = -Z. \tag{6}$$

Without loss of generality we may take the origin of z at the soil surface, and Z is then the 'water table depth'. We note that

$$P(z) = P(0) + \int_0^z \gamma \, dz, \tag{7}$$

where $P(0)$ is the vertical stress due to surface loading and γ is the apparent wet specific gravity, defined by

$$\gamma = (\vartheta + \gamma_s)/(1+e).$$

The particle specific gravity γ_s is taken to be greater than 1 in the further developments: it is about $2 \cdot 7$ for mineral soils.

Combining equations (3), (5), (6) and (7), we obtain the equation for moisture equilibrium in the vertical

$$\Psi - z + \alpha \left[P(0) + \int_0^z \gamma \, dz \right] = -Z. \tag{8}$$

With γ_s and characterizing functions $\Psi(\vartheta)$ and $e(\vartheta, P)$ known, equation (8) may be solved to yield the equilibrium moisture profile corresponding to any given value of Z.

The analysis is considerably simplified and leads to useful general results, however, if α and γ can be taken as functions of ϑ only. Soil-mechanical data and theoretical calculations indicate that the P-dependence of α is, at most, weak, and also that γ is a slowly varying function of P. The calculations suggest that the analysis treating α and γ as functions of ϑ only may be applied without serious error to, say, the top 10 m of the soil (in which the P-range is about 20 m). We make use here of the simplified analysis based on this understanding.

Philip (1969b) showed that there are then three classes of solution of equation (8) and, in consequence, three distinct types of equilibrium moisture profile. These are defined through ϑ_p, the moisture ratio at which γ assumes its maximum value. ϑ_p is designated the 'pycnotatic point' (Greek $\pi\upsilon\kappa\nu\acute{o}\tau\alpha\tau\sigma\varsigma = $ 'densest'). We have: (a) *Hydric* profiles for which the surface moisture ratio $\vartheta_0 > \vartheta_p$ and ϑ decreases with increasing depth; (b) *Pycnotatic* profiles for which $\vartheta_0 = \vartheta_p$; ϑ is constant in depth and equal to ϑ_p; (c) *Xeric* profiles for which $\vartheta_0 < \vartheta_p$ and ϑ increases with depth.

5. ILLUSTRATIVE EXAMPLE. FAILURE OF CLASSICAL CONCEPTS

The significance of these results is illustrated by reference to the soil characterized by the $\Psi(\vartheta)$ and $e(\vartheta, P)$ functions of Figs. 1 and 2 and $\gamma_s = 2 \cdot 7$ These functions are in general consonance with the experimental data on swelling clay soils. Figure 2 shows $\gamma(\vartheta, P)$ also.

Figure 3 presents a sequence of typical equilibrium moisture profiles as the water table depth increases from 0 to 250 m. The pycnotatic profile $\vartheta = \vartheta_p = 0 \cdot 547$ corresponds to $Z = 23 \cdot 4$ m. These profiles are, of course, wholly different in character from equilibrium profiles in a nonswelling soil in which ϑ always increases with z. Figure 4 compares profiles for our illustrative swelling soil and for a nonswelling one with the same $\Psi(\vartheta)$ function. For the nonswelling soil the moisture distribution is invariant with respect to the water table; for the swelling soil, on the other hand, it depends strongly on Z. Any attempt to interpret the profiles in the swelling soil through classical nonswelling concepts would be doomed to failure.

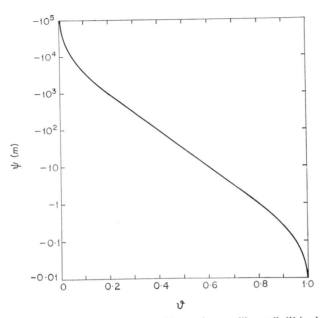

Fig. 1. The $\Psi(\vartheta)$ function adopted for the illustrative swelling soil. Ψ is the moisture potential, ϑ is the moisture ratio.

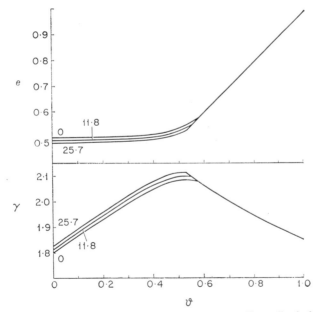

Fig. 2. The functions $e(\vartheta, P)$ and $\gamma(\vartheta, P)$ for the illustrative swelling soil. e is the void ratio, γ the apparent wet specific gravity, and P the normal stress. The numerals on the curves denote values of P in m.

J. R. Philip

It follows also that the distribution of hydraulic conductivity relative to the water table is entirely different in swelling soils from that in the non-swelling soils of conventional groundwater hydrology. Figure 6 compares these distributions for our illustrative nonswelling and swelling soils. Figure 6(*a*) shows schematically the distribution of *K* for the nonswelling

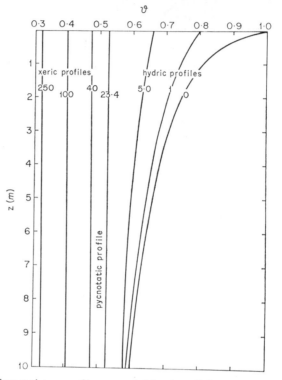

Fig. 3. Equilibrium moisture profiles computed for the soil characterized by Figs. 1 and 2 and $\gamma_s = 2\cdot7$. *z* is depth beneath the surface. The numerals on the profiles denote values of *Z*, the depth to the water table in m.

soil which corresponds to the distribution of ϑ of Fig. 4(*a*); and Fig. 6(*b*) gives for the swelling soil the profiles of *K* corresponding to those of ϑ in Fig. 4(*b*). Figure 5 shows the $K(\vartheta)$ function adopted for the swelling soil (Philip 1969*b*).

We see that serious errors are to be expected if groundwater behaviour in swelling soils is interpreted in terms of ideas and techniques established for nonswelling soils. For example, evidence of conductivity decreasing with increasing depth beneath the water table would be taken classically to imply heterogeneity, but it is clear from Fig. 6(*b*) that behaviour of this kind will be observed for any hydric profile in a *homogeneous* swelling soil. Perhaps even more disturbing to conventional expectations are the increases in K above the water table shown in Fig. 6(b).

Figure 7 illustrates another important point. At equilibrium in non-swelling soils, the surfaces of constant moisture ratio are horizontal planes, and the distribution is unaffected by surface topography. In swelling soils, however, the dependence of ϑ on elevation alone ceases to hold good, since variations in surface topography produce variations in the overburden potential at any given elevation.

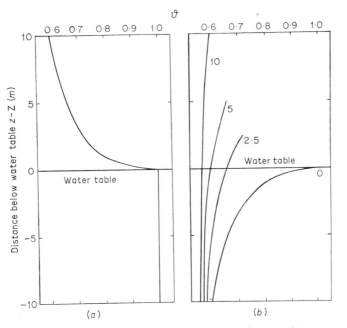

Fig. 4. Equilibrium moisture distributions relative to the water table (a) for a nonswelling soil characterized by Fig. 1; and (b) for the swelling soil characterized by Figs. 1 and 2 and $\gamma_s = 2\cdot7$. The single curve of (a) holds for all Z, the curve terminating in each case at the soil surface, i.e. at $z - Z = -Z$. In (b) numerals on the curves signify values of Z, the depth to the water table in m.

Streams, channels, lakes, swamps, puddles, and irrigation furrows may adjoin and/or overlie fine-textured soils in which the moisture ratio decreases rapidly away from the water body, as in Fig. 7(b). When little or no water movement into the soil is evident, it is often supposed that such distributions represent disequilibrium states which persist because of the very small hydraulic conductivity of the soil.

No other explanation can be offered by classical hydrological theory which neglects the consequence of swelling. However, moisture differentials of this character will exist in swelling soils *even when a true equilibrium is*

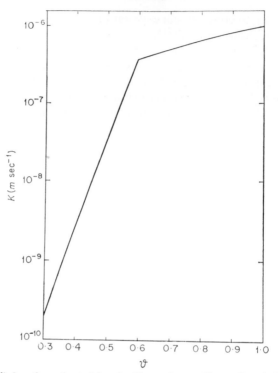

Fig. 5. The $K(\vartheta)$ function adopted for the illustrative swelling soil. K is hydraulic conductivity.

realized. In such cases the differential persists, not because of a lack of hydraulic conductivity, but because of a lack of difference in total potential.

Another contrast between swelling and nonswelling soils concerns 'specific yield'. The variation of specific yield with water table elevation and stratum thickness is basically different in the two cases (Philip 1969*b*).

6. DISCUSSION

These limitations of classical hydrological theory arise from its failure to recognize the contribution to Φ of Ω, the overburden potential*. The influence of swelling on soil-water behaviour may be summarized in the statement that the net effect of gravity is approximately $(1-\alpha\gamma)$ times that in a nonswelling soil. This factor is a function of the moisture ratio. For a

---

* Not that all authors have been unaware of overburden effects in hydrology. Schofield (1935) recognized that Φ should include an overburden contribution. Coleman and Croney (1952) introduced the 'compressibility factor' α in the course of work closely related to that reviewed here. Collis-George (1961) discussed effects of surface loading, but was apparently unaware of the Coleman-Croney studies. Rose, Stern, and Drummond (1965) were, however, influenced by them.

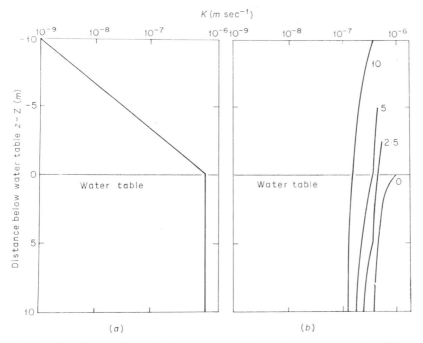

Fig. 6. Profiles of hydraulic conductivity corresponding to the moisture profiles of Fig. 4.

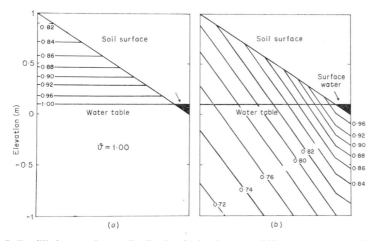

Fig. 7. Equilibrium moisture distribution in landscapes of illustrative nonswelling soil (*a*) and swelling soil (*b*). Surface water ponded to maximum depth 0·1 m. Datum of elevation taken at lowest point of soil surface. Horizontal scale is arbitrary and free to vary from point to point. Calculation of (*b*) assumes soil surface is not too steep.

8

mineral soil, it is about -1 in the normal range (the wet end of the moisture range where $e = \vartheta$), decreases to 0 as ϑ decreases to ϑ_p, and approaches $+1$ as $\alpha \to 0$ at small values of ϑ.

7. VERTICAL FLOWS IN SWELLING SOILS

These deviations from classical behaviour carry over into the phenomena of steady and unsteady vertical flows in swelling soils. The theory of the steady flows is developed by combining the one-dimensional vertical form of equation (4) with equations (3), (5), and (7). Solution of the resulting equation indicates the possible flows. The results (Philip 1969c, 1970a) are complicated. Not surprisingly, they differ profoundly from those for non-swelling soils. For example, steady upward flows may occur against a moisture gradient.

The analysis can be extended to embrace *unsteady* vertical flows, including such processes as infiltration and capillary rise. The mathematical details become rather elaborate (Philip 1969c, 1970a), and only limited calculations have been completed at this stage. It can be said, however, that, as we might expect, the overall character of unsteady vertical flows in swelling soils is significantly different from that in nonswelling soils. In keeping with the seemingly anomalous effect of gravity in swelling soils, the course of infiltration into a swelling soil has analogies with that of capillary rise into a nonswelling one; and, conversely, capillary rise into a swelling soil may exhibit classical infiltration behaviour.

REFERENCES

Childs, E. C. (1967). *Adv. Hydroscience* **4**, 73.

Childs, E. C. (1969). *An Introduction to the Physical Basis of Soil Water Phenomena.* John Wiley and Sons, London.

Coleman, J. D., and Croney, D. (1952). *Rd. Res. Lab. Note* RN/1709/JDC. DC. (unpublished).

Collis-George, N. (1961). *Soil Sci.* **91**, 306.

Gersevanov, N. M. (1937). *The Foundations of Dynamics of Soils* 3rd Edn. Stroiizdat, Moscow–Leningrad.

Miller, E. E., and Klute, A. (1967). In *Irrigation of Agricultural Lands.* (Eds. R. M. Hagan, H. R. Haise and T. W. Edminster.) p. 209. Am. Soc. Agronomy, Madison, Wisconsin.

Peck, A. J. (1971). In *Salinity and Water Use.* (Eds. T. Talsma, J. R. Philip.) p. 109. Macmillan, London.

Philip, J. R. (1964). In *Water Resources, Use and Management.* p. 257. Melbourne Univ. Press.

Philip, J. R. (1968). *Aust. J. Soil Res.* **6**, 249.

Philip, J. R. (1969*a*). *Adv. Hydroscience* **5**, 215.

Philip, J. R. (1969*b*). *Aust. J. Soil Res.* **7**, 99, 121.

Philip, J. R. (1969*c*). *Water Resources Res.* **5**, 1070.

Philip, J. R. (1970*a*). *Ann. Rev. Fluid Mech.* **2**, 177.

Philip, J. R. (1970*b*). *Water Resources Res.* **6**, 1248.

Philip, J. R., and Smiles, D. E. (1969). *Aust. J. Soil Res.* **7**, 1.

Quirk, J. P. (1971). In *Salinity and Water Use*. (Eds. T. Talsma, J. R. Philip.) p. 79. Macmillan, London.

Raats, P. A. C. (1965). Ph. D. Thesis, Univ. Illinois.

Rose, C. W., Stern, W. R., and Drummond, J. E. (1965). *Aust. J. Soil Res.* **3**, 1.

Schofield, R. K. (1935). *Trans. 3rd Int. Congr. Soil Sci*, **2**, 37.

Smiles, D. E., and Poulos, H. G. (1969). *Aust. J. Soil Res.* **7**, 285.

Smiles, D. E., and Rosenthal, M. J. (1968). *Aust. J. Soil Res.* **6**, 237.

Swartzendruber, D. (1966). *Adv. Agronomy* **18**, 327.

Youngs, E. G., and Towner, G. D. (1970). *Water Resources Res.* **6**, 1246.

Transport of Salts in Unsaturated and Saturated Soils

A. J. PECK

Division of Soils, CSIRO, Wembley, Western Australia

SUMMARY

In almost all conditions in the field, transport of soluble salts in soils results from movement (convection) of the soil solution as a whole, and molecular diffusion within the soil solution.

At very slow rates of solution flow, molecular diffusion is the dominant transport mechanism, but diffusion in solution is a very slow process. The presence of the solid and gaseous phases in soils, and exchange or adsorption of solutes result in even lower diffusion coefficients in soils than in bulk solution. In the vicinity of plant roots, molecular diffusion may be the dominant transport process at somewhat greater rates of convection due to the possible association of a relatively high concentration gradient and low nutrient concentration.

In general, molecular diffusion interacts with the convection of solutions and each process contributes to the dispersion of solutes. Thus inert solutes are mostly transported at the average velocity of the solution, but there is a superimposed dispersion of solutes about the mean position at any instant. Mathematically this dispersion may be treated as a diffusion-like process. Solutes which experience adsorption or exchange on soil surfaces travel at less than the average pore velocity. Ion exchange theories can be useful in interpreting the transport in these conditions, but there is at present, no generally satisfactory theory.

The very broad spectrum of microscopic solution velocities in structured or unsaturated soils results in a large dispersion of solutes. When most of the movement of solution occurs in only a small part of the liquid-filled pore space, inert solutes can travel appreciably faster than the pore velocity averaged over all the solution content. Negative adsorption of solute has a similar effect.

1. INTRODUCTION

The success of an irrigation project, or of dry-land farming, is dependent, amongst other factors, on the concentration of salts in the vicinity of plant roots. It is inevitable that salts are added to the soil in rain or irrigation water, and the weathering of rocks in or on the soil may make a further contribution of soluble material. These salts must be leached from the root zone by some artificial or natural process in order that salinity should not reach a harmful level.

The same processes by which salts leave the root zone are responsible for the movement within the soil profile of fertilizers, herbicides and insecticides which may be applied. Thus an understanding of the processes of transport of these soluble materials is important for optimal management of the soil for plant growth.

More generally, the transport of solutes in porous media is of interest in other technologies. Some examples are groundwater hydrology, disposal of wastes (chemical, radioactive, industrial, sanitary), chemical engineering, petroleum reservoir engineering, and mineral extraction. From these studies, and those related to agriculture, there has accumulated in the last 10 to 20 years a large body of information and a fairly detailed understanding of solute transport in porous materials.

This article is not intended as an exhaustive current review of the subject in general, or even of its essentially agricultural aspects. It is believed that the present purposes will be better met by a discussion of the basic effects and, where possible, their relative importance in the plant environment.

2. FORCE FIELDS MOVING SALTS IN SOILS

Groenevelt and Bolt (1969) have considered the nonequilibrium thermodynamics of the soil-water-salt system in which salt movement can occur in response to bulk movement of the soil solution, or to gradients of temperature, salt concentration, or electric potential. They argue that, with a temperature gradient of order 10^2 Km^{-1}, the salt flux due to the thermodiffusive effect is so small that this effect can be generally neglected relative to the others.

Since electric potential gradients are not usually *imposed* on a soil, it is reasonable to neglect also the electrophoretic transport of salt. [Note that electric potential gradients are often observed in soils, but usually these are the *result* of the tendency for differently charged ions to move at different velocities (the diffusion potential) and/or the tendency of bulk flow to separate charges in the electric double layer (the streaming potential).]

Thus the major processes involved in salt transport in soils are the convection or bulk movement of the soil solution, and molecular or ionic diffusion within the solution.

It is convenient for discussion to consider first the transport of salts through soils with essentially no bulk motion of the solution, and then to consider the role of convection. A criterion for the neglect of convection will be introduced in a later section. When the flow of water is so slow that this criterion is satisfied we refer to the soil-water as being 'quasi-stationary'.

3. TRANSPORT OF SOLUTES IN QUASI-STATIONARY SOIL-WATER

When the effects of bulk motion of the soil solution are essentially negligible, molecular or ionic diffusion is the dominant mechanism for salt transport in soils.

Diffusion of solutes in bulk solution has been studied in considerable detail (Vinograd and McBain 1941). Transport occurs according to Fick's law which, in combination with the requirement for conservation of matter, yields the equation

$$\frac{\partial c}{\partial t} = D\left(\frac{\partial^2 c}{\partial x^2} + \frac{\partial^2 c}{\partial y^2} + \frac{\partial^2 c}{\partial z^2}\right) \tag{1}$$

where c is the concentration of the solute at position (x, y, z) in orthogonal coordinates, t is time and D is the diffusion coefficient or diffusivity of the solute relative to the solvent. This equation assumes that D is a constant. In cases where D varies appreciably with the solution concentration, a modification to equation (1) is necessary.

The diffusion of salts through water in soils has been studied with increasing intensity, particularly in connection with plant nutrition (Klute and Letey 1958; Porter *et al.* 1960; Schofield and Graham-Bryce 1960; Nye 1968). Almost any recent number of *J. Soil Sci.* or *Proc. Soil Sci. Soc. Amer.* includes a paper on this topic, the total number of references being too large for individual mention here.

For our purposes the important point is that the diffusion coefficient for salt transport in a soil is almost always found to be less than that of the same molecule or ion in bulk solution, which for many aqueous solutions is of order 10^{-9} m^2 s^{-1} (Weast 1969).

(a) Factors Affecting Solute Diffusion in Soils

The diffusion coefficient for transport in soils is usually defined on the basis of unit area of the soil. Since the solution phase occupies only a fraction (equal to the moisture content) of any unit area of the soil, there is a reduced transport which is usually taken into account in a modified diffusivity often referred to as the 'effective' diffusion coefficient (Klute and Letey 1958; Porter *et al.* 1960; Gardner 1965). Some authors, however, prefer to express the role of the moisture content explicitly, and do not include this in the effective diffusivity (Gardner 1965, 1968).

Another factor included in the effective diffusion coefficient is the tortuosity of the diffusion path through soil-water. As the diffusion path in the solution exceeds the straight line separation of points in the medium, the actual concentration gradient in the solution is less than that in the medium as a whole.

These factors result in a dependence of the diffusion coefficient in soil on moisture content. As an example, the diffusivity of Cl^- in a loam was observed to be about 8×10^{-11} m^2 s^{-1} at a volumetric moisture content of 0·10 (Porter *et al.* 1960). This is a reduction by a factor about 25 from the bulk solution value.

Philip (1968) has considered the role of 'dead-end' pores in transient diffusion, and shown that the apparent diffusion coefficient after some time exceeds the initial value by an amount which depends on the ratio of dead-end to 'active' porosity. As Philip (1967) has noted, in the steady-state the presence of dead-end pore-space is of no consequence; it is simply a component of tortuosity. A somewhat similar situation exists in transport of adsorbed or exchanged ions where the transient diffusion coefficient will differ from that in the steady-state.

The reversible exchange of ions, or adsorption on the surfaces of soil particles, increases the capacity of soil to hold solutes. This effect can be taken into account in a reduced effective transport coefficient for transient diffusion (Gardner 1965; Lindstrom *et al.* 1968). By similar reasoning, some increase of the transient diffusion coefficient of negatively adsorbed ions over the steady-state diffusivity could be expected. van Schaik *et al.* (1966), however, interpret their data as indicating both steady-state and transient diffusivities of Na^+ in Na-bentonite which exceed that in bulk solution. It is difficult to reconcile these conclusions with the above model. van Schaik and Kemper (1966) claimed 'good agreement' between transient and steady-state diffusivities of negatively adsorbed Cl^-, although the transient values are the larger as we would expect.

(b) Transport of Solutes by Diffusion

When the effective diffusion coefficient is known for a particular solute and soil, and a problem can be specified adequately, it is often possible to make use of known solutions (Carslaw and Jaeger 1959) of equation (1) to predict salt transport. These solutions to diffusion problems are characterized by the dimensionless group of terms L^2/Dt. This allows a simple order-of-magnitude estimate of the distance L which a solute with diffusion coefficient D will move in time t. Thus we estimate that a salt with $D = 10^{-9}$ m^2 s^{-1} will diffuse a distance L of order 0·2 m in $t = 3·15 \times 10^7$ sec (1 year).

We may also calculate from Fick's law for steady diffusion,

$$q = -D \, \partial c / \partial x \tag{2}$$

where q is the flux density of diffusant, that with $D=10^{-9}$ m^2 s^{-1} and a concentration gradient $\partial c/\partial x = 1\cdot5 \times 10^2$ kg m^{-4} (sea water and fresh water separated by a distance of 0·2 m) the annual transport of salt would be 5 kg m^{-2}.

Note that the diffusion coefficient for a salt in soil at an intermediate moisture content will usually have a smaller value than that assumed in these examples, and so we might reasonably expect a somewhat slower transport in most practical situations.

(c) A Criterion for Neglecting Convection

A reasonable criterion for the neglect of convection is that the convective flux density of solute should be small in comparison with that due to molecular diffusion. That is, convection may be neglected provided that

$$|v|c \ll D|\partial c/\partial x| \qquad (3)$$

where v is the microscopic velocity of the solution. (Note that v generally differs from the average solution velocity. See Section 4 for a discussion of the distribution of microscopic velocities.)

Taking as orders of magnitude $D=10^{-9}$ m^2 s^{-1} and $(1/c)(\partial c/\partial x)=10$ m^{-1} (at the mid-point of the steady gradient of the above example), the criterion of equation (3) becomes $|v| \ll 10^{-8}$ ms^{-1}. Thus we conclude that at a mean velocity of about 10^{-9} ms^{-1} (corresponding to a flux density of solution of 10^{-10} ms^{-1} at a volumetric moisture content of 0·10) or less, molecular diffusion would move more salt than would convection. In nature, with periodic additions of water to the soil, we expect such extremely low seepage velocities to be rare except, perhaps, in arid regions where the mean excess of rainfall over evapotranspiration is minimal.

It will be clear from equation (3) that diffusion is more important where an appreciable solute concentration gradient is associated with a low solute concentration. This situation may occur for nutrients in the vicinity of plant roots. It does appear, however, that convection is almost always the dominant mechanism in the movement of salts over appreciable distances through soils. In the following Section we will see that molecular or ionic diffusion cannot be disregarded since its interactions with convection are important in many situations.

4. TRANSPORT OF SALTS WITH BULK MOVEMENT OF SOIL-WATER

The detailed understanding of any problem of convective salt transport in soils is dependent on a knowledge of fluid flow in porous media, but this topic is itself far too extensive to be adequately reviewed here. There are many suitable articles to which the reader is referred (Luthin 1957; Schei-degger 1957; Hagan *et al.* 1967; Bear *et al.* 1968; Childs 1969; de Wiest 1969; Philip 1969, 1970). Dr Philip has already discussed some aspects of water movement in swelling soils for this Symposium.

Fluid flow through straight pipes and capillaries may be laminar or turbulent depending on the value of the dimensionless Reynolds number (velocity × characteristic pore size × fluid density/viscosity). The situation in soils is complicated by the tortuosity of the pore-space, but it is found that for Reynolds numbers less than about 1, the flow is proportional to the hydraulic gradient (Darcy's law applies) and the regime is laminar. This covers almost every natural movement of water in soils, and we will always assume in what follows that the flow of solution is laminar.

(a) Transport in a Capillary Tube

Philip (1957, 1969) has investigated in detail the hydrodynamics of fluid flow at very low Reynolds number (Stokes flows) through pore spaces of very simple geometry. An even more simple case, however, is that of steady laminar flow in a straight capillary tube (Poiseuille flow); the distribution of fluid velocities across the tube is known classically to be parabolic. This assumes, as we do throughout this discussion, that the diameter of the tube is large in comparison with the dimensions of solute or solvent molecules. If it could be arranged then, that at some reference time there was a plane interface between two aqueous solutions of different salt concentration (but each of the same density and viscosity with solutes neither positively nor negatively adsorbed) in a capillary tube, subsequent flow would result in a parabolic distortion of the interface. Figure 1(*a*) is a schematic illustration of this distortion as it would appear at various times to an observer travelling with the 'centre-of-gravity' of the interface.

The dispersal of a salt due to convection alone could be entirely reversed, and the original concentration distribution could be recovered, simply by an equivalent amount of convection in the opposite direction. The irreversible effects of diffusion at the interface, however, are of great importance over a considerable range of flow velocities and molecular or ionic diffusion coefficients. See Fig. 1(*b*). Diffusion across streamlines interacts with the convective motion and results in a dispersion of solute which is well under-stood for Poiseuille flow (Taylor 1953, 1954; Aris 1956; Philip 1963). This dispersion can be treated as a diffusion-like process with a transport co-efficient (dispersivity) depending on the flow velocity and commonly exceeding the coefficient of a molecular diffusion in stationary solution. Thus there is a convective motion of solution yielding a displacement of the centre-of-gravity of the interface proportional to time (assuming steady flow) and a diffusion-like dispersion of solute yielding displacement proportional to $(\text{time})^{1/2}$ about the moving centre-of-gravity.

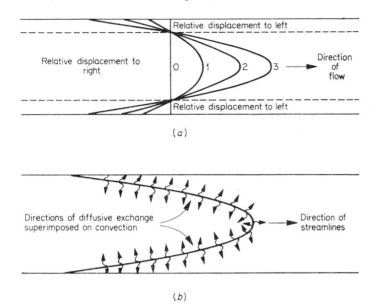

Fig. 1. Schematic illustration of the interactions of convection and molecular diffusion during Poiseuille flow. (*a*) Convective displacements, relative to the 'centre-of-gravity' of the interface, at a sequence of times 0, 1, 2, 3. The area of the interface is increased by convection which accentuates the diffusive mixing. (*b*) Diffusion transports material across streamlines into zones of greater or less, or even reversed, relative convective motion.

(*b*) Transport in Inert Porous Media

Porous media such as soils are not well represented as collections of capillary tubes since the flow paths are not canalized, but extensively cross-linked. That is, in each pore in a soil several flow paths nearly coalesce, and then diverge. The detailed pattern of fluid flow in these circumstances is almost impossible to analyse because of the complicated geometry of the pore-space which defines the fluid-solid boundary. It is quite apparent, however, that there exists in soils the spectrum of microscopic liquid velocities which is fundamental to dispersion in Poiseuille flow. In addition, the lack of canalization of flow paths in soils allows a significant dispersion of material transverse to the macroscopic flow direction.

Day (1956) observed dispersion of the interface between fresh and salt water during flow in sand, and found general agreement with a statistical theory (Scheidegger 1954) which assumes random pore size, shape and orientation.

Considering a porous medium as an assemblage of randomly oriented interconnected capillaries of uniform length, Saffman (1960) developed a theory of dispersion during steady, macroscopically 1-dimensional flow which yields longitudinal and transverse dispersivities in reasonable agreement with experimental data. The dispersivities are determined as functions of the dimensionless Peclet number (fluid velocity × characteristic pore size/molecular diffusion coefficient of solute in bulk solution). Subsequent analyses (Heller, 1963; Raats and Scotter, 1968) confirm the functional relationships between the dispersivities and the Peclet number for steady flow.

Saffman predicts that, for Peclet numbers less than about 1, the dispersivities are essentially equal to the coefficient of molecular diffusion of the solute through the medium. That is, the effects of convection on mixing at the interface are essentially negligible. Note, however, that *convection may still be dominant in solute transport*. Consider, for example, a solute with molecular diffusivity 10^{-9} m^2 s^{-1} in a medium with characteristic pore diameter 10^{-5} m (a very fine sand or silt). Then the Peclet number is less than 1, and mixing at the interface is essentially by molecular diffusion for fluid velocities less than about 10^{-4} ms^{-1}. In a period of 10^4 s convective transport would move solutes a distance of about 1 m, but in the same period of time we estimate by the order-of-magnitude method described in Section 3 that molecular diffusion would transport the solute a distance of order 10^{-3} m only. Note too, that the convective displacement increases linearly with time whereas the diffusive transport increases with (time)$^{1/2}$.

Saffman's theory predicts that both the longitudinal and transverse dispersivities increase quite rapidly so that, at a Peclet number of 10^2, they are respectively about 50 and 20 times the molecular diffusivity of the solute through the medium. As the longitudinal and transverse dispersivities differ in magnitude over a wide range of flow velocities, the dispersion coefficient is a tensor function of the Peclet number.

Saffman (1959) has also investigated the dispersal of material in porous media at very high Peclet numbers (flow velocity ≫ molecular diffusion coefficient/characteristic pore size) in which case convection along streamlines dominates the dispersion process.

We may note that, in the absence of active roots, the hydraulic or capillary conductivity of a porous medium provides an order-of-magnitude estimate of the velocity of fluid flow. (It is commonly observed that, except near the soil surface or the water table, the gradient of hydraulic potential in the field is of order 1.) Since this conductivity is itself proportional to the square of the characteristic pore size, the Peclet number is roughly proportional to the cube of the characteristic pore dimension, and high Peclet number flows are much more likely in coarse media, such as sands, than in finer materials. Furthermore, as the characteristic pore dimension varies inversely with the capillary potential, unsaturated soils and porous media can be expected to show minimal dispersion in a given time.

Usually the amount of dispersion is observed after flow for a given distance through a porous medium (Nielsen and Biggar 1961). In such cases the role of the flow velocity must be interpreted with some care since it affects both the dispersivity and the time taken for the interface to travel the fixed distance. These two factors together determine the amount of dispersion of the tracer at the interface. Thus, although the dispersion coefficient increases with velocity, it is common to observe sharper break-through curves in dispersion at higher velocities (Nielsen and Biggar 1963).

(c) Transport with Exchange in Porous Media

The diffusion-like description of dispersion in porous media may be modified to include the effects of simple reversible exchange or adsorption of solute on the medium (Banks and Ali 1964; Elrick *et al.* 1966; Elrick 1969). In many practical situations, however, chromatographic models have been applied (van der Molen 1956; Bower *et al.* 1957; Gardner and Brooks 1957; Biggar and Nielsen 1963; Gardner 1965; Biggar *et al.* 1966; Biggar and Nielsen 1967; Frissel and Poelstra 1967; Aylmore and Karim 1968). In some applications these models have been quite successful, but other investigators have attributed discrepancies between theory and experimental data to changes of the cation-exchange-capacity with pH (Thomas and Coleman 1959) and the neglect of the dispersion due to convection and diffusion (Biggar and Nielsen 1963; Green *et al.* 1968).

There does not appear to be, at present, an adequate comprehensive theory of the convective transport of a solute subject to adsorption or exchange in a soil. We may, however, draw the qualitative conclusion that adsorbed and exchanged materials are transported less rapidly than those which are not. For example, Biggar and Nielsen (1963) observed that, during displacement of Ca acetate by $MgCl_2$ in a Ca-saturated sand, Cl concentration increased to 50% of its final value with only one-quarter of the throughput of solution as did the Mg. That is, the Mg was transported through this soil at only one-quarter the rate of the Cl, which moved at essentially the average velocity of the solution. Mg was also dispersed to a greater extent, but this is to be expected for the slower-moving ion.

(d) Effects of Medium Structure and Unsaturated Flow

The preceding discussion of dispersion applies to simple media such as sands during saturated flow. Many soils, however, are characterized by a broad or even bimodal pore-size distribution. In these cases it will be apparent that sequences of larger pores will be dominant in solution transfer, and exchange of solutes between the macro- and micro-porosity may be important in transient phenomena. Similarities with molecular diffusion in aggregated media (see Section 3) will be apparent, but in the present case the transport of solutes in the macropores can be so much more rapid than that in the micropores that medium structure effects are far more important.

Biggar and Nielsen (1962*a*) report measurements of the transport of relatively inert solutes from three aggregate size fractions of a clay loam at the same flow velocity. As the aggregate size increases, and so the difference between flow in macro- and micro-pore space becomes more pronounced, there is a greater dispersion of the solute about the interface, and the 50% concentration surface travels ever more rapidly than the average solution velocity. This latter effect arises when the macropores make a relatively larger contribution to the flow than they do to the moisture content. Consequently the solution velocity calculated by a simple averaging procedure (flux density of solution/moisture content of soil) is too low.

Similar behaviour is reported (Biggar and Nielsen 1960; Nielsen and Biggar 1961) to occur with decreasing moisture content of the medium. In this case it is suggested that desaturation leaves relatively isolated volumes of water, through which there is very little convection, even in media such as sands with a narrow range of pore-sizes.

Although these experiments with aggregated and unsaturated soils yield results consistent with our qualitative understanding of inert solute transport (Nielsen and Biggar 1962), it has been suggested (Rose and Passioura 1971) that, in some cases, the dispersion may have been affected by the difference in density of displacing and resident solutions (see below). It should be noted too that the effects of aggregate size or unsaturation are reported for fixed mean flow velocity so that the Peclet number is not maintained constant.

Assuming that transport within aggregates occurs by molecular diffusion alone, Passioura (1971) has developed a theory of dispersion of inert solutes in aggregated soils which is consistent with the experimental data of Passioura and Rose (1971).

(e) *Other Effects in Convective Transport of Salts*

It would be improper not to make brief mention of several effects which may be of considerable importance to salt transport in soils in particular circumstances.

A temperature gradient, or even the gradient of solution concentration, may give rise to an unstable (more dense overlying less dense) density gradient in the soil solution. Then convective mixing can occur due to cellular motion of the soil-solution. An unstable solution density gradient can also lead to accelerated mixing during convection. Dr Wooding will discuss these effects in greater detail in his paper to this Symposium.

As Professor Quirk will discuss in his paper to this Symposium, the permeability of some soils varies considerably with the concentration of electrolytes in the soil solution. In such cases the concentration of solute may affect the whole pattern of convection, but this does not appear to have been investigated in the context of solute transport.

When the soil solution is confined to thin films over soil particles, as it is in very dense materials or soils at rather low moisture contents, electrical interactions between ions and surface charges on soil particles can restrict the movement of solute more than that of the water. This process is referred to as 'salt sieving' (Kemper 1960; Kemper and Letey 1968; Letey and Kemper 1969). As the movement of solutes is rarely, if ever, entirely halted, the result of this effect will be salt transport at less than the average solution velocity. Some similarity with transport of an adsorbed ion will be evident.

5. EXAMPLES OF APPLICATION OF SALT TRANSPORT THEORY

It is appropriate to discuss very briefly in this concluding Section some examples of the application of the theory of salt transport in soils.

(a) Leaching of Soils

In this classic problem it is usually assumed that the concentration of salts in the soil solution is initially uniform over the depth of interest, and then salt-free water is introduced at the soil surface.

Biggar and Nielsen (1967) and Gardner (1965) have reviewed much of the work which shows generally fair agreement between the form of predicted concentration profiles and those observed for various cations and anions. It is unfortunately true, however, that many of the factors required in the theories are not readily determined independently. Usually, therefore, the theory is matched to experimental data at some point.

An interesting observation, which has not been discussed in these reviews, is the increased concentration of Cl^- and NO_3^- in the soil solution near the wetting front reported by Dyer (1965). An increase in this region in the ion content per unit quantity of soil is to be expected from conservation of mass, but the increase of solution concentration suggests that there is a higher-than-average concentration of ions in the large pores which make the greatest contribution to convection. Calculations from the data indicate that the moving solution was about twice as concentrated as the original solution in the unsaturated soil. The explanation of this intriguing result appears to be the combination of maximum microscopic velocities at locations remote from particle surfaces, and the simultaneous occurrence of high anion concentrations in the same locations due to the negative adsorption effect (Kemper 1960).

A variation of the leaching problem is to introduce a slug of salt at the soil surface and to observe its dispersion as salt-free water is infiltrated. Such experiments (Day and Forsythe 1957; Corey *et al.* 1963; Aylmore and Karim 1968) illustrate the decreasing peak concentration and increasing breadth of the slug as it moves through the soil. It is usual in these experiments to presaturate the soil and maintain a constant flow velocity. Evans and Levin (1969), however, began with dry soil so that the salt could never be dispersed beyond the wetting front, and flow velocities varied in time as well as the microscopic spatial variations. Their data for three soils show that the peak of anion concentration occurs very close to the depth above which 50% of the infiltrated water is located. Following the period of infiltration, however, the salts do not move as quickly as the water. These experiments have not been adequately analysed, but they have important implications to the movement of fertilizers in soils.

Wetselaar (1962) observed leaching of NO_3^- and Cl^- from the soil surface under natural rainfall. The ion distributions he observed are closely fitted by curves presented by Gardner (1965) and adapted from the pioneering theory of Day (1956) which assumes a constant moisture content during the leaching.

Biggar and Nielsen (1962b) argue that, in field soils with a wide range of pore sizes, leaching is more efficient in terms of water usage when the soil is not continuously ponded. Thus sprinkling at a limited rate, natural rainfall, or intermittent ponding are preferable because the leaching occurs predominantly in unsaturated soil at a slow rate which allows greater exchange by diffusion of salts between regions of varying velocity. This has been confirmed by subsequent experimentation (Miller *et al.* 1965; Nielsen *et al.* 1965). Talsma (1967) notes that, in tile-drained soils, desalinization is achieved with considerably less leaching water when it is applied intermittently rather than by continuous ponding. In this case of 2-dimensional flow there are geometric effects on solution velocities in addition to the microscopic (pore-scale) effects we have discussed previously.

(b) Surface Accumulation of Salts

Soil solution moving upwards to the surface where water is evaporated results in a surface accumulation of the solutes. Gardner (1965) has developed an analysis of this problem for 'inert' ions, such as NO_3^- and Cl^- in many soils, based on the assumption that, once the soil surface is dry, the flux of water to the surface is very nearly constant. Then in the steady-state the role of solution movement towards the surface is balanced by the tendency for downward transport of solute under the concentration gradient. The analysis predicts a logarithmic distribution of solute concentration in the surface soil which is in accord with observation by Wetselaar (1961) for the distribution of NO_3^-.

REFERENCES

Aris, R. (1956). *Proc. Roy. Soc. London A* **235**, 67.

Aylmore, L. A. G., and Karim, M. (1968). *Trans. 9th Int. Congr. Soil Sci.* **1**, 143.

Banks, R. B., and Ali, I. (1964). *J. Hydraulics Div. A.S.C.E.* **90** (HY5), 13.

Bear, J., Zaslavsky, D., and Irmay, S. (Eds.) (1968). *Physical Principles of Water Percolation and Seepage.* UNESCO Arid Zone Research, Paris.

Biggar, J. W., and Nielsen, D. R. (1960). *J. geophys. Res.* **65**, 2887.

Biggar, J. W., and Nielsen, D. R. (1962a). *Proc. Soil Sci. Soc. Amer.* **26**, 125.

Biggar, J. W., and Nielsen, D. R. (1962b). *California Agric.* **16** (3), 5.

Biggar, J. W., and Nielsen, D. R. (1963). *Proc. Soil Sci. Soc. Amer.* **27**, 623.

Biggar, J. W., and Nielsen, D. R. (1967). In *Irrigation of Agricultural Lands.* Eds. R. M. Hagan *et al.* Am. Soc. Agronomy, Madison, Wisconsin.

Biggar, J. W., Nielsen, D. R., and Tanji, K. K. (1966). *Trans. Amer. Soc. Ag. Eng.* **9**, 784.

Bower, C. A., Gardner, W. R., and Goertzen, J. O. (1957). *Proc. Soil Sci. Soc. Amer.* **21**, 20.

Carslaw, H. S., and Jaeger, J. C. (1959). *Conduction of Heat in Solids.* Clarendon Press, Oxford.

Childs, E. C. (1969). *An Introduction to the Physical Basis of Soil Water Phenomena.* John Wiley and Sons, London.

Corey, J. C., Nielsen, D. R., and Biggar, J. W. (1963). *Proc. Soil Sci. Soc. Amer.* **27**, 258.

Day, P. R. (1956). *Trans. Amer. geophys. Union* **37**, 595.

Day, P. R., and Forsythe, W. M. (1957). *Proc. Soil Sci. Soc. Amer.* **21**. 477.

de Wiest, R. J. M. (1969). *Flow through Porous Media.* Academic Press, New York.

Dyer, K. L. (1965). *Proc. Soil Sci. Soc. Amer.* **29**, 121.

Elrick, D. E. (1969). *Bull. Int. Assn. Sci. Hydrol.* **14** (2), 49.

Elrick, D. E., Erh, K. T., and Krupp, H. K. (1966). *Water Resources Res.* **2**, 717.

Evans, G. N., and Levin, I. (1969). *Aust. J. Soil Res.* **7**, 21.

Frissel, M. J., and Poelstra, P. (1967). *Plant and Soil* **26**, 285.

Gardner, W. R. (1965). In *Soil Nitrogen.* Eds. W. V. Bartholomew and F. E. Clark. Am. Soc. Agronomy, Madison, Wisconsin.

Gardner, W. R. (1968). *Trans. 9th Int. Congr. Soil Sci.* **1**, 135.

Gardner, W. R., and Brooks, R. H. (1957). *Soil Sci.* **83**, 295.

Green, R. E., Yamane, V. K., and Obien, S. R. (1968). *Trans. 9th Int. Congr. Soil Sci.* **1**, 195.

Groenevelt, P. H., and Bolt, G. H. (1969). *J. Hydrol.* **7**, 358.

Hagan, R. M., Haise, H. R., and Edminster, T. W. (Eds.) (1967). *Irrigation of Agricultural Lands*. Am. Soc. Agronomy, Madison, Wisconsin.

Heller, J. P. (1963). *J. Amer. Inst. Chem. Eng.* **9**, 452.

Kemper, W. D. (1960). *Proc. Soil Sci. Soc. Amer.* **24**, 10.

Kemper, W. D., and Letey, J. (1968). *Trans. 9th Int. Congr. Soil Sci.* **1**, 233.

Klute, A., and Letey, J. (1958). *Proc. Soil Sci. Soc. Amer.* **22**, 213.

Letey, J., and Kemper, W. D. (1969). *Proc. Soil Sci. Soc. Amer.* **33**, 25.

Lindstrom, F. T., Boersma, L., and Gardiner, H. (1968). *Soil Sci.* **106**, 107.

Luthin, J. N. (Ed.) (1957). *Drainage of Agricultural Lands*. Am. Soc. Agronomy, Madison, Wisconsin.

Miller, R. J., Biggar, J. W., and Nielsen, D. R. (1965). *Water Resources Res.* **1**, 63.

Nielsen, D. R., and Biggar, J. W. (1961). *Proc. Soil Sci. Soc. Amer.* **25**, 1.

Nielsen, D. R., and Biggar, J. W. (1962). *Proc. Soil Sci. Soc. Amer.* **26**, 216.

Nielsen, D. R., and Biggar, J. W. (1963). *Proc. Soil Sci. Soc. Amer.* **27**, 10.

Nielsen, D. R., Biggar, J. W., and Luthin, J. N. (1965). *Trans. 6th Congr. Int. Comm. Irrig. Drain.* (New Delhi). Q 19, p. 15.

Nye, P. H. (1968). *Trans. 9th Int. Congr. Soil Sci.* **1**, 117.

Passioura, J. B. (1971). *Soil Sci.* (in press).

Passioura, J. B., and Rose, D. A. (1971). *Soil Sci.* (in press).

Philip, J. R. (1957). *Proc. 2nd Aust. Conf. Soil Sci.* **1**, 63.1.

Philip, J. R. (1963). *Aust. J. Phys.* **16**, 287.

Philip, J. R. (1967) *Proc. Soil Sci. Soc. Amer.* **31**, 711.

Philip, J. R. (1968). *Aust. J. Soil Res.* **6**, 21.

Philip, J. R. (1969). In *Ciba Foundation Symposium on Circulatory and Respiratory Mass Transport*. p. 25. Churchill, London.

Philip, J. R. (1970). *Ann. Rev. Fluid Mech.* **2**, 177.

Porter, L. K., Kemper, W. D., Jackson, R. D., and Stewart, B. A. (1960). *Proc. Soil Sci. Soc. Amer.* **24**, 460.

Raats, P. A. C., and Scotter, D. R. (1968). *Water Resources Res.* **4**, 561.

Rose, D. A., and Passioura, J. B. (1971). *Soil Sci.* (in press).

Saffman, P. G. (1959). *J. Fluid Mech*, **6**, 321.

Saffman, P. G. (1960). *J. Fluid Mech.* **7**, 194.

Scheidegger, A. E. (1954). *J. Appl. Phys.* **25**, 994.

Scheidegger, A. E. (1957). *The Physics of Flow Through Porous Media*. University Press, Toronto.

Schofield, R. K., and Graham-Bryce, I. J. (1960). *Nature (Lond.)* **188**, 1048.

Talsma, T. (1967). *Aust. J. Soil Res.* **5**, 37.

Taylor, G. I. (1953). *Proc. Roy. Soc. London A* **219**, 186.

Taylor, G. I. (1954). *Proc. Roy. Soc. London A* **225**, 473.

Thomas, G. W., and Coleman, N. T. (1959). *Proc. Soil Sci. Soc. Amer.* **23**, 113.

van der Molen, W. H. (1956). *Soil Sci.* **81**, 19.

van Schaik, J. C., and Kemper, W. D. (1966). *Proc. Soil Sci. Soc. Amer.* **30** 22.

van Schaik, J. C., Kemper, W. D., and Olsen, S. R. (1966). *Proc. Soil Sci., Soc. Amer.* **30**, 17.

Vinograd, J. R., and McBain, J. W. (1941). *J. Amer. chem. Soc.* **63**, 2008.

Weast, R. C. (1969). *Handbook of Chemistry and Physics*, 50th Edn. Chemical Rubber Publishing Co., Cleveland, Ohio.

Wetselaar, R. (1961). *Plant and Soil* **15**, 121.

Wetselaar, R. (1962). *Plant and Soil* **16**, 19.

Groundwater Problems of the Interaction of Saline and Fresh Water

R. A. WOODING*

Division of Environmental Mechanics, CSIRO, Canberra A.C.T.

SUMMARY

This paper reviews selected hydrodynamical aspects relevant to flow of saline groundwater in a non-reacting medium. Topics covered include macroscopic scales and dimensionless parameters, conditions for stable flow, problems of stably-stratified flows, stable and unstable mixing layers.

1. PHYSICAL PARAMETERS ASSOCIATED WITH GROUNDWATER FLOW

In the simplest model, groundwater flow occurs in a saturated semi-infinite porous medium, situated below a horizontal permeable boundary. Real media involve extensive stratification of physical properties, and the strata may be both faulted and tilted. As this paper is concerned mainly with flow effects arising from variations in fluid properties, major simplifications will be accepted for the medium description. These are usually unavoidable if analytical progress is to be possible, and represent the trend established in the literature.

(a) Macroscopic Quantities

Length scales associated with the simplified medium include the distance below the surface, or from some other horizontal boundary of significance in surface boundary-layer effects (Wooding 1960; Foster 1965; Elder 1968), and the depth H, say, of a typical layer in which the medium properties are assumed to be approximately uniform.

For groundwater flow under saturated conditions, the driving head is usually gravitational, whether due to differences in phreatic-surface level

* This paper was written while the author was at Johns Hopkins University, Baltimore, Maryland.

125

(defined as the top of the zone of saturation) or to density differences arising from non-uniform distribution of salinity.* The relative magnitude of these driving heads is of order $\Delta\rho/\rho_0$, where $\Delta\rho$ is a typical density difference, and ρ_0 is the density of fresh water. At most, the ratio is likely to be only a few per cent; one practical consequence is that the slopes of fresh-salt-water interfaces greatly exceed the phreatic-surface slopes for systems in dynamical equilibrium.

Associated with the gravitational heads are characteristic velocities which depend upon the properties of both fluid and medium. A uniform fluid of density ρ and dynamic viscosity μ, saturating a uniform, isotropic porous material of intrinsic permeability k, subject to no constraint or force other than gravity, will percolate downward with volume flow rate equal to the 'hydraulic conductivity'

$$K=kg\rho/\mu=kg/\nu \tag{1}$$

where g is acceleration due to gravity and $\nu=\mu/\rho$ is kinematic viscosity. (See, for example, Bear *et al.* 1968). By analogy, the quantity

$$\Lambda=kg\Delta\rho/\mu \tag{2}$$

represents the descending rate of flow of a liquid column of indefinite height, where the density exceeds that of a surrounding stationary fluid by the amount $\Delta\rho$.

Note that the volume-flow rate Λ is characteristic of flow differences in the presence of fluid inhomogeneities, and can be classified as a secondary flow. When the fluid is undergoing a primary flow of characteristic volume rate V (equal to K in a gravitational system) additional secondary flow can arise through viscosity differences. Assume that dynamic viscosity $\mu\equiv\mu(\rho)$, is a function of density only, and that the density change $\Delta\rho$ is small. Then the rate characteristic of the secondary flow can be written

$$\Lambda=\left(\frac{kg}{\mu}+V\frac{1}{\mu}\frac{d\mu}{d\rho}\right)\Delta\rho \tag{3}$$

comprising both gravitational and viscous-force terms. When $V=0$, (3) reduces to (2).

If the convected quantity of interest (e.g. salinity) has a finite molecular diffusivity κ in the presence of the porous medium, further scales are introduced. The increasing length $(\kappa t)^{1/2}$, where t is time, is a measure of 'diffusion thickness' at an interface. It may be compared with the displacements Kt and Λt arising from convective flow. The ratio κ/Λ is a fundamental length of the system, and κ/Λ^2 is a fundamental time.

---

* Density differences arising from non-uniform temperature distributions are not discussed here, but may be treated by identical means.

(b) Dimensionless Parameters

For a characteristic volume-flow rate V, the Reynolds number relative to the pore size d can be written as

$$Re = Vd/\nu \tag{4}$$

This must be less than $0(10)$ for Darcy's law to be valid (Hubbert 1940).

The importance of convection relative to diffusion is given by the Péclet number

$$Pé = Vd/\kappa \tag{5}$$

defined relative to the pore scale. This form of the Péclet number serves as a measure of the importance of hydrodynamic dispersion (Saffman 1960; List and Brooks 1967), longitudinal dispersion (κ_l) and transverse dispersion (κ_t) becoming significant for $Pé$ equal to $0(1)$ and $0(10)$ respectively, and increasing steadily as $Pé$ increases.

A macroscopic variant of the Péclet number is obtained by replacing d in (5) by a length dimension such as H, the depth of a porous layer. If V is replaced by Λ, the scale of the secondary flow, the result is a Rayleigh number

$$A_r = \Lambda H/\kappa \tag{6}$$

or, from (3),

$$A_r = \left(kg + V\frac{d\mu}{d\rho}\right)\frac{H\Delta\rho}{\kappa\mu} \tag{7}$$

(Wooding 1962a) which measures the significance of secondary-flow convective transport relative to diffusive transport. (In (7), the molecular diffusivity κ may be replaced by either κ_l or κ_t if either is more appropriate to the problem.)

(c) Stability Criterion

Systems in which the density ρ increases in the upward direction tend to be gravitationally unstable, i.e. a reduction in potential energy can be achieved by overturning of the fluid. A further mechanism of instability arises when a non-homogeneous fluid is driven in a direction of increasing viscosity μ (Saffman and Taylor 1958). For the unstable situation, the scale of the induced secondary flow rates is given by equation (3), and the appropriate dimensionless parameter is the Rayleigh number A_r, equation (7). By convention, the definition of A_r is taken so that positive values are associated with instability. In porous-media flows, the condition $A_r < 0$ is usually sufficient for stability. In the absence of either scale-fixing flows or boundaries, instability occurs for $A_r > 0$; however, with such a scale or scales present, the system may remain stable until A_r exceeds a positive critical value.

(d) The Stable Groundwater Environment

Flow in a stable system ($A_r < 0$) is usually sustained by particular boundary conditions, such as inflow or outflow, which change the effective head level. A valuable discussion of hydraulic concepts in systems of varying salinity is due to Lusczynski (1961).

2. FLOW WITH STABLE STRATIFICATION OF MAINLY SMALL GRADIENT

(a) Flow in a Horizontal Layer

A typical problem envisages nearly-horizontal flow with density ρ increasing slowly downward, in a layer of homogeneous porous material of depth H. The layer is bounded by an impermeable layer below and by either an impermeable boundary (Yih 1961, 1965) relevant to flow in an enclosed aquifer, or a constant-pressure condition (Knudsen 1962) above. The equation of motion is Darcy's law:

$$\frac{\mu}{k} \, q + \nabla p - \rho g = 0 \tag{8}$$

where q is the vector of volume-flow rate, p is the pressure and g is the gravity vector, other symbols being as defined previously. Since the fluid is assumed incompressible

$$\nabla . q = 0 \tag{9}$$

The slight density gradient ensures that diffusion is negligible and the transport equation reduces to the vanishing of the Lagrangian derivative

$$\frac{d\rho}{dt} = \frac{\partial \rho}{\partial t} + \frac{1}{\epsilon} \, q . \nabla \rho = 0 \tag{10}$$

where ϵ is the porosity, i.e. the density is constant at a point moving with the interstitial velocity q/ϵ of the fluid. For a steady flow, equation (10) reduces to

$$q . \nabla \rho = 0 \tag{11}$$

so that ρ must be constant along any streamline (Yih 1961). Taking k constant, Yih also shows that, if $\mu \equiv \mu(\rho)$ so that viscosity is constant along a streamline, then a relation of form $\mu q = \mu_0 q'$ transforms the system to one of constant viscosity μ_0 (cf. equation (8)).

Knudsen (1962) eliminates q between equations (8) and (9), and solves the resultant linear equation for p, assuming that the density field ρ is given. The velocity field then follows from equation (8). In the problem treated by

Knudsen the flow arises from a perturbation of an equilibrium situation:

$$\rho = \rho_0(Z) + \rho_1, \quad p = p_0(Z) + p_1, \quad \mathbf{q} = \mathbf{q}_1 \tag{12}$$

If the flow is nearly horizontal, $\mathbf{q}_1 . \nabla \rho_0$ is small and equation (11) is satisfied to second order. (In (12), Z is the vertical co-ordinate.)

For two-dimensional and axi-symmetric flows, Yih introduces a stream function ψ, observing that equation (11) gives $\rho \equiv \rho(\psi)$. In the two-dimensional case, elimination of p from equation (8) gives

$$\nabla^2 \psi = \frac{gk}{\mu_0} \frac{\partial \rho}{\partial X} = \frac{gk}{\mu_0} \frac{d\rho}{d\psi} \frac{\partial \psi}{\partial X} \tag{13}$$

where X is the horizontal co-ordinate. If the flow is confined between two horizontal impermeable boundaries, an upstream condition (at $X \to -\infty$) must be $d^2\psi/dZ^2 = 0$, i.e. $\psi \propto Z$. For the density, a linear increase with depth is a reasonable assumption for $X \to -\infty$; hence $d\rho/d\psi$ is a constant and equation (13) is linear. Yih solves this equation exactly for the case of a sink at the upper boundary, and also when the flow is partially obstructed by impermeable ridges—the latter problem by inverse methods.

(b) Extension to Diffusive Flow

List (1969) has shown that Yih's problem can still be solved exactly when the diffusion term, $\kappa \nabla^2 \rho$, is included in equation (11) provided that the upstream values of ρ at the upper and lower boundaries are maintained throughout (isopycnic conditions). A relation of form

$$\rho/\rho_0 = 1 + AZ + B\psi \tag{14}$$

is assumed, where A and B are constants. One condition relating A and B follows from the upstream density gradient; a second condition renders the mass transport equation equivalent to the first equality in equation (13). Each of Yih's solutions is then equivalent to a class of diffusive-flow solutions, depending on a Péclet number based upon layer depth.

(c) Stably-Stratified Flow Towards a Line Sink in an Infinite Medium

An exact solution of this problem is afforded by List's (1969) method. Let the horizontal line sink be located at $X = Z = 0$ (with Z-axis directed upwards) and let the basic density gradient be $-\beta \rho_0 (\beta > 0)$ where ρ_0 is the density on $Z = 0$. The nature of the solution as $|X| \to \infty$ for small Z is not immediately specified, but for $|Z| \to \infty$, the velocity tends to zero (ψ becomes constant) and the density gradient approaches $-\beta \rho_0$. Therefore, in equation (14) put $A = -\beta$. Then, with $B = (\beta/K\kappa)^{1/2}$, where $K = kg\rho_0/\mu$, both equation (13) and the mass transport equation are equivalent to

$$\partial^2\psi/\partial X^2 + \partial^2\psi/\partial Z^2 = (\beta K/\kappa)^{1/2}\, \partial\psi/\partial X \tag{15}$$

for the range $0 \leqslant X < \infty$. Suitable boundary conditions are

$$\psi(Z<0) = \psi(Z>0) + \tfrac{1}{2}Q$$

on $X=0$, where Q is sink strength. By Fourier-transform methods, an appropriate solution of equation (15) is

$$\psi = \text{constant} - \tfrac{1}{2}Q\, \frac{e^x}{2\pi i} \int_{-\infty}^{\infty} e^{-x(1+\omega^2)^{1/2}+i\omega z}\, \mathrm{d}\omega/\omega \tag{16}$$

where $(x, z) = \tfrac{1}{2}(\beta K/\kappa)^{1/2}\, (X, Z)$. For large x, the steepest-descents approximation (Watson 1944) gives

$$u = \partial\psi/\partial z \sim -\tfrac{1}{2}Q(2\pi)^{-1/2}\, x(x^2+z^2)^{-3/4}\, e^{x-(x^2+z^2)^{1/2}} + \ldots \tag{17a}$$

$$\sim -\tfrac{1}{2}Q(2\pi x)^{-1/2}\, e^{-z^2/2x}\, \{1 + O(z^2/x^2)\} \tag{17b}$$

when $z/x \ll 1$. Here $\partial\psi/\partial z = u$ is the horizontal component of flow. Integrating (17b) with respect to z over $(0, z)$ gives

$$\psi \sim -\tfrac{1}{4}Q\, \mathrm{erf}\{z/(2x)^{1/2}\} + \ldots \tag{18}$$

From equations (17b) and (18), the flow exhibits a boundary-layer appearance with thickness of order $x^{1/2}$. Koh (1964) obtains the same form using a boundary-layer approximation. List (1968) has extended Koh's work and demonstrates, in a series of elegant experiments using a Hele-Shaw cell, that the velocity profiles are indeed of the form of the equation (17b).

Substitution of equation (18) into equation (14) shows that, while the density distribution has an overall gradient of $-\beta\rho_0$, there is also a stable 'step' in density, of magnitude $\tfrac{1}{2}Q(\beta/K\kappa)^{1/2}$, at the level of the line sink. The establishment of a density deficit of one-half of this amount at large positive Z, and the corresponding excess at large negative Z, needs explanation if the sink is started in an initially uniform density gradient. A downward translation of the fluid in the half-space $Z>0$, and an upward translation in $Z<0$, could set up the required density differences. This translation could develop gradually after the start of sink flow, since the early motion is of finite (but increasing) horizontal extent, and vertical velocities are appreciable near the horizontal limits of the disturbance.

(d) Flow Induced by Diffusion at Sloping Boundaries

An unusual example of convection in a stable environment has been described by Phillips (1970). For a stably-stratified fluid in hydrostatic equilibrium, the surfaces of constant density (isopycnals) are horizontal.

However, at a sloping impermeable boundary the isopycnals must tilt to meet the boundary normally, so that the state of hydrostatic equilibrium cannot be maintained. The result is a creeping flow along the wall such that the viscous force just balances the net hydrostatic force. Along an isolated sloping wall, the convective mass flux varies with height to balance the diffusive flux within the body of the stratified fluid.

Taking a wall of slope α to the horizontal, let ξ measure distance upslope and η measure distance from the wall. For a stable linear density distribution $\rho_0(1-\beta Z)$ in the body of the fluid, where Z is the upward vertical axis, Phillips shows that the density solution is given by

$$\rho/\rho_0 = 1 - \beta Z - (\beta/\gamma) \cos \alpha \, e^{-\gamma\eta} \cos \gamma\eta \tag{19a}$$

and the velocity along the wall is

$$u = 2\kappa\gamma \cot \alpha \, e^{-\gamma\eta} \sin \gamma\eta \tag{19b}$$

(See also Wunsch 1970). Here

$$\gamma = \left(g\beta \frac{\sin^2 \alpha}{4\kappa\nu}\right)^{1/4} \tag{20}$$

is the reciprocal of a length. From equation (19b), the velocity $u = O(\kappa\gamma)$, while the depth of flow is $O(1/\gamma)$, so that the convective volume flux $\kappa \cot \alpha$ is independent of γ. The convective mass flux is

$$Q = \kappa\rho_0 \cot \alpha \left(1 - \frac{5\beta}{4\gamma} \cos \alpha - \beta\xi \sin \alpha\right) \tag{19c}$$

The effect is applicable to mass transport along fluid-filled fissures and in coarse porous media. For flow between inclined parallel walls separated by a distance H, and with the origin taken mid-way between the walls, the results obtained by Phillips can be written

$$\rho/\rho_0 = 1 - \beta Z + \frac{\beta}{z\gamma} G(\gamma H)\{F_1(\eta) + F_2(\eta)\} \tag{21a}$$

$$u = -\kappa\gamma \cot \alpha \, G(\gamma H)\{F_1(\eta) - F_2(\eta)\} \tag{21b}$$

where

$$F_1(\eta) = \frac{\cos \gamma\eta \sinh \gamma\eta}{\sin \frac{1}{2}\gamma H \cosh \frac{1}{2}\gamma H}, \quad F_2(\eta) = \frac{\sin \gamma\eta \cosh \gamma\eta}{\cos \frac{1}{2}\gamma H \sinh \frac{1}{2}\gamma H},$$

$$G(\gamma H) = \frac{\sin \gamma H \sinh \gamma H}{\sin \gamma H + \sinh \gamma H}$$

and

$$Q = \kappa\rho_0\beta H \frac{\cos^2 \alpha}{\sin \alpha}$$

$$\times \left\{1 + \frac{5}{2\gamma H} \frac{\cos \gamma H - \cosh \gamma H}{\sin \gamma H + \sinh \gamma H} + \frac{\sin \gamma H \sinh \gamma H}{(\sin \gamma H + \sinh \gamma H)^2}\right\} \tag{21c}$$

for the convective flux. The dimensionless quantity $-(\gamma H)^4$ is the Rayleigh number of the stable system. When $\gamma H \to \infty$, the expression in braces in equation (21c) tends to unity. However, as $\gamma H \to 0$ the expression tends to zero as $16(\gamma H)^8/9!$, i.e. as the square of the Rayleigh number. Phillips points out that convective transport can exceed diffusive transport by two orders of magnitude at quite small slopes. As the slope is increased from zero, the vertical component of transport quickly approaches the diffusive value for a vertical fissure.

In an unpublished study, the present author has obtained results equivalent to equation (21) for an inclined tube of circular cross-section. Let a be the radius of the tube, and take polar co-ordinates (r, θ) in the plane of a cross-section, with origin on the tube axis and the direction $\theta = 0$ upward in a vertical plane through the axis. Then

$$\rho/\rho_0 = 1 - \beta Z + \frac{\beta \cos \alpha}{\frac{1}{2}\Gamma f'(\Gamma a)} \{\mathrm{ber}_1 (\Gamma a) \, \mathrm{ber}_1 (\Gamma r) + \mathrm{bei}_1 (\Gamma a) \, \mathrm{bei}_1 (\Gamma r)\} \cos \theta$$

$$\tag{22a}$$

$$u = \frac{\kappa \Gamma \cot \alpha}{\frac{1}{2}f'(\Gamma a)} \{\mathrm{ber}_1 (\Gamma a) \, \mathrm{bei}_1 (\Gamma r) - \mathrm{bei}_1 (\Gamma a) \, \mathrm{ber}_1 (\Gamma r)\} \cos \theta \tag{22b}$$

$$Q = \kappa \rho_0 \beta \pi a^2 \frac{\cos^2 \alpha}{\sin \alpha} \left\{\frac{5}{4} - \frac{f(\Gamma a)}{\frac{1}{2}\Gamma a f'(\Gamma a)} - \frac{f(\Gamma a) + (\Gamma a)^2 g^2(\Gamma a)}{\{\Gamma a f'(\Gamma a)\}^2}\right\} \tag{22c}$$

where
$$\Gamma = 2^{1/2}\gamma, \quad f(\Gamma a) = \mathrm{ber}_1{}^2 (\Gamma a) + \mathrm{bei}_1{}^2 (\Gamma a),$$
and
$$g(\Gamma a) = \mathrm{bei}_1 (\Gamma a) \, \mathrm{ber}_1' (\Gamma a) - \mathrm{ber}_1 (\Gamma a) \, \mathrm{bei}_1' (\Gamma a),$$

the ber_1 and bei_1 being Kelvin cylinder functions of the first kind (Watson 1944) and the primes signifying differentiation with respect to the entire argument. When $\Gamma a \to \infty$, the expression in braces tends to unity as before. For $\Gamma a \to 0$, the same expression gives $\frac{7}{180}(\frac{1}{2}\Gamma a)^8$, resembling the parallel-planes case.

An important application is encountered where salt water is overlain by fresh water in a coarse porous medium. Diffusion at the interface is little retarded by the presence of the medium; roughly, a four-fold increase in rate is observed over the case when gravity is not involved.

Flooding of a saline water-table with fresh water results in diffusion at a stable horizontal interface. An experiment by the author on diffusion in sloping tubes of various angles indicated that the diffusion layer should grow in thickness as $t^{2/5}$.

3. STABLE INTERFACE FLOW

Probably the most common form of interaction between fresh and saline groundwaters arises where water of 'recent' origin encounters 'resident' water of different, usually higher, salinity. Natural gravity flows include infiltration to the water-table, either from precipitation or from water-filled channels, and seepage of groundwater to the sea or into saline lakes. A characteristic flow rate for such systems is the hydraulic conductivity K, equation (1). Artificially-induced interaction arises from injection, and sometimes withdrawal, at wells, where the characteristic flow rate V near the interface depends upon well parameters. Injection automatically generates a new interface (Muskat 1937; Bear and Jacobs 1965; Bear 1970), while withdrawal may influence an interface already present. It is possible to neglect the effect of gravity when $V \gg K$.

Two time-dependent length scales are associated with the transport of salt. The convective scale is Vt, where V may be equal to either K or Λ in gravity systems, and t is the time of transit from some origin. The diffusive scale is $(\kappa t)^{1/2}$, taking for κ the effective diffusion coefficient in the direction of maximum concentration gradient. Suppose that L is a typical path length along the streamlines—a scale for the system geometry. Then $t = L/V$, and the ratio of L to the diffusive scale is $(VL/\kappa)^{1/2}$ which is the square root of a macroscopic Péclet number. If V arises from gravitational forces, VL/κ is equivalent to a Rayleigh number, and will be designated by A_r as in equations (6) and (7).

When $|A_r|$ is large, the diffusion zone between two miscible fluids behaves like a boundary layer, of thickness $|A_r|^{-1/2}L$ in a system of dimension L (Wooding 1963, 1964). The problem then breaks into two parts, corresponding to two physical regions—the 'outer' region, away from the diffusion layer, where diffusion is actually negligible and the equations are of lower order, and the 'inner' region for which diffusion is important but boundary-layer approximations are valid. The first term in the outer solution is obtained by treating the fluids as immiscible, with a sharp interface. The first term of the inner solution is then matched to the outer expansion; both solutions are of the same order. (See Van Dyke 1964; Cole 1968). Successively higher terms, which can be found in principle to any order when the expansions exist, involve amplitudes which are increasing powers of $|A_r|^{-1/2}$.

(a) Steady Flow of Miscible Fluids

The case of steady gravity flow with an immiscible interface—the first term in the outer solution—has been solved for two-dimensional configurations involving an interface between two fluids. For a steady solution to be possible, it is necessary that one fluid remain at rest (Polubarinova-Kochina 1962, ch. 8). The motion of the other fluid, including the geometry of the interface, can then be found by conformal mapping, especially using the hodograph transformation. (See the above reference, and also Bear and

Dagan 1964; and Bear 1970). Because of the similarity in boundary conditions, the techniques used for single-fluid flows are frequently adaptable to the two-fluid case.

Using the boundary-layer approximation for the first term of the inner expansion, Wooding (1964) notes that curvature terms may be neglected to order $|A_r|^{-1/2}$ where A_r is the Rayleigh number, and obtains a general similarity solution for which the profile corresponds to that of Görtler's laminar incompressible half-jet with one fluid at rest. The thickness of the mixing layer is found to be proportional to $Z^{1/2}/\sin \alpha(Z)$, where Z is the vertical depth below the virtual origin of the diffusion layer, and α is the local slope of the interface. The density distribution and profile of flow rate parallel to the interface are related by Darcy's law as

$$\frac{u}{\Lambda} = \frac{\rho - \rho_0}{\Delta\rho} \{\sin \alpha + O(|A_r|^{-1/2} \cos \alpha)\} \tag{23}$$

if ρ_0 is the density of the stationary fluid and $\Delta\rho$ is the density difference. Thus both u and ρ change smoothly through the mixing zone. Although one fluid is assumed to be 'at rest' in the first term of the outer solution, there is actually a small entrainment flow of order $\Lambda |A_r|^{-1/2} Z^{-1/2} \sin \alpha$ which just balances the outward diffusion into the stationary fluid, and contributes to the second term of the outer solution. This flow is essential to maintain a steady state. Its existence, in the case of interface flow in a coastal aquifer, was suggested by Carrier (1958) and Cooper (1959).

An extension of the above analysis to cases where hydrodynamic dispersion is important has been made by Li and Yeh (1968). Since, with a steady interface, only the term involving lateral dispersion is retained in the boundary-layer approximation, dispersion should become important when the Péclet number defined with respect to pore size, equation (5), is $O(10)$ or greater (List and Brooks 1967; Harleman and Rumer 1963).

By transforming from spatial co-ordinates as independent variables to the velocity potential and stream function of the immiscible-interface problem, Polubarinova-Kochina (1962, ch. 8) derives a linearized version of the mass transport equation. The velocity in the convective term is taken to be that given by the potential problem, i.e. involving a step at the interface. However, this approach neglects the modification to the velocity profile (23) arising from inter-diffusion of the two fluids, which is, in fact, of the same order as the first term of the inner expansion. Also, the solution does not possess an entrainment flow and cannot be used as a basis for obtaining higher terms in a perturbation expansion. A true physical interpretation of the linearized problem is that of diffusion of a dynamically-neutral common solute between two immiscible solvent liquids.

(b) Ghyben–Herzberg Lens

This class of problems treats a biconvex lens of fresh water floating on sea-water at rest; the edges of the lens are fixed by the coast, e.g. of an idealized island (circular symmetry) or of a polder (two-dimensional flow). A system resembling one edge of a two-dimensional lens frequently occurs at the coast of a larger landform. Distributed infiltration to the upper surface of the lens from precipitation is balanced by coastal outflow. The Dupuit–Forch-heimer approximation, which assumes a hydrostatic pressure distribution, provides a simple approximate solution for the shape of the lens which is satisfactory except close to the coast (Zaoui 1965). Childs (1950), Glover (1959) and Henry (1959) solved variants of the 'edge problem'—salt water intrusion at a coast—by conformal mapping, and Bear and Dagan (1964) extended that work. Charmonman (1965) achieved a considerable simplifi-cation by taking the velocity potential and stream function as independent variables. The method has been applied by Rumer and Shiau (1968) to obtain results for flow in non-homogeneous aquifers.

With the assumption of a constant lateral-diffusion (dispersion) coefficient in a steady boundary-layer model, Wooding (1964) finds that the thickness of mixing zone in a two-dimensional Ghyben–Herzberg system is approxi-mately proportional to the square root of the radius of curvature of the interface. Thus the thickness should tend to decrease towards the coast.

Observations of mixing at the interface between fresh and salt water in the Hawaiian Islands have been discussed by Carrier (1958), who concludes that molecular diffusion is negligible compared with dispersion induced by the oscillatory tidal flow of groundwater*. Measurements made near Miami, Florida (Cooper 1959) indicate the existence of a mixing zone of order 10 m thickness. The conclusion is that, with the increase of tidal dispersion close to the coast, an increase of mixing-zone thickness should also be observed.

A single-fluid model of the oscillating tidal flow has been analysed by Carrier and Munk (1954). Their results, supported by well measurements, indicate an approximately exponential decay of groundwater tidal amplitude with distance inland, with length scale of order K/ω, where ω is tidal frequency.

(c) Flows with Injection or Withdrawal

Gravitational flow, from a steady source of dense fluid miscible with groundwater, has been discussed by Wooding (1963, 1964), Yih (1965), and Raats (1969). The problem is important in the discharge of nutrients or effluents to the soil, and is readily analysed using boundary-layer methods as described above.

---

* Dispersion in porous media due to oscillating flow has been studied in particular by Scotter, Thurtell and Raats (1967), Scotter and Raats (1968, 1969) and Kimball (1969).

For the case of release of a fluid which has lower density than the resident groundwater, the direction of convective flow is reversed, and spreading of low-density fluid occurs at the phreatic surface. A transient problem of the spreading of a groundwater lens (Galin *et al.* 1960) neglects dispersion, but is relevant to the problem.

Flow to pumping wells above a fresh-salt-water interface has received considerable study (Schmorak and Mercado, 1969). Motion of the interface towards the well (upconing) broadens the mixing zone by hydrodynamic dispersion, thus salinizing the water ahead of the mean interface. Theoretical results (Dagan and Bear 1968) appear to describe the upconing interface satisfactorily up to about half the distance of rise to the well bottom.

If a sink is immersed in the mixing zone, steady-state considerations show that the zone narrows towards the sink. This suggests the use of an inter-ceptor well below the producer. A related technique (Kunin 1964) employs an 'image' pumping well located below the interface. In a symmetrical situation, one-half of the fluid in the mixing zone appears at the producing well. However, it is considerably diluted by the freshwater intake.

4. FLOW AT UNSTABLE INTERFACES

In groundwater flow, the appearance of instability is associated with either positive upward density gradients or an increase of viscosity in the direction of flow, or a combination of both. A necessary criterion is that the secondary flow-rate scale Λ, equation (3), be positive. Since the resultant flows tend to restore stability, unstable gradients occur mainly in transient situations, such as the overflooding of a coastal aquifer by tidal movement, or the release of dense effluent to a water table. The movement of a finite saline-water body in a freshwater flow (for which Yih 1963, has treated the immis-cible case) is inherently partially unstable since the sign of Λ reverses on the interface.

Instability at an interface between immiscible fluids arises in the water-drive process used for petroleum production (Saffman and Taylor 1958; Chuoke *et al.* 1959). If an unstable horizontal interface is perturbed by superimposing a small sinusoidal displacement of wavenumber A ($=2\pi/$ wavelength), the disturbance grows initially as $\exp(\Lambda At)$, where Λ is given by equation (3), and t is time. Here the interface is treated as continuous and interfacial tension is neglected. However, these assumptions are more particularly appropriate in the miscible-fluid case.

(a) Early Growth of Instabilities

With miscible fluids the growth of the diffusion zone is a complicating factor, since the disturbance is controlled by a time-varying primary density distribution. The immiscible interface result of growth proportional to wavenumber is also modified, as the higher wavenumbers are damped by diffusion.

Numerical experiments by Elder (1968) on an unstable diffusive sub-layer at a horizontal boundary in a porous medium indicate a range of disturbance growth proportional to $\exp(C\Lambda^2 t)$, where C is a constant. This implies that the fundamental scales of Λ/κ for wavenumber and κ/Λ^2 for time are applicable. A linearized analysis by Wooding (1962a) of the initial-value problem using Galerkin's method (cf. Finlayson 1968) indicates a very brief exponential growth, followed by decreasing rates. For the first term of the series, which represents displacement of the interface, the amplitude increases as

$$\exp\left\{a(1-a)\tau - \frac{4}{3}\left(\frac{2}{\pi}\right)^{1/2} a^2\tau^{3/2} + a^3\tau^2 - \frac{16}{15}\left(\frac{2}{\pi}\right)^{1/2} a^4\tau^{5/2} + O(\tau^3)\right\} \quad (24)$$

where $a = \kappa A/\Lambda$ is the dimensionless wavenumber and $\tau = \Lambda^2 t/\kappa$ is dimensionless time. The $O(\tau^3)$ term includes the effect of interaction with higher terms. In the exponential range only $a(1-a)\tau$ is important and the coefficient is maximized for $a = \frac{1}{2}$. The maximum initial growth rate is, therefore, scaled as $\exp(\frac{1}{4}\Lambda^2 t/\kappa)$, in qualitative agreement with the scaling found in Elder's experiments. However, Elder's results show a surprisingly large exponential range, the amplitude increasing ten-fold. From equation (24) this would be possible at a much smaller wavenumber ($a \ll \frac{1}{2}$), but such a low value of a is not observed.

(b) Growth at Large Times

After sufficient time has elapsed, the interface has a 'fingered' appearance, the amplitude of the unstable waves greatly exceeding the average wavelength. Wooding (1969) obtained power-law growth rates at large times, while the observed mean wavenumber decreased with time as $t^{-1/2}$, presumably through the coalescence of neighbouring fingers—a process driven by diffusive entrainment but not well understood.

The problem of overflooding a medium saturated with fresh water by saline water should behave similarly. It is also related to the work of Wooding (1959, 1962b) and Bachmat and Elrick (1970) on convective overturning in vertical tubes filled with porous material, where fingering is again observed.

REFERENCES

Bachmat, Y., and Elrick, D. E. (1970). *Water Resources Res.* **6**, 156.

Bear, J. (1970). *Adv. Hydrosci.* **6**, 141.

Bear, J., and Dagan, G. (1964). *J. geophys. Res.* **69**, 1563.

10

Bear, J., and Jacobs, M. (1965). *J. Hydrol.* **3**, 37.

Bear, J., Zaslavsky, D., and Irmay, S. (1968). *Physical Principles of Water Percolation and Seepage.* UNESCO, Paris.

Carrier, G. F. (1958). *J. Fluid Mech.* **4**, 479.

Carrier, G. F., and Munk, W. H. (1954). *Proc. 5th A.M.S. Symp. Appl. Math.* **5**, 89.

Charmonman, S. (1965). *J. geophys. Res.* **70**, 2813.

Childs, E. C. (1950). *J. Soil Sci.* **1**, 173.

Chuoke, R. L., van Meurs, P., and van der Poel, C. (1959). *J. Petrol. Tech.* **11**, 64.

Cole, J. (1968). *Perturbation Methods in Applied Mathematics.* Blaisdell, Waltham, Massachusetts.

Cooper, H. H., Jr. (1959). *J. geophys. Res.* **64**, 461.

Dagan, G. and Bear, J. (1968). *J. Hydraul. Res.* **6**, 15.

Elder, J. W. (1968). *J. Fluid Mech.* **32**, 69.

Finlayson, B. A. (1968). *J. Fluid Mech.* **33**, 201.

Foster, T. D. (1965). *Phys. Fluids* **8**, 1249.

Galin, G. A., Karpycheva, A. F., and Shkirtch, A. R. (1960). *PMM* **24**, 826. (ASME Transl.)

Glover, R. E. (1959). *J. geophys. Res.* **64**, 457.

Harleman, D. R. F., and Rumer, R. R., Jr. (1963). *J. Fluid Mech.* **16**, 385.

Henry, H. R. (1959). *J. geophys. Res.* **64**, 1911.

Hubbert, M. K. (1940). *J. Geol.* **48**, 785.

Kimball, B. A. (1969). Microclim. Invest. Int. Rep. 69-1, USDA and Cornell Univ.

Knudsen, W. C. (1962) *J. geophys. Res.* **67**, 733.

Koh, R. C. Y. (1964). Hydraul. Water Res. T. M. 64-2, Calif. Inst. Tech.

Kunin, V. N. (1964). In *Water Resources, Use and Management.* p. 212. Melbourne Univ. Press.

Li, W.-H., and Yeh, G. T. (1968). *Water Resources Res.* **4**, 369.

List, E. J. (1968). *J. Fluid Mech.* **33**, 529.

List, E. J. (1969). *J. Fluid Mech.* **36**, 17.

List, E. J., and Brooks, N. H. (1967). *J. geophys. Res.* **72**, 2531.

Lusczynski, N. J. (1961). *J. geophys. Res.* **66**, 4247.

Muskat, M. (1937). *The Flow of Homogeneous Fluids Through Porous Media.* McGraw-Hill, New York.

Phillips, O. M. (1970). *Deep-Sea Res.* **17**, 435.

Polubarinova-Kochina, P. Ya. (1962). *Theory of Groundwater Movement.* Princeton Univ. Press.

Raats, P. A. C. (1969). *Proc. Soil Sci. Soc. Amer.* **33**, 483.

Rumer, R. R., Jr., and Shiau, J. C. (1968). *Water Resources Res.* **4**, 1235.

Saffman, P. G. (1960). *J. Fluid Mech.* **7**, 194.

Saffman, P. G., and Taylor, G. I. (1958). *Proc. Roy. Soc. A* **245**, 312.

Schmorak, S., and Mercado, A. (1969). *Water Resources Res.* **5**, 1290.
Scotter, D. R. and Raats, P. A. C. (1968). *Water Resources Res.* **4**, 1201.
Scotter, D. R. and Raats, P. A. C. (1969). *Soil Sci.* **108**, 170.
Scotter, D. R., Thurtell, G. W., and Raats, P. A. C. (1967). *Soil Sci.* **104**, 306.
Van Dyke, M. (1964). *Perturbation Methods in Fluid Mechanics.* Academic Press, New York.
Watson, G. N. (1944). *Theory of Bessel functions.* Cambridge Univ. Press.
Wooding, R. A. (1959). *Proc. Roy. Soc. A* **252**, 120.
Wooding, R. A. (1960). *J. Fluid Mech.* **9**, 183.
Wooding, R. A. (1962a). *J. Appl. Math. Phys.* (ZAMP) **13**, 255.
Wooding, R. A. (1962b). *J. Fluid Mech.* **13**, 129.
Wooding, R. A. (1963). *J. Fluid Mech.* **15**, 527.
Wooding, R. A. (1964). *J. Fluid Mech.* **19**, 103.
Wooding, R. A. (1969). *J. Fluid Mech.* **39**, 477.
Wunsch, C. (1970). *Deep-Sea Res.* **17**, 293.
Yih, C. S. (1961). *J. Fluid Mech.* **10**, 133.
Yih, C. S. (1963). *Phys. Fluids* **6**, 1403.
Yih, C. S. (1965). *Dynamics of Non-homogeneous Fluids.* Macmillan, New York.
Zaoui, J. (1965). *La Houille Blanche* **20**, 66.

The Transport of Salt in Rivers and Estuaries

I. R. WOOD

Water Research Laboratory, University of New South Wales, Manly Vale, N.S.W.

SUMMARY

In order to follow the transport of salt in rivers, estuaries and lakes, it is not only necessary to be able to analyse the flows in these systems but also to understand the diffusion processes in these flows. This paper reviews the progress in understanding these processes and in analysing cases of engineering importance.

The situations discussed are:

1. Flows where the variations in salt concentration are so small that the effect on the flow properties of the system may be neglected. This is called a well mixed flow and in this case the analysis is based on Taylor's classic papers on dispersion.
2. Flows where the salt concentration gradients acted on by the gravitational field cause internal flows which dominate the transport of salt. In this case the flow may be analysed as two distinct layers.

Where the above approximations are not reasonable the flow is called a partially mixed flow and for simple cases, the analysis used is the same as that for a well mixed flow but with a greatly increased dispersion coefficient.

1. INTRODUCTION

When salt or another pollutant is introduced into a river or estuary at a concentration higher than its surroundings the processes of molecular and turbulent diffusion reduce both the mean concentration, and the local irregularities in time and in space. The problem of predicting these reductions is one of considerable engineering importance. It is important to be able to predict the effects of a new industry or sewage treatment plant releasing a pollutant, or a power station releasing heated water, on the ecology of a river or estuary. Indeed the number of power stations permitted on a particular river may be limited by the problems of thermal pollution. Irrigation

141

diversions also change the flow regimes and give rise to return flows of considerable salinity due to the leaching of natural salts and artificial fertilizers which decrease the water quality downstream (Pels 1967). Salinity changes in an estuary are also caused by major hydraulic modifications such as the building of levee banks, dredging at the entrance or the reduction and re-routing of the fresh water entering the estuary (Harleman *et al.* 1967; Shankar and Masch 1970; Harleman and Hoopes 1963).

Ideally then, engineers and ecologists would like to know the velocity, density and the concentration of a pollutant at all times and at all positions in an estuary, river or lake. That is, it is desired to know

$$u = u(x, y, z, t)$$
$$\rho = \rho(x, y, z, t) \tag{1}$$
$$c = c(x, y, z, t)$$

where u is a local velocity, ρ the local density and c the concentration of pollutant, x, y, z, are respectively the longitudinal, transverse and vertical coordinates and t is time. In this notation $u(x, y, z, t)$ indicates that u is a function of the variables enclosed in parentheses.

If the density of fluid ρ and the velocity u were known from a solution of the equation of motion with the appropriate boundary conditions and if the pollutant in the flow moved at the same velocity as the fluid at the point where the pollutant was located, the problem would be solved. This movement of the fluid along the instantaneous streamlines is called 'convection'. In a real fluid the turbulent motion will cause movement of the pollutant between adjacent mean flow streamlines. This process is called 'diffusion' and if it were possible to relate this rate of transfer of pollutant between the streamlines to a concentration gradient and to coefficients which are a known function of position and time, it might be possible to write a computer programme to determine the movement and spreading of a dissolved substance. Even with the next generation of computers a project of this magnitude would be an extremely ambitious task and at present the physical information required for the turbulent mass transfer coefficients and for the shear stresses in an unsteady flow is not available.

If progress is therefore to be made, and decisions on many subjects cannot be postponed until there is a complete understanding of the physical phenomena, then various simplified models are necessary. For the case where the pollutant concentration is sufficiently small so as not to affect the density of the fluid, the simplified models stem from Taylor's (1922) classic paper on 'Diffusion by Continuous Movements'.

The other extreme case is where density differences dominate the flow and in this case the equations of motion and continuity for layered flow are solved.

It is proposed to first discuss, in Section 2, the dispersion of salts in rivers using the Taylor model and then, in Section 3, deal with dispersion and salinity distribution in estuaries. In the case of estuaries it is proposed to discuss three cases, the well mixed case where the Taylor model is applicable, the highly stratified estuary where layered flow theory applies, and the most common case, the partially mixed estuary, where approximate solutions can be obtained from either theory.

2. THE DISPERSION OF SALT IN RIVERS

Taylor (1922) considered the motion of particles of the same density as the fluid in a flow field where the velocity was a stationary random function of time. He was able to show that if a cloud of pollutant was released then after an initial period the cloud would spread in proportion to the square root of time.

Nearly thirty years after this analysis Batchelor pointed out that the flow at a constant speed in a long uniform pipe was one to which Taylor's analysis would apply. If a particle in the pipe was considered then its mean velocity would be the pipe discharge divided by the pipe area. At any instant, however there would be a deviation from this mean velocity according to the particle's position in the pipe cross section and the instantaneous turbulent fluctuation. The variation caused by the particle's variation in position and the turbulent fluctuation gives a random velocity variation which is independent of the longitudinal coordinate. Thus the departures from the mean velocity are a stationary random function of time.

Taylor's theory has been extended to take into account the effects of velocity distribution, radially as in a pipe, vertically as in two-dimensional flow, and laterally and vertically as in real rivers (see Taylor 1954; Aris 1956; Elder 1959; Fischer 1966; Holley *et al.* 1970).

Let us examine how Taylor's theory has been applied. The equation of continuity of concentration at a point in a laminar flow is

$$\frac{\partial c}{\partial t}+\frac{\partial}{\partial x}(uc)+\frac{\partial}{\partial y}(vc)+\frac{\partial}{\partial z}(wc)=\frac{\partial}{\partial x}\left(D_m\frac{\partial c}{\partial x}\right)+\frac{\partial}{\partial y}\left(D_m\frac{\partial c}{\partial y}\right)+\frac{\partial}{\partial z}\left(D_m\frac{\partial c}{\partial z}\right)$$

(2)

where D_m is the molecular diffusivity of the pollutant.

In this equation the first term is the local time rate of change of concentration and the remaining terms on the left hand side are those representing the convection of pollutant. The terms on the right hand side are based on Fick's law which states that the diffusion of concentration is proportional to the concentration gradient. These terms account for the fact that the mean fluid velocity cannot represent the pollutant movement because in laminar flow individual molecules have speeds and directions which differ from this mean velocity.

Now assume

$$u = \bar{u} + u', \qquad v = \bar{v} + v'$$
$$w = \bar{w} + w', \qquad c = \bar{c} + c' \tag{3}$$

where $\bar{u}$, $\bar{v}$, $\bar{w}$ and $\bar{c}$ are respectively the mean values with respect to time of fluid velocities and the pollutant concentration, and u', v', w', c' are the turbulent variations from these mean values.

Further let $\bar{u}$ = constant and hence $\partial \bar{u}/\partial x = 0$, $\bar{w} = 0$, $\bar{v} = 0$ and the mean concentration and other mean flow properties be independent of the y coordinate.

Note that the mean values of u', v' w' and c' are zero by definition. Then when the above continuity equation is integrated with respect to time and the above assumptions are used we obtain

$$\frac{\partial \bar{c}}{\partial t} + \frac{\bar{u} \partial \bar{c}}{\partial x} = \frac{\partial}{\partial x}\left(D_m \frac{\partial \bar{c}}{\partial x}\right) + \frac{\partial}{\partial z}\left(D_m \frac{\partial \bar{c}}{\partial z}\right) - \frac{\partial}{\partial x}(\overline{u'c'}) - \frac{\partial}{\partial z}(\overline{w'c'}). \tag{4}$$

It is to be noted that $\overline{u'c'}$ and $\overline{w'c'}$ are mean values with respect to time and the terms involving these mean values represent the convection of pollutant due to the difference between the mean and instantaneous velocities and concentrations. These terms are normally expressed as functions of turbulent diffusion coefficients ϵ_x and ϵ_z and the concentration gradients $\partial \bar{c}/\partial x$ and $\partial \bar{c}/\partial z$ as follows

$$\overline{u'c'} = -\epsilon_x \partial \bar{c}/\partial x, \qquad \overline{w'c'} = -\epsilon_z \partial \bar{c}/\partial z.$$

If in addition to turbulence there is a velocity gradient in the z direction then the particles of pollutant are further spread. This additional spread caused by the movement of the particles in the velocity gradient is called dispersion. It contrasts with diffusion where fluid particles move through the velocity field.

Consider the release of a pollutant in the shear flow of an open channel as in Fig. 1. Figure 1(*a*) shows an elevation of the cloud of pollutant shortly after its release and after the pollutant has spread throughout the channel depth. Figures 1(*b*) and (*c*) show an instantaneous velocity distribution and the concentration distribution shortly after the release of the pollutant.

If the average velocity in a section (the total discharge divided by the area) is defined as U and the difference in the time-averaged velocity at any z from this value is denoted by u'' then the mean velocity ($\bar{u}$) at any point may be written as

$$\bar{u}(z) = U + u''(z) \tag{5}$$

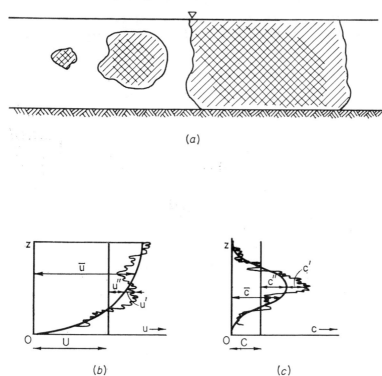

Fig. 1. (*a*) The growth of a cloud of pollutant in an open channel. (*b*) Velocity distribution in channel. (*c*) Pollutant concentration a short time after release.

Similarly for the concentration we may define an average concentration over a cross section and will get

$$\bar{c}(z) = C + c''(z) \tag{6}$$

where C is the average concentration in the section and c'' is the difference between this value and the average value at the point.

Substituting for u and c in equation (2) and neglecting molecular diffusion as being small compared to the turbulent diffusion we get after integrating over the depth and averaging over a long time

$$\frac{\partial C}{\partial t} + U \frac{\partial C}{\partial x} = -\frac{\partial}{\partial x}\overline{(u''c'')} - \frac{\partial}{\partial x}\overline{(u'c')} - \frac{\partial}{\partial z}\overline{(w'c')} \tag{7}$$

In this equation the double bar signifies an average both with time and depth and the first term on the right hand side represents the convection of pollutant by deviation from the mean velocity and the second two terms represent convection of pollutant by turbulence. In a number of flows the spread of pollutant by dispersion greatly exceeds that caused by diffusion. This is

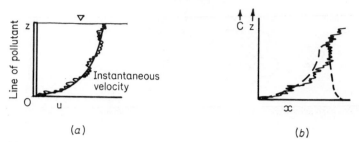

Fig. 2. (*a*) Velocity profile and line source of pollutant at $t=0$. (*b*) Appearance and concentration of pollutant after a short time. ——— Appearance of line of pollutant. – – – Average concentration of pollutant.

illustrated in Fig. 2 which shows a line of particles being released in an open channel. It is apparent that if a line of pollutant is released in a field with velocity gradient (Fig. 2*a*) then the mean concentration in a section a short time after this release (Fig. 2*b*) may be largely determined by the velocity gradient. In this case the first term on the right hand side of equation (7) would be more important than those dealing with turbulent diffusion (terms 2 and 3 on the right hand side of (7)). Thus to a reasonable approximation equation (7) becomes

$$\frac{\partial C}{\partial t} + U\,\frac{\partial C}{\partial x} = -\frac{\partial}{\partial x}\left(\overline{u''c''}\right) \tag{8}$$

or if we move with the mean velocity of the fluid by defining a new variable

$$\zeta = x - Ut$$

then we get

$$\frac{\partial C}{\partial t} = -\frac{\partial}{\partial \zeta}\left(\overline{u''c''}\right) \tag{9}$$

If now we write

$$\overline{u''c''} = -D\,\frac{\partial C}{\partial \zeta} \tag{10}$$

then the solution of equation (9) is of the same form as Taylor obtained.

The cases when the assumption used in equation (10) is appropriate can be deduced from equation (4). Assume the concentration gradients are so small that they do not affect the flow. In this case the particles of pollutant behave in the same manner as particles of water and it is reasonable to assume that the diffusion coefficient for the flux of momentum ϵ_m is the same as that for the flux of concentration ϵ_c. Thus ϵ_c can be obtained from measurements of the known velocity distribution.

Further if it is assumed that the pollutant is sufficiently spread in the vertical direction such that the dispersion of the pollutant in the x direction by the turbulent fluctuations in the z direction and the velocity gradient is relatively much greater than that caused by the turbulent fluctuations in the x direction, then equation (4) without the viscous terms may be written as

$$\frac{\partial \bar{c}}{\partial t} + \bar{u}\frac{\partial \bar{c}}{\partial x} = \epsilon_z \frac{\partial \bar{c}}{\partial z} \tag{11}$$

Yotsukura and Fiering (1964) show that this equation enables a programme to be written which for given initial conditions for the cloud of pollutant $c = c(x_0 z_0 t)$ and a known uniform velocity distribution enables the spread of the cloud to be followed as it travels downstream (i.e. $c = c(x, z, t)$).

As the cloud spreads the average concentration in any vertical is reduced and the variation becomes very small. In this case the small variations in the z direction are ignored and the problem becomes less complicated as the solution sought is one in which c is now only a function of two variables $(C = c(x, t))$. For this case Fischer and others show that

$$D = \int_0^d u'' \int_0^z \frac{1}{\epsilon_z} \int_0^z u'' \, dz \, dz \, dz \tag{12}$$

Thus D is independent of x and t and the dispersion equation can be written as

$$\frac{\partial C}{\partial t} = D\frac{\partial^2 C}{\partial \zeta^2} \tag{13}$$

where D is a known constant. The solution of this equation gives a Gaussian distribution of C with spread proportional to $t^{1/2}$. Values of D can be deduced from the known velocity distributions in a pipe or a channel and these values are in reasonable agreement with the predicted values.

In the case of natural streams Fischer (1967, 1968) has shown that the major contributor to dispersion is velocity differences across the stream and he obtained equation (14).

$$D = -\frac{1}{A}\int_0^b u''h \int_0^y \frac{1}{\epsilon_y h} \int_0^y \int_0^h u'' \, dz \, dy \, dy \, dy \tag{14}$$

where: A is the flow area, b the width of the river, y the transverse direction, h depth of flow at any y and ϵ_y the turbulent transverse mixing coefficient. Holley *et al.* (1970) gave a simpler approximate form of equation (14). In uniform streams Fischer's calculations agree with measured values but in markedly non-uniform streams can be in error by a factor of 4 which affects predictions by a factor of 2. Fischer (1969*a*) presents a method of evaluating the influence of stream curvature in a meandering stream.

Thus, after an initial mixing time the dispersion of small quantities of an additive to a river flow can be calculated for engineering purposes provided the velocity distribution in the river is known and the flow reasonably steady.

3. DISPERSION AND SALINITY DISTRIBUTION IN ESTUARIES

Mass transfer processes in estuaries are vastly more complex than those in the simple uniform flow discussed above. In a normal tidal estuary the salinity intrusion is affected by the tidal flow in the estuary, the geometry of the estuary and the fresh water discharge. If the river discharges into an almost tideless sea with a large fresh water flow, there is a distinct interface between the salt and the fresh water as in Fig. 3(a). Above the interface the fresh water flows with almost no contamination and below the interface the salinity is practically that of the sea. There is no net flow within the wedge when it is in a stationary position. Nevertheless, the shear stress at the interface forces a circulation in the wedge with salt water flowing in along the bottom of the wedge and out close to the interface.

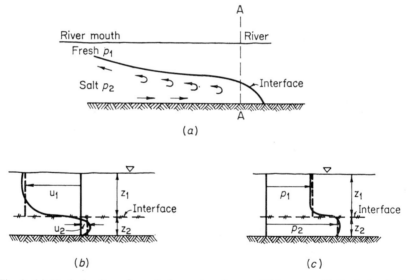

Fig. 3. (a) Typical salt wedge entering a river from a tideless sea. (b) Typical velocity distribution at Section A–A ———. Idealized velocity distribution – – –. (c) Typical density distribution at Section A–A ———. Idealized density distribution – – –.

Under these conditions of small tide and large fresh water discharges the large density difference at the interface suppresses the turbulent fluctuations in the region of the interface and little or no mixing results. Some estuaries have this completely stratified character only at certain times, while under conditions of high tide, waves, turbulence induced by wind action and wind induced currents the wedge is almost completely destroyed.

At the other end of the spectrum when the tidal prism (the volume exchanged during a tide) is large compared to the freshwater inflow, the estuary becomes well mixed and all the vertical salinity gradients are reduced (Fig. 4).

In the limit when these vertical gradients tend to zero it is appropriate to discuss a theory similar to that already discussed for the dispersion of a pollutant in rivers.

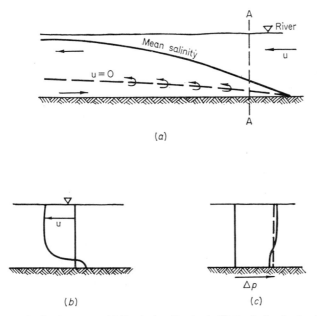

(a)

(b)   (c)

Fig. 4. The well mixed estuary. (*a*) Typical well mixed. (*b*) Typical velocity distribution. (*c*) Typical density distribution.

This well mixed case and the case of a highly stratified estuary will be discussed before proceeding to the more normal partially mixed estuary.

(*a*) The Well Mixed Estuary

In this case, when the vertical density gradients are extremely small, the main difference between the dispersion in a river and that in an estuary is caused by the tidal oscillation and the variation of the cross section of the estuary both with distance and time. If the variations in cross sectional areas are small and the cross sectional area is constant in time (i.e. the cross section must have the same area at high and low tide) then Okubu (1964) shows that

$$\frac{\partial \bar{C}}{\partial t} + U_f \frac{\partial \bar{C}}{\partial x} = \frac{1}{A} \frac{\partial}{\partial x} \left(A D_x \frac{\partial \bar{C}}{\partial x} \right) \tag{15}$$

In this equation U_f is the fresh water discharge divided by the estuary cross section and $\bar{C}$ is the mean concentration at the section of area (A) averaged over a tidal cycle (T) and it is assumed that

$$\frac{1}{T}\int_0^T \int_A u''c'' \, dA \, dt = D_x A \frac{\partial \bar{C}}{\partial x} \tag{16}$$

where D_x is the dispersion coefficient at section x and x is measured upstream from the ocean outlet. It remains to determine the value of the averaged dispersion coefficient.

For this idealized estuary with no fresh inflow the effects of oscillation can be illustrated qualitatively in a very simple manner (Holley 1969). If there were no diffusion there would be no dispersion. This is illustrated by the movement of the line of particles defined by the broken line in Fig. 5. If, however, the process is diffusive then there will be a continuous exchange of particles between different levels in the flow and this will lead to the dispersion of the particles. This is illustrated by the movement of the particles

Fig. 5. Motion of a line of particles in an oscillating flow with diffusion modelled by an exchange of the particle positions at times $t = T/4$ and $t = \frac{3}{4}T$.

represented by ● in Fig. 5. It is apparent from this figure that the amount of dispersion is a function of the mixing during a tidal period. Now if the time for complete mixing in a section is T_s and that of the tidal cycle is T then the amount of mixing in a tidal cycle is a function of the number of times the fluid is exchanged in a tidal period (i.e. T/T_s) and the magnitude of this term is an indication of the dispersion at the end of a tidal period.

Now the turbulent eddy transfer coefficient has the dimensions of length squared divided by time. Thus an indication of the time for complete mixing in a vertical section may be written as $T_z = d^2/\epsilon_z$ where d is the fluid depth. For the complete mixing in the transverse direction we have $T_y = b^2/\epsilon_y$ where b is the width of the channel. In most tidal estuaries $b \gg d$ and ϵ_z is of the same order as ϵ_y. Thus $T_z \ll T_y$ and hence $T/T_z \gg T/T_y$. Thus the dispersion coefficient due to the oscillating flow will result mainly from the vertical shear. This is in complete contrast to the case of a uniform flow in a wide river where the dispersion coefficient is dominated by the transverse shear.

Holley *et al.* (1970) derived an expression for the ratio of the dispersion coefficient in an oscillating flow to the dispersion coefficient in a steady flow as a function of the time of tidal oscillation and the critical mixing time T_z. Fischer (1969*b*) points out that the maximum contribution to the dispersion coefficient due to the flow oscillation depends on the mean square velocity distribution, a shape factor for velocity and depth distribution and the tidal period. It has a value of 50 m² sec⁻¹ for a typical estuary.

For the case of a slug of pollutant injected into an estuary he shows that the dispersion coefficient due to the net steady flow may be calculated from the steady flow velocities and added to the coefficient caused by the oscillation. Unfortunately, this only holds for a slug of pollutant in a coordinate system moving with the mean velocity. It does not necessarily hold for the case of a salinity intrusion where there is no mean velocity.

At the present time it appears that there is no method of estimating the total dispersion coefficient even in the most simple of estuaries. However, computer programmes have been written which, from the tidal variations at the estuary mouth and the geometry and frictional characteristics, compute the tidal flows in the estuary and put these flows into a second programme which solves the diffusion equation. If sufficient prototype information is available to adjust the dispersion coefficient to obtain computer prototype verification then Shankar and Masch (1970) show that the method may be used to predict the changes in salinity caused by changes in the geometry or the fresh water inflow into a well mixed estuary.

(b) The Highly Stratified Estuary

When the river bed is relatively smooth and the river discharge is relatively large compared to the tidal volume, the interface between the fresh and the salt water is sharp and the flow may be treated as a two layered system (Fig. 3). This is the most obvious case of a layered flow but, as measuring techniques have improved, more and more investigators have discovered that bodies of fluid consist of layers of uniform fluid separated by sharp interfaces and a great deal of work is being carried out on the formation and flow of these layers (Woods 1968; Turner and Kraus 1967*a* and *b*; Turner 1968; Yih 1965; Wood 1969; Thorpe *et al.* 1969).

The flow in the salt wedge is one of the simpler of these flows and the equations of continuity and momentum for each layer were presented by Schijf and Schonfeld (1953) for the case where the flow is gradually varied such that the pressures in each layer were hydrostatic and where there was no transport across the interface. This case is illustrated in Fig. 3 and the equations are

$$\frac{\partial z_1}{\partial t} + \frac{\partial}{\partial x}(z_1 u_1) = 0 \tag{17}$$

$$\frac{\partial z_2}{\partial t} + \frac{\partial}{\partial x}(z_2 u_2) = 0 \tag{18}$$

$$\frac{\partial u_1}{\partial t} + u_1 \frac{\partial u_1}{\partial x} + g \frac{\partial}{\partial x}(z_1 + z_2) + \frac{T_i}{\rho_1 z_1} = 0 \tag{19}$$

$$\frac{\partial u_2}{\partial t} + u_2 \frac{\partial u_2}{\partial x} + (1-\alpha)g \frac{\partial}{\partial x}(z_1 + z_2) + \alpha \frac{\partial z_2}{\partial x} + \frac{T_b - T_i}{\rho_2 z_2} = 0 \tag{20}$$

where u_1 and u_2 are the average velocities in each layer; T_i and T_b the interfacial and bottom shear stresses; z_1 and z_2 the layer depths, ρ_1 and ρ_2 the densities of layers; x the distance along the estuary; and $\alpha = (\rho_2 - \rho_1)/\rho_1$.

These equations have been solved numerically and the solution is always started from the case where there is no tide and a constant river discharge. In this case the salt layer (called a salt wedge) is stationary. For this case of an arrested salt wedge a large amount of experimental data based on prototype data and measurements in three laboratory flumes has been presented by Keulegan (in Ippen 1966). These results enable the shape and length of an arrested saline wedge to be obtained.

It is interesting to note that Stommel and Farmer (1952) show that simple one-dimensional theory enables the depth of the salt wedge at the river mouth to be predicted and this prediction is in remarkable accord with experimental measurements. However, the length of the saline wedge and the transfer of salt across the interface are determined by friction and have been obtained experimentally or from prototype data.

Now in order to solve for the migration of the salt wedge up and down the river as the water surface at the river mouth changes with the tide the conditions at each end of the problem must be known. Far upstream the salt wedge disappears, the shear stress at the interface changes to the shear stress at the river bed and we are left with the equations for one layer only. Going still further upstream the tidal range disappears and we are left with conditions in the river and these are the boundary conditions in the upstream region of the problem.

The conditions at the downstream end of the channel are less well defined. The variation in the sea level is known but there are problems in determining the variation of the layer depth with time. In the presence of the variation of sea level at the mouth of the channel the internal flow will not adjust itself to critical conditions (the steady flow conditions at the river mouth) at each moment. Nevertheless the assumption of an immediate adjustment of the saline wedge depth at the river entrance has been used as a working hypothesis and does seem to give reasonable results. In the case where there is mixing across the interface, the density of the inflowing salt water also needs to be specified.

With these boundary conditions, the complete equations or an approximation to the complete equations have been solved numerically by Vreugdenhil (1970) and Boulot and Daubert (1969) using a finite difference method and a complete solution has been obtained.

Solutions of this type depend critically on the selection of values of the interfacial shear T_i, the bottom shear T_b and the entrainment across the interface. If, however, there is freedom to select these values the migration of the salt wedge can be closely simulated and the effects of changes to the estuary can then be investigated using this numerical model with a reasonable degree of confidence.

(c) The Partially Mixed Estuary

The majority of estuaries cannot be classified as completely mixed or highly stratified with a sharp interface. Indeed in most estuaries there are salinity gradients in both the horizontal and vertical directions. In this case two approaches are possible. First, the flow may be idealized as a two layer flow with an interface assumed to be present at the depth of the mean salinity as in Fig. 4. Indeed, this is in effect what Vreugdenhil (1970) has done for the Rotterdam waterway as described in the previous section. Although there are enough free constants (the frictional coefficient at the interface and bed and the quantities of salt and fresh water exchanged through the interface) to obtain prototype verification the replacement of vertical density distribution with two distinct layers as in Figs. 3b and 3c has not been justified.

The second and apparently more usual approach is to modify the dispersion coefficient and to treat the estuary as if it were well mixed.

In a partially mixed estuary there are vertical density gradients at each section. In this case, changes in hydrostatic pressure (caused by longitudinal and vertical salinity gradients) generate internal flows and these are inextricably coupled to the mixing process produced by tidal shear flows. Tidal velocities greatly exceed the flows generated by the density differences (density currents) but these weak currents greatly increase dispersion. This has been demonstrated in a remarkable manner in a series of laboratory experiments with an idealized estuary reported by Harleman (in Ippen 1966). It was shown in these experments that dispersion coefficients with a density difference could be as much as three orders of magnitude greater than those for similar experiments without the density differences.

Approximate values of this apparent dispersion coefficient were derived for a series of large scale experiments at the Waterways Experiment Station (Ippen 1966) and for actual estuaries (Harleman and co-workers 1963, 1966, 1967). This approach involves using equation (15) as derived by Okubu (1964) but assuming that the inflow into the estuary varies with a very much

11

longer time scale than the tidal cycle. This implies that the distribution of salinity is almost the same at times differing by one tidal period (i.e. $\partial \bar{C}/\partial t$ is small) and there is a balance between the dispersion of salinity due to the tidal motion and the convection of salt water with the fresh water flow. That is

$$U_f \frac{\partial \bar{C}}{\partial x} = \frac{\partial}{\partial x}\left(D_x \frac{\partial \bar{C}}{\partial x}\right) \tag{21}$$

This may be integrated to give

$$U_f \bar{C} = D_x \frac{\partial \bar{C}}{\partial x} + \text{constant} \tag{22}$$

The integration constant is assumed zero since far upstream $\bar{C}$ and $\partial \bar{C}/\partial x$ will tend to zero. Harleman assumed that for a simple uniform channel entering the ocean the form of dispersion coefficient is

$$D_x = D_0 B/(x+B)$$

where D_0 is the averaged dispersion coefficient at the ocean outlet and B is a constant. Substituting into equation (22) and integrating they obtained $\bar{C}/\bar{C}_0 = \exp[-U_f(x+B)^2/2D_0B]$, where $\bar{C}_0$ is the ocean concentration at $x=0$.

For the simple estuaries measurements show that the salinity distribution moves up and down with the tide without change in form (Fig. 6) and this fact was used to justify the salinity distribution at low water slack tide to deduce the constants B' and D_0' which apply to this low water salinity distribution.

Dimensionless numbers formed from these terms are D_0/U_fB' and $2\pi B'/U_0T$ where U_0 is the maximum flood tide velocity and T is the tidal period. These dimensionless numbers were shown by Harleman and Abraham (1966) to depend on the ratio of the tidal amplitude a' to the mean

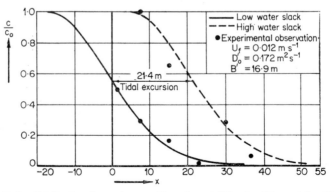

Fig. 6. Salinity distribution for waterways Experimental Station Flume (after Harleman and Abraham 1966).

depth at the outlet to the ocean h' and a number called the estuary number. This number was defined as $P_t F_0^2 / Q_f T$

where P_t is the tidal prism (i.e. the volume of sea water entering the estuary), F_0 the Froude number and equals $U_0 / \sqrt{gh'}$ and Q_f the freshwater discharge. The relationships obtained between these numbers for the Waterway Experimental Station and the Rotterdam Waterway are shown in Figs 7 and 8.

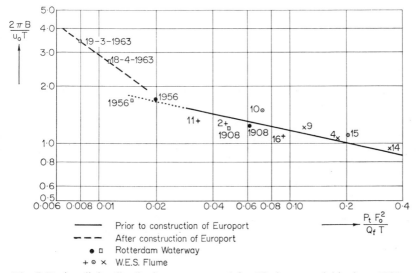

Fig. 7. Basic salinity distribution parameters (after Harleman and Abraham 1966).

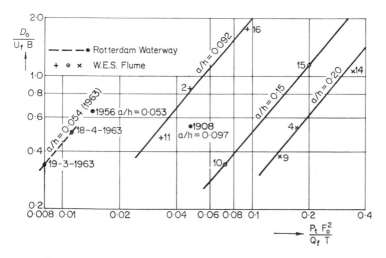

Fig. 8. Basic salinity distribution parameters (after Harleman and Abraham 1966).

The effects of changes in the estuary geometry such as the depth and tidal prism and/or changes in the fresh water discharge may be predicted from these curves. It would, of course, be necessary to carry out the tidal calculations for each new change in geometry in order to determine the values occurring in the estuary number. Errors must be expected where the changes are more complicated than the simple deepening of the estuary channel or the diversion of some of the fresh water. This has been shown by the departures from the predicted curves once the complicated Europort was built at the mouth of the Rotterdam Waterway (Fig. 7).

4. CONCLUSIONS

It can be seen from this review that the dispersion of salt in rivers and the behaviour of saline wedges in estuaries is understood in a qualitative manner. If sufficient prototype data are collected a numerical model of the behaviour of the dispersion of salt or any pollutant in a river or estuary can be made to produce the prototype data. This is done in the same manner as in a normal hydraulic model. That is, in a numerical model the bottom friction and interfacial friction or the dispersion coefficient is varied in order to obtain prototype verification, while in a normal distorted hydraulic model the bottom is roughened and wire mesh is placed through the interface in order to obtain the interfacial shears and mixing necessary to get prototype-model verification.

In both cases the model is then used to predict what will happen when major changes are made in the prototype. In the present stage of the art there seems little to choose between the two methods although there appears to be slightly more hope of gaining further understanding by pursuing the numerical approach and this is the reason for concentrating on this approach in this review.

REFERENCES

Aris, R. (1956). *Proc. Roy. Soc. London A* **235**, 67.

Boulot, F., and Daubert, A. (1969). *Proc. 13th Congr. Int. Assoc. Hydraulic Res.* **3**, 353.

Elder, J. W. (1959). *J. Fluid Mech.* **5**, 554.

Fischer, H. B. (1966). *Int. J. Air. Wat. Poll.* **10**, 443.

Fischer, H. B. (1967). *J. Hydraulics Div. A.S.C.E.* **93** (HY6), 187.

Fischer, H. B. (1968). *J. Sanit. Eng. Div., A.S.C.E.* **94**, (SA5), 927.

Fischer, H. B. (1969a). *Water Resources Res.* **5**, 496.

Fischer, H. B. (1969b). *Proc. 13th Congr. Int. Assoc. Hydraulic Res.* **3**, 173.

Harleman, D. R. F., and Abraham, G. (1966). Delft Hydraulic Laboratory Report Pub. No. 44.

Harleman, D. R. F., and Hoopes, J. A. (1963). *Proc. 10th Congr. Int. Assoc. Hydraulic Res.* **1**, 109.

Harleman, D. R. F., Luis, F., and Parthencades, E. (1967). *Proc. 12th Congr. Int. Assoc. Hydraulic Res.* **4**, 164.

Holley, E. R. (1969). *J. Hydraulics Div. A.S.C.E.* **95** (HY2), 621.

Holley, E. R., Harleman, D. R. F., and Fischer, H. B. (1970). *J. Hydraulics Div. A.S.C.E.* **96** (HY8), 1691.

Ippen, A. T. (1966). *Estuary and Coastline Hydrodynamics.* McGraw–Hill, New York.

Okubu, A. (1964). *Studies in Oceanography.* p. 216. Univ. of Washington Press, Seattle.

Pels, S. (1967). The Winston Churchill Memorial Trust Report No. 2.

Schijf, J. B., and Schonfeld, J. C. (1953). *Proc. Minnesota Int. Hydraulics Conv.* p. 321.

Shankar, N. J., and Masch, F. D. (1970). Tech. Rep. Office Wat. Resc. Res. Dept. Int. and Texas Wat. Dev. Board. Rpt. Hyd. 16-7001. C.R.W.R. 49.

Stommel, H., and Farmer, H. G. (1952). *J. Marine Res.* **11**, 205.

Taylor, G. I. (1922). *Proc. London Math. Soc.* **20**, 196.

Taylor, G. I. (1954). *Proc. Roy. Soc. London A* **223**, 446.

Thorpe, S. A., Hutt, P. K., and Soulsby, R. (1969). *J. Fluid Mech.* **38**, 375.

Turner, J. S. (1968). *J. Fluid Mech.* **33**, 639.

Turner, J. S., and Kraus, J. B. (1967a). *Tellus* **19**, 88.

Turner, J. S., and Kraus, J. B. (1967b). *Tellus* **19**, 98.

Vreugdenhil, C. B. (1970). *La Houille Blanche* No. 1, 35.

Wood, I. R. (1969). *Proc. 13th Congr. Int. Assoc. Hydraulic Res.* **3**, 271.

Woods, J. D. (1968). *Meteor. Mag.* **3**, 271.

Yih, C. S. (1965). *Dynamics of Non-homogeneous Fluids.* Macmillan, New York.

Yotsukura, N., and Fiering, M. B. (1964). *J. Hydraulics Div. A.S.C.E.* **99** (HY5), 83.

PART IV   Biology and Salinity

Salinity and the Whole Animal

W. V. MACFARLANE

Waite Agricultural Research Institute, University of Adelaide, South Australia

SUMMARY

Land mammals have neuroendocrine controls and cellular pumping mechanisms to maintain inter- and intracellular electrolyte concentrations. Sodium conservation is highly developed. In the ocean and in arid hot areas the salinity of water reaches four or more times that of the body fluids. Either such water is not consumed or kidneys are developed to excrete the surplus electrolyte. Amongst sheep and cattle, 180–220 mmol l^{-1} NaCl is the concentration chronically tolerated in drinking water. Sheep and goats do not drink in winter, so that saline water is not a nutritional problem, until summer. Camels live satisfactorily when drinking 1850 mmol l^{-1} NaCl (5·5%) but sheep accept only 220 mmol l^{-1} NaCl (1·3%). Animals evolved in the desert (jerboas, quokkas, camels) are more salt tolerant than swamp-based animals like bovids. There are renal and cellular adjustments to the high salt intakes but all members of a breed or species do not make the adjustment as well as others.

The toxicity of Na salts is complex. They may reduce plasma K levels, which leads to circulatory inadequacy. High plasma and cellular Na also reduces appetite, causes drowsiness, incoordination, spasticity, and finally autogenous firing of neurones.

Potassium salts come mainly from plants and large quantities of K can readily be excreted. Potassium retention (in kidney damage) causes spontaneous firing of nerves and muscles. With 10–15 meq l^{-1} K in plasma there are heart irregularities and fibrillation. Calcium salts in hard saline waters are not readily absorbed but rather cause water loss through diarrhoea. When Ca is absorbed it facilitates conduction in nerve and muscle, increases the force of skeletal and heart muscle contraction, and facilitates nerve-muscle transmission. Stones of Ca oxalate, carbonate or phosphate may form in the kidney or renal tract in dry regions.

Magnesium is not readily absorbed. When Mg^{++} ions are taken up, however, they counteract Ca^{++}. Magnesium blocks nerve-muscle junctional transmission and brings about paralysis. It is used as an anesthetic in some animals. Magnesium may form part of renal stones.

There are species limits to the salinity of water that can be tolerated without strain. Some species have high intrinsic tolerance to salinity but most animals require weeks of gradual exposure, before an equilibrium is reached. The degree to which growth, fertility and efficiency are reduced by saline waters is determined by species or breed of animal; and the effects are modulated by food, air temperature, age and lactation.

1. INTRODUCTION

Animal life probably differentiated in the weakly saline water of the Cambrian seas (Macallum 1926). This concentration of salts at 200–300 mosmol l^{-1} accompanied snails, insects, amphibians, reptiles, birds and mammals that left the sea for dry land. It persisted as the private bath of extracellular fluid which is pumped around the body to perfuse all cells. Extracellular fluid remained a bland Na solution with a low K content, but its proteins helped in gas transport, osmotic regulation and transport of hormones and metabolites.

2. ELECTROLYTES AMONG LAND MAMMALS

Immigration of animals to the relative desert of dry land required not only low permeability of the skin, but also auto-regulation of salinity in the body fluids. As the oceans filled with salts washed from the land they too became biological deserts with osmotic concentrations of 1100–1500 mosmol l^{-1}— 4 or 5 times greater than the salinity of the cell media of mammals. In the ocean, mechanisms rarely persisted in mammals to allow drinking of salt water. Only some desert animals, like the camel, kangaroo rat or quokka survive while drinking water as salt as the sea (Schmidt-Nielsen 1964). The salt-handling mechanisms for desert life presumably evolved because salt became concentrated in the water supplies, or salts were stored in halophytic vegetation. In the dry two-thirds of Australia there are many ringworm-like circles of salt formed at the edges of drying ponds or salt lakes.

Heavy rainfall, in mountains or the wet tropics, leaches salts (Na, I) from the soils. Tropical plants (Table 1) may have only about 1 % of the Na found in temperate zone plants (Howard *et al.* 1962). Herbivores such as the vegans of the New Guinea highlands (Macfarlane *et al.* 1968) or rabbits and sheep, adapt renal and endocrine functions to salt-leached environments (Blair-West *et al.* 1968*b*).

Two sources of salt water result from human intervention: underground waters with high Na, Mg and Ca as Cl, HCO_3 or SO_4 or artesian waters in bore drains or troughs evaporated to toxic salinity levels (Moule 1945).

Manmade saline water arises also from irrigation, which combines leaching of soil electrolytes with increased runoff of salts to river systems (Table 1).

TABLE 1

Composition of river and sea water, and mammalian plasma

	River water meq l⁻¹ Murray River*		Mammalian plasma meq l⁻¹	Sea† water meq l⁻¹
	summer	winter		
Na	10	1·4	145	470·2
K	0·1	0·06	5	9·9
Ca	1·7	0·4	5	10·2
Mg	2·5	0·5	2	53·6

* Average composition of Murray water near Murray Bridge 1965–69, by courtesy of Mr D. Pearce, E. and W. S. D. Adelaide.
† Barnes, H. (1954) Salinity 3·43 %.
The composition of plasma lies between river water and sea water. Both fluids must be selectively modified by an animal to become plasma.

3. ELECTROLYTES AND BODY COMPOSITION OF MAMMALS

Conventional analysis of the mammalian body by weight is convenient but it does not help understanding of the functions of salt (Fig. 1 (2)). Since biological molecules vary in size, mass as such gives little biochemical information. Measurement of electrolytes in body compartments is useful in assessing movements between fluids and cells. A better functional analysis, however, records the number of molecules or atoms present (Table 2). In an adult animal of 100 kg (pig or a large human), water is the most common molecule (Fig. 1 (1)). After burning off C, H, O, N and water, ash remains as about 4% of the live body weight. Calcium salts of bone occur mainly as apatite, a complex of $Ca(OH)_2$ and $Ca_3(PO_4)_2$. Sodium can enter the mineral lattice, so that less than half of bone Na is exchangeable. Similarly, hydroxides in apatite can be replaced by F or Cl directly from drinking water or toothpaste. There is about 2% of $Mg_3(PO_4)_2$ also in bone. Only one-fourth of the body's ash is Na and K (Table 2).

By volume, a mammal of 100 kg carries about 38 litres of water in cells and gut (Fig. 1 (4)) which dissolves some 5000 meq of exchangeable K, 150 meq of Na and about 150 meq Mg (Ussing et al. 1960). Intracellular anions are mainly PO_4, some Cl, less HCO_3, and protein with about 17 negative charges per molecule (Fig. 1 (3)). In bony tissues there are 3000 meq Na and 400 meq K. In the 25 litres of extracellular fluid Na predominates at about 3600 meq 100 kg body weight⁻¹. There are some 130 meq of K and

COMPOSITION

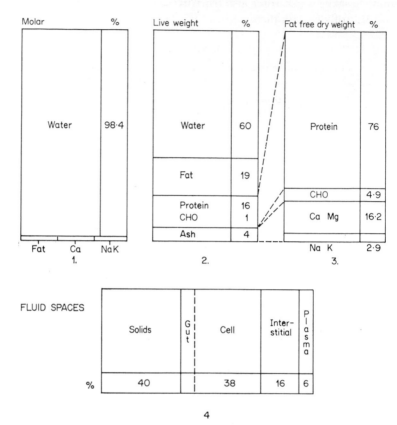

Fig. 1. Body composition is expressed as composition by weight, as distribution of fluid in gut, cell, interstitial and plasma spaces, and as the number of molecules in the body. The diagrams illustrate the different ways of regarding the electrolyte and water content of animals. Molecular or ionic concentration are the only satisfactory measures, and they indicate the osmotic relations between compartments.

of Ca in extracellular fluid, along with 45 meq of Mg (Edelman and Liebman 1959). Potassium is separated from Na by the semipermeable membrane of cells so there is a trans-membrane potential of −85 mV.

A third way of looking at a mammal is in molar terms (Table 2). Each mol, equivalent or osmol represents $6·01 \times 10^{23}$ particles. By number, water comprises 98·3% of the body, about 3333 mol 100 kg^{-1} (Fig. 1 (1)). Fat molecules number 24 ± 12 mol. Protein and carbohydrate molecules are not numerous (0·0006 mol %) but their large molecular weights raise their proportion by weight to 17%. There are about 24 mol of Ca salts, 6·7 mol of K and 5·3 mol of Na salts. The living processes, therefore, take place in a water medium where only 1·7% of the number of molecules provides the form and most of the function. Only 1 % of the molecules by number or 4 % by weight are electrolytes, mostly Ca salts in the skeleton, and 0·3 % of all molecules are Na and K salts.

TABLE 2

Body composition by weight and number of molecules: 100 kg mammal

	Body content			Turnover 24 hr^{-1}		
	kg %	Mol	Mol %	kg	Mol	Mol % of content
Water	60·0	3333·0	98·3	6·0	333·0	10·0
Fats	19·0	24·0	0·7			
Proteins	16·0	0·1	0·0003	0·6	3·0	12·0
Carbohydrates	1·0	<0·1	0·0003	0·001	0·05	0·008
Calcium salts	3·2	23·0	0·7	0·001	0·05	0·008
Na, K salts	0·8	12·0	0·35	0·04	0·8	6·7
Oxygen (O$_2$)	0·002	0·06	0·002	0·7	21·3	357·0
Energy (kcal)	240000	—	—	2400	—	10·0

Approximate composition by weight and number of molecules of 100 kg mammals resting in a thermoneutral environment (e.g. large sheep, man or pig). The turnover of molecules is expressed as a fraction of the body content of those molecules, and the energy turnover is related to the average energy content. There is a close relationship between the proportion (about 10 %) of molecules, of water, carbon and electrolyte turned over each day, and the energy turnover.

The number of molecules present may be obtained by multiplying the second column (mol) by $6·0 \times 10^{23}$, giving a total of $2·04 \times 10^{27}$ molecules of which about $2·1 \times 10^{26}$ turn over daily.

TABLE 3

Comparison of electrolyte content of plants and animals

	Na		K		Ca		Mg	
	% DM	meq kg^{-1} DM	% DM	meq kg^{-1} DM	% DM	meq kg^{-1} DM	% DM	meq kg^{-1} DM
Grass, temperate	0·14	61	2·0	512	0·40	200	0·24	198
Grass, tropical*	0·007	3	2·5	740	0·40	200	0·18	148
Herbs, temperate	0·17	74	3·1	795	1·4	700	0·75	618
Daily requirement for growth								
Pig	0·09	39	0·25	64	0·5	250	0·05	41
Young ruminant	0·08	35	0·50	128	0·27	135	0·07	58

DM = dry matter

Based on Underwood (1966)
* Howard, Burdin, and Lampkin (1962)

Food content of cations and the requirement of these mineral elements in food, for growth in an omnivore (pig) and ruminants. These values relate to temperate zone pastures, for which median compositions are given, and for equatorial grassland, which is very low in Na.

W. V. Macfarlane

Turnover of electrolytes. Calcium exchangeability and turnover is very low (0·008 % day^{-1}) but it is higher (8·0 % day^{-1}) for other cations (Table 2). About 40 % of body Na, however, is bound firmly in bone and 35 % of bone Na is exchangeable. Ruminants turn over about 20 % each day of body K because of the high levels of K in plant food (Tables 3, 4) while an omnivore turns over only 6–10 % daily. The Na turnover by man is 6–8 % of content daily except amongst vegetarians (Macfarlane *et al.* 1968).

TABLE 4

Electrolyte content of water, milk, meat, vegetables and grains

| | Milk | | | | | |
	mature human milk meq l^{-1}	mature cows milk meq l^{-1}	Oats grain meq kg^{-1}	Sweet potato meq kg^{-1}	Beans meq kg^{-1}	Mutton meq kg^{-1}
Na	7·5	33	1	2	0·5	76
K	12	37	88	135	174	45
Ca	17	68	27	15	31	2
Mg	3	11	120	10	55	3

The molar concentrations of electrolytes in typical forms of food and milk give an indication of the possible surpluses of electrolyte (e.g. excess K in vegetables, Na in cows milk or Mg in oats) or of deficits (Na in vegetables, Ca in meat) in dietary components, in their normal edible form. The units (kg) relate to wet weight not dry weight.

Herbivores ingest excess K relative to meat-eating animals (Table 4). Carnivores consume a dietary ratio of Na : K like that of their own body composition. Aboriginals cook kangaroos in the skin and retain extra-cellular Na with the cell K, since there is no bleeding-out of the animal, whereas modern slaughtering drains 1000 meq 100 kg^{-1} of Na and some Fe from the animal.

4. REGULATION OF ELECTROLYTE CONTENT AND TURNOVER

The turnover of electrolytes is a product of intake, storage and excretion. These phases are separately regulated by physico-chemical, nervous or endocrine controls.

Intake. The newborn mammal normally has an intrinsic drive to take milk and thus electrolytes (Richter 1956). Human milk provides 5–10 meq Na l^{-1} and cows 20–40 meq l^{-1}. Potassium is similar in concentration to Na whereas Ca reaches 70 meq l^{-1} in cows milk, but is low (17 meq l^{-1}) in human milk (Table 4).

If the Na content of pasture is low, adequate endocrine adjustments for re-use of Na are usually made (Blair-West *et al.* 1968*a*). When, however, an animal loses Na in milk or sweat or becomes deficient because of growth or grain feeding (Table 4) Na supplements can increase growth and well being.

Salt hunger develops when Na intakes are low and this appetite is specific for Na salts (Denton 1967, 1969). The international salt trade developed to meet human fashions in relatively recent times (mainly during the last 500 years), although interest in salt has been increasing over the last 3000 years. Salt was adopted in early Roman times as the salarium for troops who often fought in hot country. Increased desire for salt probably arose on a grain-based dietary that has spread increasingly in the last 7000 years (Clark 1969). Sodium selection, however, is specific and derives from taste receptors and their central neurones with no learning component initially (Richter 1956). Rabbits, sheep, cattle (Denton 1967, 1969) and man (Macfarlane *et al.* 1968) can maintain good health and reproduction on very low Na intakes. A taste for salt is readily acquired, to become an appetite drive well beyond physiological needs for growth or maintenance and it is probably linked with hypertension. There is no well-defined upper limit for Na intake, though high concentrations (10%) of NaCl will induce vomiting in man by irritation of the stomach. Sheep grazing saltbush take in 3000 meq a day yet they can sustain good function on about 1000th of that quantity (Macfarlane *et al.* 1967).

Distribution.   Electrolytes may be ingested in solution or in solid form. In ruminants the rumen contains about 10 litres of fluid per 100 kg, slightly hypotonic to plasma. Ingested salts are diluted in this fluid. There is some active transport requiring ATP and butyrate to move Na from rumen to blood. Rumen K at 50–200 meq l^{-1} diffuses down its concentration gradient to 5 meq l^{-1} in the plasma. There is a constant recycling of salts through glands into and out of the gut.

Intestinal cells use the extensive cell membranes of the gut for ion transport. This is mainly an active process with two components (Barry *et al.* 1969):

1.   Sodium is moved with an anion into the intestinal cells. In the membrane there is a Na^+, K^+ activated ATP'ase (Skou 1960, 1965) which by splitting ATP yields energy to move Na into the cell on a lipoprotein carrier in exchange for K. Sodium then diffuses out into interstitial fluid and plasma for circulation. A similar mechanism pumps excess Na out of nerve or muscle.

2.   An electrogenic pump is also active in gut and gland cells. With this, Na^+ is separated from anions and is actively transported into the cell as a cation, thus creating a potential difference. This transport is linked with glucose transport. From the intestinal cells Na^+ diffuses to the intercellular

space for further distribution (Curran and Solomon 1957; Parsons 1967).

Active transport across intestinal cells moves Ca into the blood and vitamin D is required for this process. The colon pumps Ca and K back into the intestine for egestion.

Interstitial fluid pervades all body cells (Table 1). From extracellular fluid, K at 5 meq l^{-1} is moved into cells by active transport against a 26 : 1 gradient. Again membrane-bound, ouabain-inhibited $Na^+–K^+$ ATP'ase is active and Na is pumped outward from low intracellular to high extracellular concentrations. There is also a Mg^{++} activated $Na^+–K^+$ ATP'ase (Schmidt and Dubach 1970) in kidney and other tissues. It is not sensitive to ouabain and it moves molecular NaCl. Calcium is extracellular, except during excitation of heart, muscle or nerve when some Ca penetrates cells to couple excitation with contraction in muscle, to facilitate secretion or to release transmitter substances (Hubbard et al. 1969). It is then actively transported outward across mitochrondrial, reticular and cell membranes. When active transport of Na is blocked by ouabain, cells swell as water moves osmotically into cells. Proteins have little osmotic effect, but the electrolyte concentrations in cell water (300 mosmol l^{-1}) exert 7 atm pressure. Small changes of electrolytes thus have large effects on cell osmotic pressure, normally a few mm of water pressure above that of interstitial fluid (Tosteson 1964).

The uptake of electrolytes from the intestine, and their concentrations in plasma or cells are sustained mainly by active transport, though passive or assisted ion fluxes also occur. The pumps in turn are subject to nervous and endocrine regulation. Surplus electrolyte is dismissed from the body by selective transport mechanisms in sweat glands, kidney, gut or tear glands.

Central control of sodium intake and output.   The drive to eat salt has some representation in the hypothalamus. Wolf (1964) reduced salt appetite by destruction of dorso-lateral neurones of the hypothalamus; but definition of Na-sensitive areas is still imprecise. Elimination of excess Na from increased extracellular volume is not yet understood though a Na-excreting hormone has been postulated. Sodium salts in the third ventricle of goats and rats (Andersson et al. 1969; Dorn and Porter 1970) lead apparently to Na excretion though the mechanism is not known.

Fluid volume and excretion.   Intracellular concentrations remain remarkably constant ($\pm 1 \%$) though their control is more at the cell membrane than centrally (Tosteson 1964). The extracellular fluid lies in the flowstream between the gut and output at the kidney. A close balance is achieved, but failure of heart, liver or kidney can lead to Na accumulation and oedema, an increase of extracellular fluid.

(*a*) *Volume regulation*. Stretch receptors in the atrium of the heart (and possibly liver or lung receptors) respond to the volume of plasma by transmitting information on pulse pressure to the brain stem (Gauer 1967). A fall of blood volume is translated in the hypothalamus to the neurosecretion of vasopressin. Vasopressin increases the amount of cyclic AMP in the distal kidney cells, which increases permeability of the collecting duct so more water is returned to circulation (Handler *et al.* 1965). Sodium also is retained by central mechanisms and renal monitors which release aldosterone. Aldosterone increases enzyme concentrations in kidney tubules so that they pump more Na from the kidney lumen back into the blood stream (Edelman 1967). The retained water and Na increase the volume of extra-cellular fluid (Fig. 2).

(*b*) *Concentration control*. At least three mechanisms increase reabsorption of Na from the gut, sweat glands or the kidney:

1. Direct action of electrolytes on the adrenal. A 1 % fall in Na concentration or a 0·5 meq l^{-1} rise in plasma K concentration releases aldosterone (Blair-West *et al.* 1968*a*) from the glomerular layer of adrenal cells.

2. Renal mechanisms. Reduction in filtration and slow tubular passage result in increased Na reabsorption (Wesson 1957). Sodium concentration, blood pressure or osmotic gradients act on the juxtaglomerular monitoring and gland cells between the glomerular arterioles and the loop of the distal tubule. The gland cells release an enzyme, renin. This splits a decapeptide, angiotensin I from plasma α-globulin, then a lung enzyme forms an octapeptide, angiotensin II, which releases aldosterone from the adrenal cortex. It also causes smooth muscle to contract and thus raises arterial blood pressure. Renin, angiotensin and aldosterone concentrations in plasma are closely related (Blair-West *et al.* 1968*a*) but there may be a further renal factor in sodium control.

3. Central mechanisms. From the anterior pituitary, ACTH is released during physiological strain and weakly activates the aldosterone system. The brain also acts through renal nerves to release renin.

In these ways the control of Na is linked with circulation, blood pressure and the homeostasis of fluid and electrolytes.

Potassium concentrations in the blood vary little since there is rapid excretion of any increased plasma K. The mechanisms of K control are still obscure. The Na–K pumps in cell membranes are important and include the K-secreting cells of the distal renal tubule and colon, which increase activity under vasopressin in ruminants. Sweat glands, particularly in ruminants also secrete K. Aldosterone in man and dog increases K secretion by the kidney but not in ruminants (Macfarlane *et al.* 1967).

Calcium is mainly immobilized in bone but some ionic (4 meq l^{-1}) and bound Ca is present in extracellular fluids. The gill-arch system of fish persists in mammals as thyroid and parathyroid glands to maintain endocrine

12

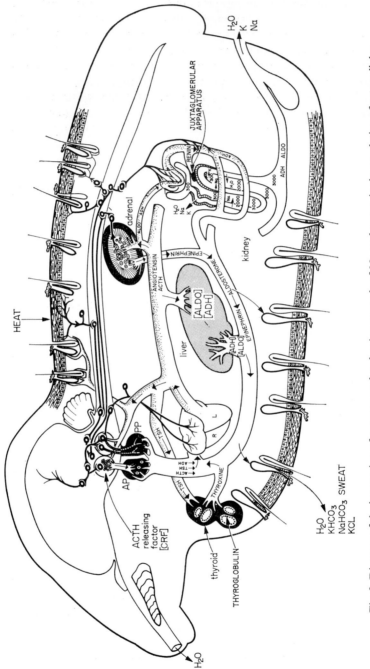

Fig. 2. Diagram of the interaction of nervous and endocrine controls of Na and water, in the regulation of extracellular fluid volume and concentration.

When water is lost in evaporative cooling by sweating or panting, blood volume falls, and this is registered in the nervous system. Neuroendocrine activation of the pituitary releases vasopressin (to reduce urine flow) and renin (from the kidney to lead to angiotensin II and Na reabsorption). The adrenal glands respond directly to Na and K concentrations in plasma, as do some cells in the hypothalamus.

control of Ca. Parathormone is a polypeptide which removes bone Ca enzymatically and raises Ca in the blood. The ultimobranchial cells of the gill-arch lower plasma Ca by a polypeptide, calcitonin (Copp 1965) which encourages deposition of Ca in bone. The direct monitoring of Ca by parathyroid cells is regulatory, much as the glomerular layer of the adrenal responds directly to Na-K concentrations.

Release of Ca from the kidney is largely under the influence of parathormone which increases both PO_4 and Ca excretion and in dry hot areas these may crystalize as renal stones. Milk drains up to 1·5 eq Ca daily from high production cows (Table 4).

Magnesium. The control of Mg uptake, cellular distribution and excretion is still not adequately understood. Most Mg is held in the hydration cells of apatite crystals in bone. Low plasma Mg follows a large output of Ca and this leads to tetany, rigidity and disturbances of movement. Excess Mg in the plasma produces immobility and coma, through the blocking by Mg, of release of acetyl choline vesicles from nerve endings (Hubbard *et al.* 1969). The balancing of Mg in the body appears to be linked with the deposition or mobilization of Ca (Harma *et al.* 1961) while Ca^{++} and Mg^{++} compete for reabsorption.

Increased demands for Na and Ca arise during lactation or sweating. Man secretes a high-Na sweat (5–110 meq l^{-1}). Cattle come next in rank order of sweat production but they secrete more K than Na in the sweat (Macfarlane 1964; Johnson 1969). These losses may increase intake of electrolytes.

5. EXCESSIVE SALT INTAKE

Excessive intake of electrolyte most commonly arises from high concentrations in food or drinking fluid (Heller 1933; Moule 1945; Garner 1961). The consequences of taking salts are different when they come from solid sources rather than from solutions. If the Na content of food is high, salt can be washed out by increased intake of water. When salt is taken with water, there is conflict between the need for water and the salt load to be excreted.

Hypernatraemia. Human infants fed cows milk during hot weather may fail to excrete the excess Na (Danks *et al.* 1962) so plasma Na rises to 200 meq l^{-1}. This causes coma, irritability, fits, and death or brain damage. This sequence follows seawater ingestion, but it is rare in man without dehydration and renal failure (Katzman 1966).

Ingestion of solid electrolytes. When ruminants lick salt from a solid block the electrolytes are dissolved in saliva and there is little effect beyond an increase of thirst. Sheep may take 4000 to 5000 mmol NaCl daily yet maintain weight and health. A temporary rise of blood osmolality stimulates the drinking (ventrolateral) areas of the hypothalamus. Water intake rises but this is less in Merino than in Leicester sheep eating salt-bush (Macfarlane *et al.* 1967). In both breeds urine is diluted to about 1000–1200 mosmol l^{-1} by drinking 10 to 18 litres of water daily. The kidney is not driven to its concentration limit at 3800 mosmol l^{-1} in sheep. Presumably it is more efficient to drink water to wash out salts than to perform the osmotic work of concentration to 3000 mosmol l^{-1}. Wilson *et al.* (1969) find that saltbush is not preferred by sheep but is eaten when grass is not available. *Atriplex nummularia* contains about 3900 meq kg^{-1} Na and 900 meq kg^{-1} of K. *Kochia* has similar concentrations although some species accumulate more K than Na. As the salt content of water rises, there is relatively less physiological reserve to cope with high Na or K intakes from saltbush. The upper limit of salinity in water for sheep eating salt is about 80–98 mmol NaCl (0·5–0·6%, Wilson 1966).

When solid salt is taken by man, it passes into the glandular stomach. Salt tablets can produce vomiting and remain often undissolved. The ruminant not only has copious saliva but also the saliva-salt mixture passes onto squamous rumen epithelium, where salt is diluted without causing irritation.

In man ingestion of 20–40 g NaCl reduces, then raises, plasma volume. If renal function is poor, plasma Na concentration rises, and this leads to weakness, a feeling of toxicity, circulatory failure and central nervous dysfunction. Ordinarily, however, if water is available the salt can be washed out in a massive Na diuresis.

When KCl is ingested in 20–40 g doses, apart from the immediate effect on the stomach and osmotic disturbances of circulation, there is a rise in plasma K. At 8–12 meq l^{-1} plasma K depolarizes nerves and muscles, increases excitability and this leads to twitching of muscles while the spontaneous firing of nerves is felt as pins and needles over the skin area. Extra heart beats intrude on the normal rhythm. Death usually results from tachycardia, venticular fibrillation and heart standstill (Hoffman and Cranefield 1960). If the kidney is adequate and water is available the K can be washed out.

The osmotic effects of large doses of Ca or Mg salts are considerable since these are poorly absorbed divalent cations. After some uptake the transport mechanisms in the gut become saturated so that ions remain in the gut, with water drawn from the plasma. This induces diarrhoea which discharges some of the excess electrolytes.

Saline fluids.   When drinking-water contains salts the toxic effects are greater than those induced by solid electrolytes. Even NaCl is more toxic, unless fresh water is available for diuresis.

Sea water. Marine mammals use small amounts of sea water (Krogh 1939) but seals and whales mostly live on fish and crustacea with lower osmolalities than sea water. Metabolic water comes from oxidized food hydrogen. Sea mammals live on this without high renal concentrating powers, since they do not lose water as sweat. In marine birds (like cormorants, Schmidt-Nielsen 1960) a specialized tear-gland excretes salt and a similar gland is present in land lizards. Active cellular transport (Fänge and Schmidt-Nielsen 1958) concentrates NaCl to levels above those of sea water.

Only 300–500 ml day^{-1} of sea water (a 1200 mosmolar solution of Na, K, Ca, Mg, Cl and HCO_3) is tolerated by man (Harvey 1957; Laddell 1965). Above that intake, there is dehydration as tissue water is drawn upon to excrete excess electrolytes (McCance *et al.* 1951). Potassium rises in the plasma also. Men can cross the Atlantic in cooler latitudes using fish and sea water in the manner of whales. When there is little sweat, a balance can be met on 400 ml sea water daily even with the human kidney, which concentrates only to 1400 mosmol l^{-1}. Laddell (1947) showed that naval subjects on rafts who drank sea water were in negative balance when more than 400 ml of sea water per day were ingested. Drinking of sea water reduced appetite and produced the lassitude, weakness, nausea, confusion and delirium associated with Na toxicity.

Wild animals. In some desert animals the kidney copes with sea water. The high renal work capacity and urine concentration to 6 or 7 osmol l^{-1} of kangaroo rat (*Dipodomys*), gerbils and some small marsupials, allows these animals to live on seeds or insects without drinking water (Schmidt-Nielsen 1964). Food and metabolic water maintains function. The camel also maintains appetite and excretes excess electrolytes when drinking sea water. This is partly due to the kidney, though its concentrating power is less than that of sheep. Camels tolerate raised extracellular Na, so that a plasma Na of 200 meq l^{-1} does not disturb either circulation or nerve and muscle function though 185 meq l^{-1} is fatal to man. Maloiy (personal communication) has shown that the dromedary at rest and cool, maintains food intake and body weight while drinking 1850 mosmol l^{-1} (5·5 % NaCl), a greater concentration than that of a tropical ocean. A camel drinking 195 g day^{-1} NaCl averaged 3 litres fluid intake, and 4 litres output of urine. The 5 kg food yield about 3 litres of water, so there were 6 litres of water to meet respiratory, urine, sweat and faecal loss. Of the 3340 mmol NaCl taken daily 1600 mosmol NaCl go to each litre of urine. This would leave 1400 mosmol in urine for other salts, urea and minor solutes to make up the 3000 mosmol l^{-1} urine produced by the camel. This renal work regulates plasma Na to 150 meq l^{-1}.

With high protein intake, high sweating rates, lactation or heavy work, undoubtedly the camel would have difficulty in surviving on the higher salinities of water. It is, however, a very efficient organism for the heat, drought and salt waters of the desert.

Domestic animals. In Australia livestock die periodically after drinking salt waters in hot regions. Moule (1945) reported 2% mortality amongst sheep that drank water evaporated to 410 mmol l⁻¹ (2·4% NaCl). Ohman (1939) found a 7% death rate amongst cattle 9 days off water, when they drank 260 mmol l⁻¹ bore water (1·5% NaCl). Cattle are more affected by high salinities than sheep, and saline water is even more toxic to equines than to cattle.

(*a*) *Sheep.* In 1957, Pierce began to study the effects of saline drinking-water on sheep in South Australia. Sheep were initially in pens and later at pasture (Pierce 1957, 1968). Sheep varied greatly in their responses to salt in drinking water. Some animals were left out of trials because they could not adapt to saline water. But animals exposed to increasing salinities similar to the salt of drying ponds during summer, adjusted to increasing salinity, some more than others. There is probably a genetic background to salt tolerance. The need for more water during summer, and for even more during lactation (Pierce 1968; Macfarlane and Howard 1970), the breed of sheep and its age (Macfarlane *et al.* 1967) all affect the salt intake and its effects.

Merino wethers are more thirsty when drinking 100–150 mmol l⁻¹ NaCl especially during summer. In winter, sheep need not drink unless food is very dry. Sheep drinking 150 mmol l⁻¹ NaCl begin to loose appetite and thus weight. Merino sheep chronically drinking 260 mmol l⁻¹ NaCl suffer inappetance, wasting, diarrhoea and inflammation of the intestine (Pierce 1957). At a salt level about 270 mmol l⁻¹ milk output and wool growth were reduced. There were signs of central nervous disturbance, with incoordination, weakness and final convulsions. Plasma electrolyte changed little although Na, K and Cl showed a small decrement (Pierce 1968). In the field Macfarlane *et al.* (1967) found that sheep eating saltbush had high water turnovers but reduced plasma Na proportionally to water intake.

Maloiy (personal communication) found that Somali fat-tail sheep were similar to Merinos in their tolerance of 220 mmol l⁻¹ NaCl, while Turkana goats ate well and maintained weight on 257 mmol l⁻¹ salt in drinking water containing 220 mmol l⁻¹ NaCl (1·3%). The period of build-up to this concentration was 3 or 4 weeks. Old ewes, however, adjusted less well than young sheep and had more reproductive difficulties.

When Mg or Ca was present in small quantities in the water, the tolerance to NaCl was reduced. For instance, 1·2% NaCl with 0·1% MgCl₂, or 0·9% NaCl, 0·2% NaHCO₃ and 0·2% Na₂CO₃ were accepted without loss of weight by penned wethers (Pierce 1968). Sodium bicarbonate 0·5% was also tolerated. The animals could not adjust to 0·7% NaCl plus 0·5% MgCl₂.

(*b*) *Cattle.* Cattle have a high water turnover and relatively low renal concentration to a maximum around 2500 mosmol l⁻¹ (Macfarlane 1964). They maintain weight on 160 mmol l⁻¹ NaCl (1%) (Weeth *et al.* 1960). Potter (1969) mentions that pigs seem to live in equilibrium with 160 mmol l⁻¹ NaCl, while horses do not function well on more than 120 mmol l⁻¹ (0·7% NaCl). Somali donkeys on saline waters in a temperate climate (Maloiy peronal communication) lost body weight at 255 mmol l⁻¹ NaCl (1·5%). Food intake was reduced at 210 mmol l⁻¹ drinking water. The osmolality of urine, however, remained at 1100–1400 mosmol l⁻¹. These desert-based donkeys, therefore, have much the same salt tolerance as Merino sheep and surpass horses in acceptance of salt.

The kidney and salt tolerance mechanisms.   Potter (1961, 1968) found that initially sheep ate little when drinking 220 mmol l⁻¹ NaCl but after several weeks appetite was recovered, and over years there was increase in faecal Na output. Tissue and body fluid Na remained within the same limits as in sheep drinking salt-free water. At high Na intakes there was, however, more water turnover and faster rumen emptying. Rumen Na concentration rose, and K fell. The normally high-K, low-Na secretion from the apocrine sweat glands of sheep was reversed. On 220 mmol l⁻¹ the kidney increased filtration fraction (Potter 1961) and the clearance of solute-free water was negative, as in the camel. Potter (1963) observed that filtration rose from 55 ml min⁻¹ on salt-free water to 80 ml min⁻¹ on drinking 220 mmol l⁻¹ NaCl as in the camel. Urine volume was four times greater on salt.

Total body water increases with salt intake, and there is an expansion of extracellular volume (Macfarlane *et al.*, 1967; Jones *et al* 1970), as is usual with high rates of water turnover from any cause.

Oral NaCl seems uniformly to increase filtration rate, but when 1660 mmol l⁻¹ NaCl (10%) was infused intravenously, filtration did not change in Merinos (Potter 1968). In Dorset Horn ewes, however, there was a rise in filtration after intravenous 10% NaCl. When sheep drinking rainwater received 48 g hr⁻¹ NaCl intravenously they became confused, the heart was irregular and they died in 3 days. Infusion of Na reduced plasma K levels and the syndrome was reversed by giving 10 g of KCl. In sheep accustomed to 220 meq l⁻¹ NaCl, an infusion of 1660 mmol NaCl caused less rise in plasma Na and less fall in K than in controls. Thus adaptive responses to Na intake take place, but the full cellular background is obscure. Potter (personal communication) has found enlarged adrenal cortices in sheep on longterm intake of 220 meq l⁻¹NaCl. Aldosterone output would be minimal in such animals so that the adrenal hypertrophy suggests functional strain comparable with the effects of other toxic stresses.

The effects of Na on smooth muscle in arterioles has been investigated for many years, and in man and rat some vascular hypertension can be relieved by low Na diet. Sheep drinking 220 meq l⁻¹ NaCl, however, had the same arterial pressures as those on rainwater (Potter 1969). Questions such as the status and sensitivity of the renin-angiotensin-aldosterone control system during chronic salt intake appear not to have been examined. When kidneys are damaged or mineralocorticoids are present Na raises blood pressure. In sheep taking saline water (Potter 1969) there was some reduction in rumen microbial synthesis associated with the rapid passage of substances from the rumen. Lambs on saline water appeared less fat than control lambs.

Renal lithiasis. Kidney and bladder stones form in man and animals from uric acid, silica, or from Ca, Mg oxalates, carbonates or phosphates. A matrix of mucoprotein is associated with precipitation of salts in layers. Stones are not inevitably connected with high concentrations of electrolyte in water, but they are common when Ca is available. Salt water or NaCl in food has been used to increase water flow-through and thus reduce stone formation (Udall 1959).

REFERENCES

Andersson, B., Dolman, M. F., and Olsson, K. (1969). *Acta Physiol. Scand.* **75**, 496.

Barnes, H. (1954). *J. exp. Biol.* **31**, 582.

Barry, R. J. C., Eggerton, J., and Smyth, D. (1969). *J. Physiol.* **204**, 299.

Blair-West, J., Cain, M., Catt, K., Coghlan, J. P., Denton, D. A., Funder, J. W., Scroggins, B. A., and Wright, R. D. (1968a). *Progress in Endocrinology.* Experpta Med. Int. Cong. Series No. 184, 276.

Blair-West, J. R., Coghlan, J. P., Denton, D. A., Goding, J. R., Wintour, M., and Wright, R. D. (1968b). *Nature* (Lond.) **217**, 922.

Clark, G. (1969). *World Prehistory.* p. 122. Cambridge University Press.

Copp, D. H. (1965). *Recent Progress Horm. Res.* **20**, 64.

Curran, P. F., and Solomon, A. K. (1957). *J. gen. Physiol.* **41**, 143.

Danks, D. M., Webb, D. W., and Allen, Jean (1962). *Brit. med. J.* **2**, 287.

Denton, D. A. (1967). In *Handbook of Physiology.* (Ed. C. E. Code.) **6**, 433. Am. Physiol. Soc., Washington.

Denton, D. A. (1969). *Nut. Abst. Rev.* **39**, 1943.

Dorn, J., and Porter, J. C. (1970). *Endocrinol.* **86**, 1112.

Edelman, I. S. (1967). *Amer. J. Physiol.* **213**, 954.

Edelman, I. S., and Liebman, J. (1959). *Amer. J. Med.* **27**, 256.

Fänge, R., and Schmidt-Nielsen, K. (1958). *Amer. J. Physiol.* **195**, 321.

Garner, R. J. (1961). *Veterinary Toxicology.* Bailliere, Tindall and Cox, London.

Gauer, O. H. (1967). *Les Concepts de Claude Bernard sur le Milieu Interieur.* p. 29. Masson, Paris.

Handler, J. S., Butcher, R. W., and Orloff, J. (1965). *J. biol. Chem.* **240**, 4524.

Harma, S., North, K. A. K., MacIntyre, I., and Fraser, R. (1961). *Brit. med. J.* **2**, 1253.

Harvey, G. R. (1957). *Lancet*, March 9th, 533.

Heller, V. G. (1933). Bull. Okla. Agric. Exp. Sta. No. 217.

Hoffman, B. F., and Cranefield, P. F. (1960). *Electrophysiology of the Heart.* McGraw-Hill, New York.

Howard, D. A., Burdin, H. L., and Lampkin, G. H. (1962). *J. agric. Sci.* **59**, 251.

Hubbard, J. T., Llinas, R., and Quastel, D. M. .J (1969). *Electrophysiological Analysis of Synaptic Transmission.* Arnold, London.

Johnson, K. G. (1969). Thesis, University of Queensland.

Jones, G. B., Potter, B. J., and Reid, C. S. W. (1970). *Aust. J. agric. Res.* **21**, 927.

Katzman, R. (1966). *Ann. Rev. Med.* **17**, 197.

Krogh, A. (1939). *Osmotic Regulation of Aquatic Animals.* Cambridge University Press.

Laddell, W. S. (1947). *Brit. med. Bull.* **5**, 9–12.

Laddell, W. S. (1965). In *Physiology of Human Survival.* (Eds. O. G. Edholm and A. L. Bacharach.) p. 267. Academic Press, New York.

Macallum, A. B. (1926). *Physiol. Rev.* **6**, 316.

Macfarlane, W. V. (1964). *Handbook of Physiology—Environment.* **4**, 509. Am. Physiol. Soc., Washington.

Macfarlane, W. V., and Howard, B. (1970). *The Physiology of Digestion and Metabolism in Ruminants.* Oriel Press, Aberdeen.

Macfarlane, W. V., Howard, B., and Siebert, B. D. (1967). *Aust. J. agric. Res.* **18**, 947.

Macfarlane, W. V., Howard, B., Skinner, S. A., and Scroggins, B. A. (1968). *Proc.* 14*th Int. Physiol. Congr.* p. 854.

Macfarlane, W. V., Kinne, R., Walmsley, C. M., Siebert, B. D., and Peter, D. (1967). *Nature* (Lond.) **214**, 979.

McCance, R. A., Crosfill, J. W. L., Ungley, G. C., and Widdowson, E. M. (1951). Med. Res. Council Report, No. 291.

Moule, G. R. (1945). *Aust. Vet. J.* **21**, 37.

Ohman, A. F. S. (1939). *Aust. Vet. J.* **15**, 37.

Parsons, D. S. (1967) *Brit. med. Bull.* **23**, 252.

Pierce, A. W. (1957). *Vet. Rev. Annot.* **3**, 37.

Pierce, A. W. (1968). *Aust. J. agric. Res.* **19**, 577.

Potter, B. J. (1961). *Aust. J. agric. Res.* **12**, 440.

Potter, B. J. (1963). *Aust. J. agric. Res.* **14**, 518.

Potter, B. J. (1966). *J. Physiol.* (Lond.) **184**, 605.

Potter, B. J. (1968). *J. Physiol.* (Lond.) **194**, 435.

Potter, B. J. (1969). Water Res. Foundn. Aust., Report No. 29, 8.1.

Richter, C. (1956). *L'instinct dans le Comportement des Animaux et de l'Homme.* Masson, Paris.

Schmidt, U., and Dubach, U. C. (1970). *Nephron.* **7**, 447.

Schmidt-Nielsen, K. (1960). *Circulation,* **21**, 955.

Schmidt-Nielsen, K. (1964). *Desert Animals.* Oxford University Press.

Skou, J. C. (1960). *Biochem. Biophys. Acta.* **42**, 6.

Skou, J. C. (1965). *Physiol. Rev.* **45**, 596.

Tosteson, D. C. (1964). *The Cellular Function of Membrane Transport.* Prentice-Hall, New York.

Udall, R. H. (1959). *Amer. J. vet. Res.* **23**, 1241.

Underwood, E. J. (1966). *The Mineral Nutrition of Livestock.* FAO and Comm. Agr. Bureau, Rome.

Ussing, H. H., Kruhoffer, P., Thaysen, J. H., and Thorn, N. A. (1960). *Handbuch der Experimentallen Pharmakologie.* Springer Verlag, Berlin.

Weeth, H. J., Haverland, L. H., and Cassard, D. W. (1960). *J. animal. Sci.* **19**, 845.

Wesson, L. O. (1957). *Medicine,* **36**, 281.

Wilson, A. D. (1966). *Aust. J. agric. Res.* **17**, 155.

Wilson, A. D., Leigh, J. H., and Mulham, W. E. (1969). *Aust. J. agric. Res.* **20**, 1123.

Wolf, C. (1964). *Psychonomic Sci.* **1**, 211.

Salinity and Animal Cells

P. W. GAGE

School of Physiology and Pharmacology, University of New South Wales,
Kensington, N.S.W.

SUMMARY

Biological cells exist in a saline environment which differs in ionic composition from the intracellular solution. Potassium is more concentrated inside, whereas sodium is more concentrated outside, cells. In the resting state, cell membranes are much more permeable to potassium than to sodium ions and this results in an electrical potential across the membrane, negative inside. The transmission of electrical signals, communication between cells, and the conversion of environmental energy to electrical signals, all depend on an inflow of sodium ions into cells as a result of an increase in the sodium permeability of the cell membrane. The intracellular concentrations of sodium and potassium ions are regulated by metabolically 'fuelled' ionic pumps. Because membrane potentials are essentially ionic diffusion potentials, the concentration gradients of sodium and potassium ions are of fundamental importance in the generation of electrical signals which are hence very sensitive to the concentration of these ions in the extracellular saline.

1. INTRODUCTION

Water is essential to life as we know it. About two-thirds of the total mass of a mammalian organism consists of water which is the solvent and medium of transport for all body solutes. Even small changes in total body water can cause serious changes in cellular function principally because of changes in solute concentration. These effects are related to the architecture of cells of which every organism is composed.

A cell may be described for present purposes as an aqueous protein gel composed of 10 to 20% solids and 80–90% water separated from an extracellular solution by a thin semipermeable membrane. This membrane is a bimolecular lipoprotein sandwich, 50 to 100 Angstroms thick, which acts as a diffusion barrier. Body water consists of two components, intracellular and extracellular. In primitive animals the extracellular solution is environmental water, fresh or salt, and is not contained within the organism. In

179

more sophisticated animals the extracellular solution is contained within the animal and a considerable amount of energy and biological machinery is devoted to maintaining its composition precisely.

In these higher animals there is an invariable difference in the concentration of salts on either side of the cell membrane. The sodium concentration is about ten times higher outside the cell than inside whereas the concentration gradient for potassium is in the opposite direction. Why these concentration gradients should exist in all cells is not clear. They certainly contribute to an electrical potential across most cell membranes and, in excitable cells, it is the change in this resting membrane potential which allows an electrical signal to be transmitted. It is interesting that the ratio of the concentrations of sodium and potassium ions across cell membranes is similar in land creatures and some primitive sea creatures. Presumably our ancestors could survive on land only when they had developed machinery to purify and circulate an artificial 'seawater'. As mentioned already, a large part of the complexity of higher animals is caused by the requirement of maintaining a good substitute for seawater.

The existence of ionic concentration gradients across a membrane which is not equally permeable to all ions results in an electrical potential. Since one of my interests is the electric activity of cells, and the influence of the extracellular saline on this activity, I will devote most of this paper to that aspect of cellular activity. If the reader wishes to read a fuller treatment of the topics briefly outlined here, two particularly lucid books are available (Hodgkin 1964; Katz 1966). Many methods of communication and energy transduction which we know about depend on ionic batteries across membranes. In other words, the differing concentrations of ions in the saline environment in combination with permeability 'switches' in cell membranes allow electrical pulses to be generated and transmitted. As will be seen, if the salinity of the external environment is allowed to alter, these pulses may be changed in amplitude or sometimes suppressed.

2. RESTING MEMBRANE POTENTIAL

A steady electrical potential can be recorded across the surface membrane of most cells. It is now generally believed that this potential is a consequence of the ionic concentration gradients and the differences in the ease with which different ions can diffuse through the membrane. Ions diffuse through membranes at a minute fraction of the rate at which they diffuse in water because of the non-polar nature of the lipid in the membrane. In the resting, non-active state the membrane is much more permeable to potassium than to sodium ions (by a factor which varies from cell to cell but is generally in the range of 20 to 100). Because the concentration of potassium ions is higher inside than outside the cell there is a net outward movement of potassium ions. This is not balanced by an inward movement of sodium ions because they cannot cross the membrane as rapidly as potassium ions. It is this net outward movement of positively charged ions which makes the inside of the cell negative with respect to the outside and is responsible for the membrane potential. In skeletal muscle cells this potential can be as high as one-tenth of a volt. If the membrane were permeable only to potassium ions, the membrane potential would be given by the Nernst equation

$$Em = \frac{RT}{F} \ln \frac{[K]_o}{[K]_i},$$

where Em = the membrane potential, R is the gas constant, T is temperature in degrees Kelvin, F is Faraday's constant and $[K]_o$ and $[K]_i$ are the external and internal potassium concentrations, or more correctly, activities. When the external potassium concentration is high the membrane potential does fit with this prediction. At lower concentrations however, the membrane potential deviates from a simple Nernst relationship because the membrane is not completely impermeable to sodium ions so that a small inward movement of these ions lowers the potential. At higher extracellular potassium concentrations the inward movement of potassium ions, though much less than the outward movement, is considerably greater than the inward sodium movement which therefore has little effect on potential. The relationship between extracellular potassium concentration and membrane potential in a single skeletal muscle fibre (Hodgkin and Horowicz 1959*b*) is shown in Fig. 1. The straight line is given by the Nernst equation. If allowance is made for sodium permeability, the following equation, modified by Hodgkin and Katz (1949) from Goldman's (1943) constant field equation, can be used:

$$Em = \frac{RT}{F} \ln \frac{P_{Na}[Na]_o + P_K[K]_o}{P_{Na}[Na]_i + P_K[K]_i},$$

where P_{Na} and P_K are the sodium and potassium permeability of the membrane. If the ratio P_{Na}/P_K is taken as 0·01, the curved line in Fig. 1 can be obtained from the above equation. There is clearly an acceptable agreement between the experimental points and the theoretical relationship. Experiments with radio-isotopes confirm that the ratio of permeabilities of sodium and potassium is of the order of 0·01 (Hodgkin and Horowicz 1959*a*). The idea that resting membrane potentials are essentially diffusion potentials has been challenged from time to time but no alternative theory as consistent with experimental findings has been formulated. There seems no reason therefore to abandon the concept of membrane potentials as diffusion potentials. The fact that membrane potentials, at least in nerve and muscle tissues, are very sensitive to extracellular potassium but not sodium con-

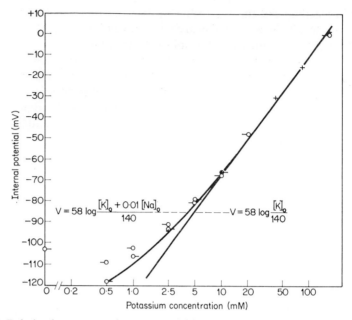

Fig. 1. Relation between membrane potential (ordinate) and the extracellular potassium concentration (abscissa: note log scale). The straight line is drawn according to the Nernst equation (inset right) assuming an intracellular concentration of 140 mM. The curved line is derived from the equation (inset left) assuming $P_{Na}/P_K = 0.01$ and internal potassium as before. At low external potassium concentrations the points fit the curved line rather than the straight line (Hodgkin and Horowicz 1959b).

centrations cannot be questioned. The result of this can be seen in people whose serum potassium rises for some reason, e.g. in diabetic coma. Muscle fibres of the heart are depolarized and the heart stops. It is very important therefore, that the potassium concentration of an organism's extracellular saline be controlled within fairly narrow limits.

3. ACTION POTENTIALS

Information is transmitted in nerve or muscle cells by brief electrical pulses known as action potentials. These pulses last about one three-hundredth of a second and are uniform in height (one- to two-tenths of a volt). The brain is a complex, closely packed network of nerve cells signalling each other with these pulses. Before the advent of intracellular recording techniques it was thought that action potentials consisted of a drop in the normal membrane potential to zero. As early as 1902 Bernstein had suggested that cell membranes are permeable only to potassium ions and this leads to the resting membrane potential. This hypothesis remains essentially intact. He attributed an action potential to a loss of this selective potassium permeability so that the membrane becomes equally permeable to all ions. This would predict that an action potential would consist of a 'short circuit' of the membrane. However, this theory was discarded when it was discovered that the polarity of the membrane potential actually reversed during an

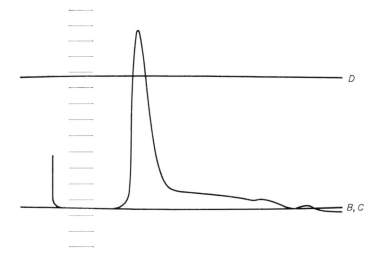

Fig. 2. Resting potential and action potential of a skeletal muscle fibre. The ordinate scale indicates steps of 10 mV, negative downwards. Line *D* shows the zero potential level outside the fibre. The straight horizontal line *B* shows the negative resting potential inside the fibre (recorded with a glass microelectrode) and the upward wave form (*C*) is an action potential which at its peak crosses the zero level showing that the inside of the fibre becomes positive. (Nastuk and Hodgkin 1950).

action potential (Fig. 2). Hodgkin and Katz (1949) suggested that this was due to an increase in the permeability of the membrane to sodium ions. In support of this hypothesis they produced evidence which showed that the height of an action potential depended critically on the concentration of sodium in the external saline.

The probability of propagation or spread of an action potential depends on its height so that nerves become less excitable in saline containing low sodium concentrations but action potentials are not completely abolished until the sodium concentration is reduced below 30% of the normal concentration. When the sodium concentration was progressively lowered and osmotically replaced with dextrose the height of action potentials progressively decreased. This is shown in Fig. 3. There is a linear relationship between the peak height of an action potential and the logarithm of the sodium concentration. If, during an action potential, the membrane became more permeable to sodium than potassium ions for a short time, this kind of relationship might be expected. There is now a wealth of evidence in support of this theory, most of it furnished by Hodgkin and Huxley (see Hodgkin 1964). By controlling the potential across an area of membrane electronically, a technique known as 'voltage clamp', it is possible to record two membrane resistance or conductance changes with separate time

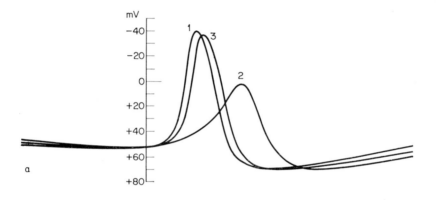

Fig. 3. Action of sodium-deficient saline on action potentials. (1) Action potential in normal seawater; (2) after 16 minutes in 33 % seawater, 67 % isotonic sucrose; (3) after 13 minutes back in seawater. The ordinate shows potential, outside with respect to inside, the opposite of the present convention. (Hodgkin and Katz 1949).

courses. (Membrane conductance can be converted to membrane permeability.) For example, when the potential across the membrane of a squid nerve is 'clamped' at a depolarized level (more positive than the resting potential) the following conductance changes can be recorded. The sodium conductance starts at a very low value, rises rapidly to about 25 mmho cm^{-2} and then declines exponentially. The potassium conductance does not change at once but rises in an S-shaped curve to a steady level. For a short time therefore sodium ions can cross the membrane much more easily than potassium ions so that positive charge builds up on the inside of the membrane. This causes a reversal of the membrane potential. The sodium permeability then switches off (inactivates) and the membrane potential is restored to its normal polarity by efflux of potassium ions. Evidently a cell gains sodium and loses potassium during an action potential, but these imbalances are then corrected by finely controlled 'pumps' which will be discussed later.

A difference in time course of sodium and potassium conductance does not necessarily mean that these ions move through spatially separate channels. The differential permeability of a single channel in a membrane could change with time following a depolarizing stimulus giving sodium and potassium conductance changes with different time courses. Such a time-dependent change in differential permeability could reflect a sequence of changes of molecular structure in parts of the membrane. Very little is known of the reason for the large increases in membrane permeability during an action potential. All we know is that the relative permeabilities of excitable membranes are changed transiently by membrane depolarization.

In some invertebrates, for example barnacles and crayfish, action potentials in muscle fibres are caused by an increase in calcium not sodium permeability so that it is calcium not sodium which carries the inward current. In man, action potentials in some parts of the heart and in smooth muscles are associated with an increase in calcium permeability. Thus both the sodium ion concentration and the calcium ion concentration in the extracellular medium are important for the maintenance of action potentials in whole animals.

When an action potential has occurred at a site of local depolarization it travels away along the membrane of the cell. The way in which this happens is by local circuit current flow. In an active region the membrane potential approaches $+40$ mV and in surrounding non-active membrane is -90 mV. These differences in membrane potential cause 'local circuit' current which flows away from the active region inside the cell and towards the active region in the extracellular saline. This flow of current depolarizes the inactive membrane and triggers another explosive increase in sodium permeability. In this way action potentials spread rapidly along the cell surface. It was clearly shown by Hodgkin (1937) many years ago that it was necessary to have an extracellular current conductor, normally saline, for spread or propagation of an action potential to occur. The extracellular saline is important therefore not only in its concentration of sodium ions but also as a current conductor.

4. ION PUMPS

In cells in which the concentration gradient of an ion is not opposed by an equal electrical force, net flux of that ion in the direction of the net force

13

must result if these are the only forces acting. In muscle or nerve cells, the sodium concentration is much higher outside than inside the cell. The electrical potential across the membrane is negative inside. Both these forces favour an influx of sodium ions and there should be a continuous trickle of these ions into the cells. One might expect, but does not find, a gradual accumulation of sodium ions. At first it was thought that membranes were completely impermeable to sodium ions but experiments with radio-isotopes showed that sodium did in fact pass through the membrane though much less readily than potassium ions. It was necessary to postulate the existence of an 'uphill' efflux of sodium ions balancing the passive influx. An efflux of sodium ions against both an electrical force and a concentration gradient requires energy and this is supplied by hydrolysis of the phosphate bonds of 'energy rich' phosphate compounds such as adenosine triphosphate (ATP). A magnesium-dependent enzyme, adenosine triphosphatase is found at sites where this transport of sodium occurs. The activity of this enzyme is increased by the presence of sodium and potassium in the medium. The process whereby a cell continuously uses metabolic energy to maintain an efflux of sodium is called active sodium transport or the sodium pump. This mechanism has been shown to exist in many different types of cells, e.g. giant axons of the squid, red blood cells, skeletal, cardiac and smooth muscle and in nerve cells. Active transport of sodium is also involved in conservation of sodium in the kidney and in the elaboration of saliva and other gastro-intestinal secretions.

Very little is known of the mechanisms whereby sodium is actively ejected from a cell to maintain the internal concentration constant. However, some of the characteristics of the process have been defined and seem to be similar in most tissues. Hodgkin and Keynes (1955) used radio-isotopes to measure sodium and potassium fluxes in *Sepia* (cuttlefish) axons and found:

(a) Sodium efflux is roughly proportional to the internal sodium concentration.

(b) Sodium efflux is almost completely inhibited by metabolic inhibitors which block the production of ATP and thus deprive the pump of its source of energy.

(c) Potassium influx is also inhibited by the same metabolic inhibitors. There is an equal decrease in sodium efflux and potassium influx.

(d) Sodium influx and potassium efflux, which are essentially passive fluxes driven by electrochemical gradients, are not affected by metabolic inhibitors.

(e) Sodium efflux is reduced to about 30% by removal of extracellular potassium and increases when the potassium concentration is increased.

(*f*) The active fluxes (sodium efflux and potassium influx), but not the passive fluxes, are very sensitive to temperature. A reduction in temperature drastically reduces the active fluxes and the Q_{10} of the effect is 3 to 4.

The results show that there is an active uptake of potassium coupled to the active extrusion of sodium ions. But the persistence of 30% of the sodium efflux when potassium influx has been abolished by removing the external potassium indicates that the coupling cannot be mandatory under all conditions. In fact, some recent observations of changes in membrane potential associated with activity of the sodium pump have been explained by postulating that the pump can be electrogenic, i.e. that sodium ions can be transferred alone so that a potential is generated directly. Limitations of the present context restrict this discussion to the statement that the question remains open.

The sodium pump thus plays a very important role in animal cells surrounded by sodium and potassium ions which are not in electrochemical equilibrium across the membrane. Clearly the resting membrane potential could not be maintained if potassium were allowed to leak out of a cell. If the sodium pump is inhibited in skeletal muscles there is no immediate change in membrane potential. However, after several hours when there has been sufficient time for appreciable amounts of potassium to be lost, the membrane potential is found to be diminished and progressive depolarization occurs. The cells also swell. An important function of the sodium pump is to maintain cell volume constant.

5. CELL VOLUME

Cell membranes are very permeable to water. Therefore, unless water is actively transported, there can be no concentration gradient of water across the cell membrane if a cell is to maintain a constant volume, because animal cells do not have sufficient tensile strength to balance an osmotic pressure by allowing an increase in hydrostatic pressure. It is generally found that the total concentration of solutes is much the same inside and outside a cell. Let us now consider what would happen if the sodium pump stopped. The concentration of sodium ions inside the cell would rise and the potassium concentration would fall. This would lead to a fall in membrane potential and the intracellular chloride concentration would rise. If potassium and chloride ions are distributed according to a Gibbs–Donnan equilibrium, as seems to apply in skeletal muscle, the intracellular chloride concentration would be expected to rise for this reason also. Thus, because of this increase in sodium and chloride concentration the intracellular osmotic pressure would rise and water would enter the cell which would swell and eventually burst.

6. SYNAPTIC POTENTIALS

An action potential in a cell spreads as far as it can go along the surface membrane and then is confronted by a ravine, or synaptic cleft, between it and the next cell. Communication across this gap is generally achieved, not by a trans-synaptic flow of current, but by rapid secretion of a chemical transmitter which affects the target cell or postsynaptic membrane. The first transmitter to be identified was acetylcholine which is secreted in response to an action potential at the ends of peripheral motor nerves. Transmitters produce an electrical signal in target cells by increasing the permeability of their membranes to ions in the ambient saline.

The depolarization caused by acetylcholine is due to an increase in the permeability of the postsynaptic membrane to sodium ions and the permeability to potassium ions is increased at the same time. The electrical effect of acetylcholine on the postsynaptic cell has been likened to an electrical 'shunt' or 'short circuit' across the postsynaptic membrane. The concentration of ions, particularly sodium, in the external saline is very important in determining whether synaptic transmission will be effected. The transmitter causes an influx of sodium ions, the magnitude of which depends on the extracellular sodium concentration. This influx of sodium ions deposits positive charge on the inner surface of the membrane which is thus depolarized. If this depolarization is sufficiently large (more than 10–20 mV) an explosive increase in sodium permeability will occur and the action potential so generated will travel away from the synaptic region and traverse the cell. In this way transmission is accomplished from cell to cell.

Synaptic transmission is even more sensitive to the concentration of calcium ions, than to the concentration of sodium ions. In fact, calcium is an essential co-factor for the secretion of transmitters. An example of this may be seen at the giant synapse in the stellate ganglion of squid (Fig. 4). When calcium is removed from the external fluid, the size of the postsynaptic potential soon falls and transmission eventually ceases. The process is reversible—restoration of calcium allows transmission to continue. It has been shown conclusively at many synapses that calcium acts by modulating transmitter secretion.

Several divalent cations, e.g. magnesium, can reduce transmitter secretion by competing with calcium. Thus it is possible to block synaptic transmission by raising the concentration of magnesium in the extracellular saline and this seems to be generally applicable to all synapses.

Changes in the amplitude of the action potentials which trigger the secretion of transmitters also affect the amount of transmitter which is released.

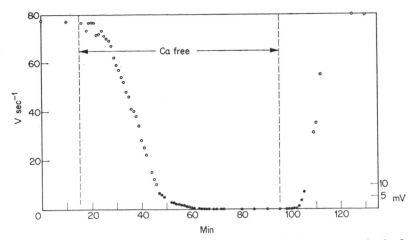

Fig. 4. Calcium action on synaptic transmission at the squid giant synapse. At the first interrupted vertical line the artificial seawater (containing 9 mM Ca) was replaced by a solution containing no calcium. Open circles show maximum rate of rise of postsynaptic potentials. Filled circles show amplitude of postsynaptic potentials. At the second interrupted vertical line the perfusion fluid was switched back to the seawater containing 9 mM Ca (Miledi and Slater 1966).

Larger action potentials cause the release of more transmitter than smaller action potentials. Since the size of an action potential depends on the concentration of sodium ions, these ions can affect synaptic efficacy both by modifying the size of action potentials (and hence transmitter release) and the size of synaptic potentials which depend on an influx of sodium.

7. GENERATOR POTENTIALS

Many forms of energy, e.g. heat, light and sound, are converted to electrical signals by specialized cells called receptors. In other words, these cells act as transducers. The following sequence of events seems to be similar in many different types of receptors. A physical stimulus causes a depolarization of the receptor by increasing the permeability of the membrane to sodium (and perhaps other) ions. This depolarization (the generator potential), which is proportional in amplitude to the intensity of the stimulus, leads to a burst of action potentials, the frequency of which is proportional to the amplitude of the generator potential. It is the frequency or time distribution of action potentials in this burst which is believed to convey the information about the intensity of the stimulus. The sequence of events may be summarized. A physical stimulus of intensity I causes a generator potential of amplitude A, and A is a function of I. This generator potential gives rise to action potentials of frequency F, and F is a function of A and hence a function of I. Thus receptors use both amplitude and frequency modulation in conveying information about the input. The intermediate steps in these processes can be very complicated. For example, in visual receptors, light leads to a series of chemical events which in turn produce a generator potential by some unknown process.

The ionic mechanisms of generator potentials have not been well defined. Certainly in those receptors which have been investigated sodium ions are involved. For example, generator potentials in Pacinian corpuscles (vibration-sensitive receptors) which have been perfused with sodium-free solutions are about 10 % of the normal amplitude. It is generally thought, by default perhaps, that generator potentials involve a non-specific increase in the permeability of the surface membrane to all ions. The small size of the receptors and the inaccessibility of the sites where the permeability changes occur have precluded a more exact study.

8. CONCLUSION

This review has dealt mainly with the effects of salinity on the electrical activity of nerve and muscle cells which form the bulk of the cell population of larger animals. The basic unit of electrical signalling is the action potential which is initiated by depolarization (a synaptic potential or generator potential) and consists itself of a brief reversal of membrane potential. The importance of the external salinity depends on the fact that cells transmit information electrically and generate current flows by switching on concentration cells, usually sodium for depolarization or chloride for hyperpolarization. To recharge the 'battery' after current has been drawn from it, 'trickle chargers' or ionic pumps driven by metabolic energy are turned on and extracellular salinity is regulated precisely by a delicate balance between an organism's intake, storage, and excretion of salts and water.

The role of calcium ions has not been emphasized here because it does not contribute in many cells to the actual currents. However, calcium is essential for the maintenance of the normal ionic permeabilities of cell membranes; for the secretion of neurotransmitters and some, if not all, hormones; for contraction in muscle; for some enzyme reactions including formation of thrombin; for the cohesion of cells; and for bone and teeth formation.

Maintained concentration gradients of sodium and potassium ions are necessary for normal membrane potentials and action potentials. Therefore accurate control of the extracellular salinity is essential for intercellular communication. The wide-ranging effects of alterations in extracellular ion concentrations are well known to clinicians and many of the signs they observe can be explained in terms of the cellular effects briefly discussed here.

The nature of the ions involved in electrical activity is more or less established. Reasonable hypotheses have been formulated to explain the role of electrochemical forces in the generation of membrane potentials. What is now needed is information about the membrane itself. Why is a membrane differentially permeable to different ions and how does the selective permeability change during activity?

REFERENCES

Goldman, D. E. (1943). *J. gen. Physiol.* **27**, 37.

Hodgkin, A. L. (1937). *J. Physiol.* (Lond.) **90**, 183.

Hodgkin, A. L. (1964). *The Conduction of the Nervous Impulse.* Liverpool University Press, Liverpool.

Hodgkin, A. L., and Horowicz, P. (1959*a*). *J. Physiol.* (Lond.) **145**, 405.

Hodgkin, A. L., and Horowicz, P. (1959*b*). *J. Physiol.* (Lond.) **148**, 127.

Hodgkin, A. L., and Katz, B. (1949). *J. Physiol.* (Lond.) **108**, 37.

Hodgkin, A. L., and Keynes, R. D. (1955). *J. Physiol.* (Lond.) **128**, 28.

Katz, B. (1966). *Nerve, Muscle and Synapse.* McGraw-Hill, New York.

Miledi, R. and Slater, C. R. (1966). *J. Physiol.* (Lond.) **184**, 473.

Nastuk, W. L. and Hodgkin, A. L. (1950). *J. Cell. Comp. Physiol.* **35**, 39.

Salinity and the Whole Plant

J. B. ROBINSON

Department of Agriculture, Adelaide, South Australia

SUMMARY

The deficiencies in present knowledge concerning the behaviour of ionic species within the plant are discussed, with particular reference to the leaf; and a possible experimental approach to these problems is developed. Briefly, a distinction must be made between ions entering plant tissue and subsequent partition of ions between extracellular and cellular compartments. With techniques at present available the dynamic state of the extracellular compartment with respect to any particular ion can be determined. Using tissue slices, and duplicating the native state of the leaf cell, information on the ionic and water relations of the leaf cell could be obtained. Extrapolation of such data to the native state may enable distinction to be drawn between the 'osmotic' and 'specific ion toxicity' theories of salt damage.

1. INTRODUCTION

Salinity damage to many species of plants can be associated with well defined soil solution parameters, e.g. osmotic pressure, content of sodium, chloride, boron, lithium, carbonate or bicarbonate. The limits of these soil and water properties are considered in detail in Richards (1954) and Chapman (1966) and will not be considered here.

Rather the mechanism by which salinity damage to plants is caused will be considered as a problem in whole plant and, more particularly, leaf ion physiology.

Most work on salinity in relation to plant growth has been concentrated on sodium (Na) and chloride (Cl). The expression of salinity damage which has been related to these ions may, broadly, be described in the following ways.

(*a*) *Growth or yield decrement.* At levels of substrate salinity that cause no obvious damage to the plant, growth or economic yield may be quite severely restricted.

(*b*) *Leaf damage.* At higher levels of substrate salinity obvious leaf symptoms appear. These may be expressed as cupping; yellowing;

bronzing; tip, marginal, or veinal necrosis; premature abscission and fall; or whole twig dieback. Often Na and Cl cause different types of damage to any one species. These are often similar to responses to drought conditions.

(c) *Succulence*. Increased leaf thickness is often observed in response to substrate salinity. Authorities differ in attributing this to enlargement of mesophyll cells or to cell wall thickening (e.g. Jennings 1968).

(d) *Miscellaneous*. Germination may be inhibited and at the cellular level certain enzyme functions may be impaired.

2. IONIC RELATIONS OF LEAVES

Most forms of obvious salinity damage are expressed at the leaf level. To understand the mechanism by which such damage is caused some consideration of the ionic relations of leaves is necessary.

In general salinity damage has been attributed to osmotic stress to the plant or to a 'toxic' build-up of ions in the leaf *in toto*. For example, toxic levels of Na, Cl, B, etc. are documented for many plants (see Chapman 1966). These levels are expressed as a percentage of the leaf dry weight and tell us little about the mechanism of damage. Oertli (1968) has pointed out that the leaf must be considered to have both extracellular and cellular compartments and he has considered the dangers inherent in examining responses in the O.P. of 'expressed cell sap' to substrate salinization, which Bernstein (1961, 1964) recognized with respect to roots, but not when considering aerial parts. Perhaps it would be fruitful to construct a model of the leaf as a two compartment ionic system, to formalize this and enter in the known values of some of the parameters required by the model, with the aim of defining the type of information that must be collected if we are to understand the mechanisms of salinity damage.

On the basis of structural information it is possible to draw a compartmental model of the plant leaf. Any ion entering the leaf in the transpiration stream, *via* the xylem, will be discharged into an aqueous extracellular compartment which, in a tissue containing a high percentage air space such as the mesophyll, is likely to be contained largely within the cell walls. This compartment will be equivalent to the Free Space (cf. Briggs *et al.* 1961). Partition of ions between the Water Free Space and Donnan Free Space can be ignored for the purposes of this rather general discussion of leaf ion physiology and no errors are likely to result from such a simplification.

From this extracellular compartment ions may move to one or more cellular compartments as shown diagrammatically in Fig. 1. Possible ion fluxes are entered and each should be considered separately.

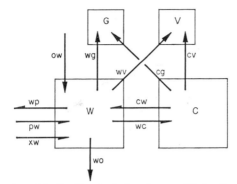

Fig. 1. Compartmental model of leaf (see text) showing possible ion fluxes into and between the extracellular compartment (*W*) and the cellular compartment (*C*) together with possible fluxes from the leaf to the outside, *via* salt gland (*G*) and vesicular hairs (*V*).

ϕxw. This is equivalent to total ion movement into the leaf with the transpiration stream. In magnitude it is the product of the gross leaf transpiration rate and the concentration of the relevant ion in the xylem sap. These values can be measured with some difficulty, and may be estimated without destructive sampling of the whole plant, as transpiration data can be collected simply and xylem sap can be collected from pressure bomb exudates of perennial plant parts (e.g. Atkinson *et al.* 1967).

ϕwc, ϕcw. These are fluxes between the extracellular compartment and cellular compartment. They are likely to depend upon the concentration of the relevant ion in the extracellular compartment, the permeability and/or ion pumping ability of the cells comprising the cellular compartment. These are difficult fluxes to measure, and are impossible to measure or estimate without destructive sampling of the leaf. Attempts have been made to describe the uptake properties of the cellular compartment with respect to Cl, Na and K using slices of leaves (Robinson and Smith 1970; Smith and Robinson 1971; Rains and Epstein 1967; Osmond 1968) and such data may survive extrapolation to the intact leaf.

ϕpw, ϕwp. These fluxes represent phloem entry to and outputs from the leaf and are also difficult to measure. Estimation of *net* efflux or influx of an ion appears to be feasible. On a whole leaf basis total xylem input of an ion can be estimated (see above, ϕxw), in a leaf with no salt glands and where leaching (see later) has been ruled out any excess or deficiency over a known time period will represent a net influx or net efflux and the phloem is the most likely pathway. Radio-isotopes could be used to point out those ions that are redistributed by the phloem, but to derive flux data from leaf applications of isotopes would be a formidable task as very accurate data would be required concerning pool sizes in the extracellular and cellular compartments of the leaf to derive meaningful estimates of specific activity.

ϕow, ϕwo. These fluxes represent 'foliar absorption' by and 'leaching' of ions from the leaf. Foliar absorption has been implicated in the rapid expression of salinity damage in plants irrigated by overhead sprays of water containing Na or Cl (e.g. Eaton and Harding 1959), and must be considered as a leaf ion input. The pathway of entry to the leaf is under question. Franke (1967) implicates specific structures, the ectodesmata, in movement across the cuticle. Other workers consider that the stomates are the primary site of entry to the leaf (see Malcolm 1968). Leaching of ions from leaves is also well documented (e.g. review by Tukey 1970). These two fluxes are amenable to simple measurement. It is worth emphasising that such fluxes are unlikely to be directly to or from the cellular compartment, rather they will be between the extracellular compartment and the leaf surface. The apparent movement of ions from the leaf surface into the leaf against 11 to 14 fold concentration gradients (Ehlig and Bernstein 1959) probably represents diffusion from the outside into the extracellular compartment either actively, against an electrochemical potential gradient, or passively down such a gradient, concentration *per se* being relatively unimportant.

ϕwg, ϕcg. These fluxes will apply in specialized species possessing salt glands (e.g. some mangroves, and *Limonium*). Which of these fluxes occurs is doubtful. Electron microscopic evidence quoted by Hill (1967) is available, showing extensive plasmadesmatal development between the salt glands and neighbouring cells in *Limonium*, suggesting that the gland may draw upon the leaf mesophyll symplast during secretion. Atkinson *et al*. (1967) suggest that the gland in the mangrove *Aegialitis* draws upon the extensive intercellular spaces in the palisade layer of cells between the veins and the salt glands, in competition with the salt accumulation systems in other leaf cells. Some data presented by these authors suggest that Cl passes directly to the salt glands through the extracellular compartment. In short, the net efflux of ions from the leaf *via* salt glands can be measured, but in any system to be investigated some preliminary work would be required to decide which of the fluxes (ϕwg or ϕcg) is involved.

ϕwv, ϕcv. In many halophytes (e.g. *Atriplex*) large vesicular hairs are present on the epidermis of leaves. These apparently form a separate compartment from the mesophyll and serve as a salt sink. Osmond (1968) considers that transport to these cells occurs directly from the free space of the leaf in which case ϕwv is the important flux for the purposes of this discussion.

Electron microscope studies (Osmond *et al.* 1969) show plasmadesmata between the mesophyll and the basal cells of the vesicular hairs suggesting that ϕcv is the important flux in this situation. Again, this could be checked quite simply in any experimental situation. Thus the possible fluxes into and from the leaf, and between the various compartments of the leaf, are amenable to experimental investigation, some directly and some indirectly.

The size of, and the concentrations of ions within the extracellular and cellular compartments of the leaf have so far been neglected.

The extracellular compartment (W) will have a fixed volume (Wv) unless:

(a) the airspaces of the leaf become injected with water;
(b) the cell walls of the leaf become thicker (which may occur during the increase in succulence of plants subjected to a saline root environment) and can hold more water;
(c) the leaf continues to grow as in the mangrove, *Rhizophora* (Atkinson *et al.* 1967).

The concentration of an ion within the extracellular space may be represented as W_c. The total quantity of any ion within the extracellular space which may be represented as W_Q will vary as a function of the fluxes into and from W.

$$\text{viz. } \frac{dW_c}{dt} = \underbrace{(\phi xw, \ cw, \ pw, \ ow)}_{\text{influxes}} - \underbrace{(\phi wc, \ wo, \ wg, \ wp)}_{\text{outfluxes}}$$

If W_v remains constant, as would be expected in a mature leaf, the significance of this relationship becomes obvious: any positive change in W_Q will result in a concentration increase in the extracellular compartment with respect to the ion under consideration. This in essence is the point made by Oertli (1968)—that whole leaf or expressed cell sap analyses are of doubtful value and may conceal compartmentalized increases in concentration. It is possible to derive approximate values for W_v with the usual reservations due to inaccuracies in technique. Leaf slices may be immersed in isotopically labelled solutions of ions, whereby the rapidly labelled volume (following thorough blotting) or the rapidly exchangeable volume (again following thorough blotting) will give an approximate value for W_v, if it is assumed that photosynthesis is maintained at a rate sufficient to prevent injection of air spaces with uptake solution. (Smith and Robinson, unpublished data, suggest about 200 μl g^{-1} for *Citrus* leaves which seems high and might indicate injection of air spaces.)

Direct measurement of W_Q or W_c is equally difficult. Data obtained in attempts to estimate the rapidly accessible fraction of ions in freshly cut leaf slices have been rendered doubtful by the large quantities of ionic species released from cut cells (Robinson, unpublished experiments). Perhaps the most successful approach to estimation of W_c has been that employed by Fenn *et al.* (1968) who have used the pressure bomb to drive fluid back through the leaf petiole, coming apparently from the extra-cellular compartment. Their data are presented in Table 1. The Cl concentration in the early drops of exudation fluid is likely to represent the xylem Cl level and that in subsequent drops may be tentatively ascribed to the extra-cellular compartment.

TABLE 1

Chloride level in forced xylem exudates from leaves of avocado trees growing in substrates containing different levels of chloride (Data of Fenn *et al.* 1968)

Fraction of xylem liquid exuding from petiole (drop number)	Chloride in drop (meq l^{-1})	
	Substrate chloride	
	Trace	20 meq l^{-1}
1	1·5	25
10	1·7	300
20	1·5	315

These data suggest that quite large increases in W_c occur following root zone salinization if it is assumed that no ion leakage from the cellular compartment takes place under the high pressures employed. In this context the effect of hydrostatic pressure on K fluxes in *Valonia* reported by Gutknecht (1968) is worth noting.

Another approach to the value of W_c involves reversing the pressure and driving solution through the leaf and out through the stomates which could give ratios of ions within the extracellular compartment but no absolute values for either W_c or W_Q (Robinson and Smith, unpublished experiments). Oertli (1968) has used virtually this approach with intact barley plants, collecting forced 'guttation' fluid from hydathodes. In these experiments the osmotic pressure of the exudate was measured and found to be higher than the xylem exudate of cut leaves where direct passage through the xylem can be assumed. The osmotic pressure of the forced guttation varied with the salinity of the root medium.

From analyses of xylem sap, a minimum value for W_c can be derived. Thus the minimum Cl content of W for the two mangrove species growing in sea water studied by Atkinson *et al.* (1967) would be equivalent to the xylem sap concentrations presented in Table 2, if it is assumed that Cl enters the extracellular compartment of the leaf as fast or faster than it is seques-tered by other compartments. This assumption may be useful.

TABLE 2

Xylem sap chloride levels in mangroves
(Data of Atkinson *et al.* 1967)

Mangrove	Sap Cl (meq l^{-1})
Rhizophora	17
Aegialitis	100

Clearly it is possible to obtain some quantitative measurements of the following parameters of the extracellular compartment.

(a) W_v, by normal Free Space methods (Smith and Robinson, unpublished experiments).

(b) W_c, by a bomb technique (Oertli 1968; Fenn *et al.* 1968).

(c) W_c (minimum), by pressure cell expression of xylem sap (Scholander *et al.* 1966; Atkinson *et al.* 1967).

It is also clear that any increase in concentration of an ion in the extracellular compartment of the leaf will have far-reaching effects on the ionic relations of the cellular compartment and the water relations of the cellular compartment. These effects are likely to influence the metabolism or membrane properties of this compartment.

As mentioned earlier, both osmotic stress to the plant and specific ion toxicity to leaf cells have been proposed as the likely causes of salinity damage to the plant. If the leaf cell environment can be defined in the way proposed above, it may prove possible to use leaf slices as a means of investigating the response of the ionic relations, water relations and metabolism of the cellular compartment to artificial extracellular solution (see Robinson and Smith 1970; Smith and Robinson 1971).

The cellular compartment of the leaf will also have measurable volume (C_v), ion concentrations (C_c) and content (C_Q). Growth or increase in succulence is likely to increase C_v, net influxes of ions will increase C_Q (and C_c in the absence of growth or increase in succulence). The relationship between the osmotic pressures of W and C will determine whether water will move from C to W and cause local water stress. The relative concentrations of the Ca, K and Na levels in the extracellular compartment will have important effects upon the ion fluxes and membrane properties of the cellular compartment (Robinson and Smith 1970; Smith and Robinson 1971).

Thus a rational experimental approach to the mechanism of salinity damage to leaves is possible and would appear to be worthwhile. Table 3 contains some known values for the parameters discussed above. The large

TABLE 3

Some collected data showing gaps in our knowledge of ionic relations of leaves

Experimental plant	Xylem content	Transpiration rate ml leaf⁻¹ day⁻¹	ϕxw μeq leaf⁻¹ day⁻¹	ϕwp	ϕpw	W_Q	W_v	W_c	ϕwc	ϕcw	ϕwg	C_Q	C_v	C_c
Rhizophora[1]	17 mM (Cl)	1	17	?	?	+	+	0	?+	?	n.a.	+	?+	?0
Aegialitis[1]	100 mM (Cl)	1	100	?	?	0	0	0	?	?	100	0	0	0
Avocado[2]														
Nonsalinized	15 mM (Cl)	?	?	?	?	0	0	b	?	?	n.a.	+	?+	+
Salinized	25 mM (Cl)	?	?	?	?	+	?0	c	?	?	n.a.	+	?+	+
Citrus[3] (slices)	0–100 mM (Cl)	n.a.	n.a.	n.a.	n.a.	+	0	+	+[a]	?	n.a.	+	?0	+
Barley[4]														
day 1	10 mmho cm⁻²	?	?	?	?	+	?0	d	?	?	n.a.	?+	?0	?+
day 4	18 mmho cm⁻²	?	?	?	?			e	?+	?	n.a.			

[a] 0–10 μeq g⁻¹ hr⁻¹   ?+ suspected rise
[b] 15 meq l⁻¹   + rise
[c] 300 meq l⁻¹   ? unknown
[d] 8 mmho cm⁻²   0 no change
[e] 30 mmho cm⁻²   ?0 suspected no change
   n.a. not applicable under experimental conditions

[1] Atkinson *et al.* (1967)
[2] Fenn *et al.* (1968)
[3] Robinson and Smith (1970)
[4] Oertli (1968)

number of missing values emphasizes the lack of information in individual cases.

3. THE IONIC RELATIONS OF THE ROOT-SHOOT SYSTEM

The compartmental model described for the leaf must be extended, at least in a general way, to the rest of the plant to enable meaningful discussion of the behaviour (within the plant) of the various ions which have been implicated in salinity damage.

Briefly, ions present in the soil solution enter the Free Space of the root and reach the xylem, either carried in the water mass flow caused by transpiration, by diffusion, or by active transport into or from the symplasm of the root. Ions may be diverted into and held by the vacuoles of the root cells or, once in the xylem stream, diverted from the transpiration stream into cells of the root or aerial parts of the plant, prior to discharge into the leaf. Ions may be re-exported into the soil solution by the cells of the roots (see review by Laties 1969). Some examples may be cited which provide evidence on these aspects of sodium and chloride movement.

The simplest proposition is that ion movement occurs through the Free Space of the root, to the xylem, following mass flow of soil solution. This is a doubtful possibility on the basis of the following evidence.

(a) The Casparian strip (suberization in the radial and transverse walls of the endodermis surrounding the stele) is alleged to present a barrier of free water movement through the cell walls to the stele (Slatyer 1967). But Pitman (1965b) suggests that the endodermis provides no real barrier to diffusion of Na and K in barley roots. Further data are obviously required in any particular study.

(b) Electrical resistances and potentials can be measured between the root medium and the xylem exudate of de-topped plants (e.g. Bowling *et al.* 1966) suggesting that a strong diffusion barrier to ions exists between the xylem and the outside.

(c) Xylem mass flow has minimal effects upon the transport of ions from the solution to the xylem until very high rates of flow or external concentration are maintained (Russel and Shorrocks 1959).

On the basis of this evidence an ion pathway to the xylem *via* the symplast of root cells is more likely. Evidence for *active* transport against an electro-chemical potential gradient between the bathing medium and the xylem has been presented by Bowling *et al.* (1966).

These authors, using concentration and potential data from de-topped castor oil plants, indicate that NO_3, Cl, SO_4, H_2PO_4 and HPO_4 are actively

14

transported into the xylem, and that movement of Na, Ca, and Mg is passive (down an electrochemical potential gradient); K is likely to be at passive equilibrium. A more complex interpretation of these results by Jennings (1967) requires that more data be obtained on the fluxes across the various membranes within the root to show unequivocally that transport is active. A further complication is raised by the evidence of Anderson and House (1967) who presented electron micrographs showing membranes within the xylem elements of maize roots 10 cm behind the root tip. It may be that 'secretion' of ionic species into the xylem is, rather, movement into the vacuoles of xylem elements which subsequently break down and release their contents to the xylem stream, although the rate of ion movement into the xylem stream is perhaps too high to reconcile with this idea.

However, there is good evidence that plants are able to prevent entry to the xylem of some ions even though the ions in question be present at considerable concentrations in the root environment; e.g. the low concentration of chloride in the xylem sap of *Rhizophora* (17 mM) in comparison with *Aegialitis* (100 mM) when both are growing in sea water (Atkinson *et al.* 1967; see Table 3). This may reflect diversion of ions entering the cytoplasm of root cells to the vacuoles of these cells, alternatively the permeability of the root cells may be low. Ions may in fact be excluded as proposed by some authors (e.g. Scholander *et al.* 1966) or they may be re-exported to the root environment by pumps, rather than be allowed to enter the xylem.

Pitman (1965*a*, 1965*b*, 1966) relates the monovalent cation selectivity of barley and mustard to active cation transport at the plasmalemma into the cytoplasm of some root cells, and considers that cation movement in the xylem is achieved by active transport of anions into the stele. A non-selective (passive) pathway may exist through the extracellular compartment of the root which may assume importance at high external concentrations and particularly during conditions of high transpirational demand.

The commonly used citrus rootstocks, rough lemon (*Citrus jambhiri*) and trifoliate orange (*Poncirus trifoliata*) appear to differ in the amount of sodium allowed to reach the aerial plant parts. Both take up approximately equal amounts of Na^{22} labelled Na from similar culture solutions, but a much lower percentage of the label reaches the upper leaves in trifoliate orange (El-Gazzar *et al.* 1965). However, it is not clear whether similar rates of transpiration were maintained in these experiments. Better evidence would be provided by determination of the Na level in the xylem sap of the two plants. Nonetheless the Na content (% dry weight basis) of four-month-old leaves of Eureka lemon scions worked on a range of rootstocks grown under identical conditions does vary widely (sour orange, 0·19; sweet orange, 0·12; rough lemon, 0·15; grapefruit, 0·22; trifoliate orange, 0·05) which is reasonable evidence for variation in the amount of Na allowed to enter the xylem. There is also a wide variation, within the genus *Citrus*, in the ability to cope with high Cl levels in the root environment (e.g. Peynado and Young 1969). This appears to reflect the ability of the roots to prevent Cl reaching the tops of the plants. Both rough lemon and trifoliate orange are poor Cl 'excluders'. Movement of ions from the root to the leaf in the xylem stream will be largely unimpeded, except for diversion into the living cells of the stem which must be considered. Experimental data on the ion uptake properties of cells of plant stems are scarce. But at least with perennial crops, the concept of 'salt load' in perennial parts appears to have some meaning. Stone fruit trees may survive the first and second growing seasons in a saline root environment, but express severe symptoms of salt damage early in the following growing season (Bernstein *et al.* 1956). Both sodium and chloride appear to be involved, but in different ways, in stone fruit salinity damage. Sodium movement to the leaves appears to be restricted (Hayward *et al.* 1946; Brown *et al.* 1953) and high leaf chloride can be associated with damage (Wadleigh *et al.* 1951). However, Bernstein *et al.* (1956) found evidence for sodium release from perennial wood (perhaps due to senescence of heart wood cells) after two years on saline substrates. Evidence for restriction of Cl movement to the leaves in the first season was also obtained. The data of Greenway and co-workers (Greenway 1962*a*, 1962*b*; Greenway *et al.* 1965, 1966) provide detailed information on the fate of Na and Cl in barley plants subjected to various salinity stresses. Salt content of the whole plant was variety dependent, tolerant varieties taking up less Na and Cl than a sensitive variety. Growing parts of the tops of the plant had lower Na and Cl contents due to growth and to low rates of retranslocation of Na and Cl from older parts of the tops.

Thus in both annual and perennial species two levels of 'protection' appear to exist. The first, at the root, where there is some regulation of the ions allowed to enter the xylem stream. The second, in the aerial parts, involves restriction of the mobility of ions preventing redistribution between mature and growing organs. Such protection may break down: at the root level, if the plant is subjected to high transpirational demand whereupon the passive unregulated pathway to the xylem becomes important; and in the tops, if usually immobile ion pools become available for retranslocation.

4. GENERAL REMARKS

The need for an integrated experimental approach to the ionic relations of the whole plant and hence the mode of salinity damage has been established above. For many species, isolated bits of information are available. But all the information needed is not available for a single annual species or a single perennial species.

Variation between plant species in the ability to tolerate salinity stress (e.g. bean vs. lucerne, Eaton 1966) on the basis of the above discussion may be a consequence of:

(*a*) exclusion of the ion at the root level;

(*b*) sequestration of the ion in the vacuoles of the growing root;

(*c*) sequestration of the ion within root or aerial parts able to tolerate considerable extracellular or cellular concentrations of the ion;

(*d*) retranslocation of the ion to the root for excretion to the medium;

(*e*) ability of the cellular compartment of the leaf (and possibly other plant parts) to:

   (i) tolerate a large build-up of the ion in the cell or vacuole of the cell;

   (ii) tolerate relatively high levels of local water stress, following large increases in concentration within the extracellular compartment of the organ;

(*f*) maintenance of a constant increase in the size of the cellular or extracellular compartments through growth or increase in succulence with a resultant 'dilution' of the ion in these compartments;

(*g*) maintenance of favourable levels of K and Ca in relation to Na in the extracellular compartment of the organ, thus maintaining membrane structure and function;

(*h*) scavenging excessive quantities of the ion entering the leaf, directly by salt glands or indirectly with specialized structures such as vesicular hairs;

(*i*) loss of excessive quantities of the ion entering the aerial parts of the plant, through leaching or leaf drop.

It would be naïve to expect that only one of these possibilities would explain the difference in salt tolerance between any two plants. Just as it would be naïve to expect that knowledge of the important factors would allow instant control of salt damage.

REFERENCES

Anderson, W. P., and House, C. R. (1967). *J. exp. Bot.* **18**, 544.

Atkinson, M. R., Findlay, G. P., Hope, A. B., Pitman, M. G., Saddler, H. D. W., and West, K. R. (1967). *Aust. J. biol. Sci.* **20**, 589.

Bernstein, L. (1961). *Amer. J. Bot.* **48**, 909.

Bernstein, L. (1964). *Amer. J. Bot.* **50**, 360.

Bernstein, L. (1969). *Proc. First Int. Citrus Symp.* **3**, 1779.

Bernstein, L., Brown, J. W., and Hayward, H. E. (1956). *Proc. Amer. Soc. Hort. Sci.* **68**, 86.

Bowling, D. J. F., Macklon, A. E. S., and Spanswick, R. M. (1966). *J. exp. Bot.* **17**, 410.

Briggs, G. E., Hope, A. B., and Robertson, R. N. (1961). *Electrolytes and Plant Cells.* Blackwell Scientific Publications, Oxford.

Brown, J. W., Wadleigh, C. H., and Hayward, H. E. (1953). *Proc. Amer. Soc. Hort. Sci.* **61**, 49.

Chapman, H. D. (Ed.) (1966). *Diagnostic Criteria for Plants and Soils.* Univ. of California, Berkeley.

Eaton, F. M. (1966). In *Diagnostic Criteria for Plants and Soils.* (Ed. H. D. Chapman.) p. 98. Univ. of California, Berkeley.

Eaton, F. M., and Harding, R. B. (1959). *Plant Physiol.* **34**, 22.

Ehlig, C. F., and Bernstein, L. (1959). *Proc. Amer. Soc. Hort. Sci.* **74**, 661.

El-Gazzar, A., Wallace, A., and Hemaidan, N. (1965). *Soil Sci.* **99**, 387.

Fenn, L. B., Bingham, F. T., and Oertli, J. J. (1968). *Calif. Avocado Yrbk.* 113.

Franke, W. (1967). *Ann. Rev. Plant Physiol.* **18**, 281.

Greenway, H. (1962a). *Aust. J. biol. Sci.* **15**, 16.

Greenway, H. (1962b). *Aust. J. biol. Sci.* **15**, 39.

Greenway, H., Gunn, A., Pitman, M. G., and Thomas, D. A. (1965). *Aust. J. biol. Sci.* **18**, 525.

Greenway, H., Gunn, A., and Thomas, D. A. (1966). *Aust. J. biol. Sci.* **19**, 744.

Gutknecht, J. (1968). *Science* **160**, 68.

Hayward, H. E., Long, E. M. and Uhvits, R. (1946). U.S.D.A. *Tech. Bull.* **922**.

Hill, A. E. (1967). *Biochim. biophys. Acta* **135**, 454.

Jennings, D. H. (1967). *New Phytol.* **66**, 357.

Jennings, D. H. (1968). *New Phytol.* **67**, 899.

Laties, G. G. (1969). *Ann. Rev. Plant Physiol.* **20**, 89.

Malcolm, C. V. (1968). *Hilgardia* **39**, 69.

Oertli, J. J. (1968). *Agrochimica* **12**, 461.

Osmond, C. B. (1968). *Aust. J. biol. Sci,* **21**, 1119.

Osmond, C. B., Lüttge, U., West, K. R., Pallaghy, C. K., and Shacher-Hill, B. (1969). *Aust. J. biol. Sci.* **22**, 797.

Peynado, A., and Young, R. (1969). *Proc. First Int. Cit. Symp.* **3**, 1793.

Pitman, M. G. (1965a). *Aust. J. biol. Sci.* **18**, 10.

Pitman, M. G. (1965b). *Aust. J. biol. Sci.* **18**, 987.

Pitman, M. G. (1966). *Aust. J. biol. Sci.* **19**, 257.

Rains, D. W., and Epstein, E. (1967). *Aust. J. biol. Sci.* **20**, 847.

Richards, L. A. (Ed.) (1954). *Diagnosis and Improvement of Saline and Alkaline Soils.* U.S.D.A. Handbook No. 60.

Robinson, J. B., and Smith, F. A. (1970). *Aust. J. biol. Sci.* **23**, 953.

Russell, R. S., and Shorrocks, V. M. (1959). *J. exp. Bot.* **10**, 301.

Scholander, P. F., Bradstreet, E. D., Hammel, H. T. and Hemmingsen, E. A. (1966). *Plant Physiol.* **41**, 529.

Slatyer, R. O. (1967). *Plant Water Relationships.* Academic Press, London and New York.

Smith, F. A., and Robinson, J. B. (1971). *Aust. J. biol. Sci.* (in press).

Tukey, H. B. Jr. (1970). *Ann. Rev. Plant Physiol.* **21**, 305.

Wadleigh, C. H., Hayward, H. E. and Ayers, A. D. (1951). *Proc. Amer. Soc. Hort. Sci.* **57**, 31.

Salinity and Plant Cells

L. C. CAMPBELL and M. G. PITMAN

School of Biological Sciences, University of Sydney, N.S.W.

SUMMARY

This paper discusses regulation of ionic content by plant cells and possible ways salinity may disrupt cell function and development. Selective uptake of K relative to Na has some importance but in general, plants seem less dependent on ionic balance than do animal cells. The effect of salinity and osmotic pressure on the activity of mitochondria and chloroplasts is discussed in relation to electron transport processes. It is suggested that some of the effects of salinity on cell activity can be explained in terms of membrane structure.

1. INTRODUCTION

We are surrounded by the seas where plants grow vigorously in 500 mM NaCl, yet many land plants are killed or damaged by concentrations one-tenth this level. This difference is one of the interesting anomalies of plants and salinity.

Salinity has its effect at the cellular level. The parts of the cell that carry out its functions, the mitochondria, ribosomes, chloroplasts etc. are adapted to working in a limited range of ionic concentrations. To some extent the plant cell can control these conditions by means of ion transport processes at the cell membrane. The seaweed *Valonia* for example, contains high levels of K and low Na; replacing the cell sap with a solution high in Na kills the cell. The low permeability of the membranes to ions is, of course, particularly important for regulation of content but can be destroyed by lack of Ca, by high H or in some cases by Na. This effect on the membrane seems to be an important way salinity can affect the cell.

This paper considers the effects of salinity on plant cells and discusses the action of NaCl in terms of membrane properties, of enzyme reactions and of the responses of cell organelles.

2. POTASSIUM, SODIUM AND CHLORIDE LEVELS IN PLANT CELLS

(a) Mechanisms for K and Na Uptake

Plant cells possess mechanisms for taking up K in preference to Na. The efficiency of uptake of K relative to Na can be shown by calculating the selectivity, $S_{K, Na}$, defined as

$$S_{K, Na} = \frac{K \text{ in plant}}{Na \text{ in plant}} \Big/ \frac{K \text{ in solution}}{Na \text{ in solution}}$$

Table 1 gives examples of K and Na concentrations in some seaweeds, freshwater algae and higher plant roots. Many marine plants have very high selectivity for K; for *Chaetomorpha* $S_{K, Na} = 970$. Higher plants show lower selectivity, in the range 5 to 20. It is interesting to note that even mangroves are not highly selective for K.

Cell potential differences have been measured for many of these plants. The tissues were growing in the listed medium and were in flux equilibrium with it, so that the potential differences can be used to determine whether K or Na are at electrochemical equilibrium. In all cases the expected Na levels are much higher than observed and many of the expected K levels are lower than observed. The difference in K and Na appears to require active transport inwards of K and outwards of Na.

The presence of an active K influx is confirmed by the effects of inhibitors of respiration, which reduce tracer K uptake. In a few cases reduction of both K influx and Na efflux by the inhibitor ouabain has been reported (Raven 1967; MacRobbie 1962). This inhibitor is specific for K/Na transport in many animal systems.

Using certain giant algal cells it is possible to measure concentrations of ions in the cytoplasm separately from the vacuole. From such experiments, and from measurements of tracer exchange, it can be shown that the selectivity for K is set up at the outer cell membrane, the plasmalemma. Figure 1 shows the K and Na distribution in cells of *Nitella translucens* and the location of active transport processes. Location of transport processes in other plants has not been established so clearly but it is most likely that variations of this basic system are involved in determining selectivity for K and Na.

(b) Chloride Levels in Plant Cells

Many plant cells contain high levels of Cl without any ill effect. Marine algae commonly contain about 500 to 600 mM Cl and in holophytes Cl may be at much higher concentrations. Since the cells contain high levels of K

TABLE 1

Sodium and potassium in plant cells

Plant cell	Concentration				$S_{K,Na}$	Potential difference E_{ov} (mV)	Predicted cell concentration (mM)		Reference
	external (mM)		cell content (mM)						
	K	Na	K	Na			K	Na	
Chaetomorpha darwinii	11	500	540	25	970	+10	7	300	Dodd *et al.* (1966)
Griffithsia pulvinata	10	490	550	50	539	−50	71	3520	Findlay *et al.* (1969)
Nitella translucens	0·1	1·0	75	65	11·5	−120	11	110	Spanswick and Williams (1964)
Barley root	0·22	9·0	34	68	22·5	−110	17	750	Pitman and Saddler (1967)
cells	2·8	8·1	80	23	10·0	−87	86	250	
Mangrove roots	11	500	1040	320	14	—	—	—	Atkinson *et al.* (1967)

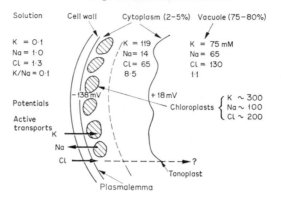

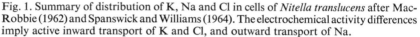

Fig. 1. Summary of distribution of K, Na and Cl in cells of *Nitella translucens* after Mac-Robbie (1962) and Spanswick and Williams (1964). The electrochemical activity differences imply active inward transport of K and Cl, and outward transport of Na.

and Na some negative ion is necessary in the cell to maintain charge balance. In marine situations this ion is mainly chloride, but in non-saline conditions plants tend to balance K and Na in the vacuoles with organic acids.

Figure 1 showed that plant cells have an inward active transport of chloride; this process operates when Cl is present but can and does transport other univalent anions such as NO_3 and organic acids. One possible effect of high Cl is that it interferes with transport of organic acids within the cell and between cells. Transport of organic acids into mitochondria is involved in respiration so high Cl levels could affect mitochondrial activity.

It has been shown very clearly (Carter and Lathwell 1967) that Cl (from KCl) does *not* interfere with phosphate uptake to roots. In experiments in our own laboratory it has been found that NaCl levels up to 100 mM do not reduce the rate of phosphate uptake to barley or mustard seedlings.

(c) *K, Na and Cl Levels in Organelles*

Within the cytoplasm further degrees of selectivity are possible, as mitochondria and chloroplasts possess mechanisms for ion transport. Estimation of levels of ions in organelles is difficult, as exchange can take place between organelles and isolating medium. Again, damage to organelles during isolation may cause loss of ions. Measurements of content also need to be made in parallel with some test of physiological activity.

In vivo estimates have been made in some plants where the chloroplasts are in a discrete layer, and the content of this layer could be determined. For example, the cytoplasmic phase of *Chara australis* contains enough Cl to give an average concentration of 100 mM, but Coster (1966) found that microelectrodes in the cytoplasm showed a Cl activity of only 14 mM. Most of the Cl must have been in organelles (mainly chloroplasts) and not free in the cytoplasm. Similarly, using *Nitella translucens*, MacRobbie (1962) found that concentrations in the chloroplast layer of the cytoplasm were 340 mM K and 120 mM Na, whereas Spanswick and Williams (1964) found that the flowing cytoplasm which did not contain chloroplasts contained 120 mM K and 14 mM Na. From their results it is inferred that the chloroplasts contain more K, Na and Cl than the bulk of the cytoplasm.

Some estimates of content of extracted organelles are given in Table 2. The most reliable estimates for chloroplasts are probably those for *Limonium* where extraction was made in a non-aqueous medium. Clearly, levels of Na and Cl are related to the conditions of plant growth. Chloroplasts from plants grown in saline conditions contained much more Na and Cl than those from plants grown in low salt conditions. In general these figures support the view that chloroplasts can accumulate ions.

Estimates of mitochondrial content are less useful as their content is closely related to the extracting medium. The values given here are characteristic of those in the literature and show that mitochondria can contain high concentrations of ions. Other measurements of ion uptake in relation to oxidative phosphorylation show that ion transport is integrally related to mitochondrial activity.

Since organelles contain relatively large amounts of protein and other changed molecules, it seems highly probable that a proportion of the ions are bound to the charged components or else their concentration is controlled by Donnan fixed charges. Ion content and the fixed charges will be important in the control of osmotically induced volume charges.

(d) Factors Affecting K and Na Levels in Plant Cells

The overall impression from these results is that most cells can cope with high Na levels in the medium by preferential uptake of K. From the point of view of this Symposium, we need to consider how high Na levels might be expected to break down this selectivity and under what conditions. Alteration of membrane permeability or of K and Na transport would both affect selectivity by changing the size of the 'leak' relative to the 'pump'.

The ratio of K/Na in the solution seems more important in determining the levels of K and Na in plant cells than the absolute concentrations. Roots of barley seedlings grown in solutions containing a constant ratio of K : Na (1/3) but increasing total concentration were found to contain K and Na in the same proportion (2·7–3·3 : 1) at least up to 80 mM total concentration (Pitman 1965*b*). However, changing the ratio of K/Na in the solution from 1/3 to 3/1 changed the ratio of K/Na in the roots from 2·7 to 13. These results partly explain why plant sensitivity to a particular concentration of NaCl is greater at low than at high K concentration of the medium (Greenway 1963).

TABLE 2

Ionic concentrations in organelles

Origin	Concentration (mM)					Reference
	Na⁺	K⁺	Mg²⁺	Ca²⁺	Cl⁻	
Pea						
seedling	320–520*	—	—	—	560*	Livne and Levin (1967)
mitochondria						
Potato						
mitochondria	139*	251*	89*	15*	—	Campbell (unpublished data)
Limonium vulgare						
chloroplasts						
saline	960	540	200	168	1250	Larkum (1968)
non-saline	50–500	200–300	—	—	250–750	Larkum and Hill (1970)
Beta vulgaris						
chloroplasts	390	500	120	26	130	Larkum (1968)

* Calculated assuming 2·5 μl of mitochondrial water per mg of mitochondrial protein

Levels of both Ca and H ions appear to be important in controlling selectivity. Figure 2 shows the effect of Ca level on $S_{K, Na}$ in roots of mustard plants. Similar reductions in $S_{K, Na}$ were found for barley (Pitman 1965*a*).

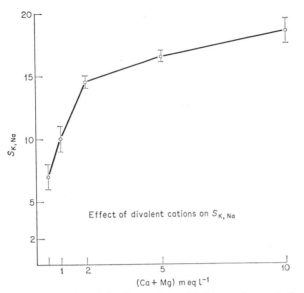

Fig. 2. Increased concentration of divalent cations added to a culture solution containing 0·5 mM K + 1·5 mM Na resulted in increased $S_{K, Na}$ in roots of mustard plants (Pitman 1966).

In these situations H and Ca appear to affect membrane permeability resulting in loss of selectivity for K. Uptake of K and Na by low salt barley roots from a solution of 2·5 mM KCl + 7·5 mM NaCl + 0·5 mM CaSO₄ is accompanied by an efflux of H. When H efflux was large, selectivity ($S_{K, Na}$) was low.

H efflux (μeq g^{-1} hr^{-1})	0	1·0	4·0
$S_{K, Na}$	0	1·4	0·3

Selectivity is also reduced in solutions of low pH, or when roots are losing H from inside the root to the outside. Thus in a solution of pH 4·0, $S_{K, Na}$ for initial uptake was 0·37 but in a solution of pH 5·0 it was 0·8. Calcium is also important: omission of Ca from a solution at pH 4·0 resulted in a net efflux of K from the tissue to such an extent that $S_{K, Na} = -4·5$, the efflux being predominantly due to increased leakage rather than reduced influx (Pitman 1969).

High concentrations of Na can increase membrane permeability though the same K concentration has no effect. Figure 3 shows loss of tracer Rb from *Vicia faba* roots in either 50 mM KCl or 50 mM NaCl. Hyder and

Greenway (1965) showed that Ca could relieve the reduction in growth in barley seedlings due to high NaCl levels, but that extra K did not, so it appears that K/Na ratios are not the only factor relevant to salinity damage.

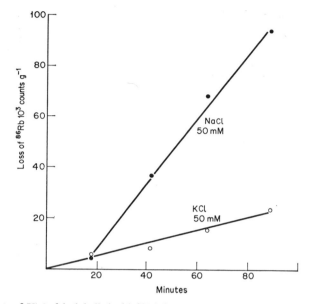

Fig. 3. Roots of *Vicia faba* labelled with ^{86}Rb from 10 mM KCl + 0·5 mM CaSO$_4$ were put into 50 mM NaCl (●) or 50 mM KCl (○) at $t = 0$, and loss of tracer measured. After a short lag there was rapid loss from roots in NaCl solution.

Other factors within the plant may be more important in determining cell content than the levels around the roots. For example when solution concentration is high, the proportion of Na taken up increases markedly with transpiration. As plants (with few exceptions) are unable to excrete Na except by leaf-drop, the cells in the leaf may be exposed to a more saline environment than cells in the root. This problem is discussed in more detail by Dr Robinson.

3. SALINITY AND ORGANELLES

(a) In vivo Studies

Studies of the effects of salinity on organelles in the plant suffer from the difficulty of controlling the level of saline stress. One problem is that there is an interaction of the level and duration of stress, which is more variable and more extended for whole plants than for isolated organelles. Salinity at the whole plant level may have diverse effects and it is difficult to localize the action to, say, a chloroplast reaction instead of a non-chloroplast parameter which in turn mediates its effect on the chloroplast. Thus Gale and Poljakoff-Mayber (1970) found reduced growth in saline media (NaCl or Na_2SO_4) was due to increase in stomatal resistance to CO_2; chloroplast function did not appear to be the limiting factor.

Despite the complex nature and limitations of *in vivo* studies on organelles, Gale *et al.* (1967), in an elegant approach were able to demonstrate that high salinity had an adverse effect on the light reaction of photosynthesis in cotton plants.

(b) Effects on Ultrastructure

Chloride and sulphate salinities have been examined with respect to changes in ultrastructure in two plants with dimorphic chloroplasts, corn (Lapina *et al.* 1968) and *Atriplex halimus* (Blumenthal-Goldschmidt and Poljakoff-Mayber 1968). Salinities ranged from -1 to -23 atm osmotic pressure for the halophytic *Atriplex*, and from 0 to $-4 \cdot 4$ atm for corn which has a lower salt tolerance.

The essential features of the corn experiments were: (i) that the chloroplast membrane suffered abnormalities even under mild salinity stress; (ii) that these deformations were not simply due to water potential and (iii) the results implied that Cl was the active ion.

However, for *Atriplex* there was no fundamental difference between sulphate and chloride salinities except that at iso-osmotic concentrations chloroplasts were less swollen in Na_2SO_4 than in NaCl salinization (Blumenthal-Goldschmidt and Poljakoff-Mayber 1968). These observations are summarized in Table 3. It is worth noting that the saline conditions may introduce artefacts in the methods of preparation of samples for electron microscopy.

(c) Salt Effects on Mitochondria and Respiration

It has already been mentioned that organelles contain high concentrations of K and Cl, as well as Donnan type fixed changes. It can be shown that these ions are actively transported into the organelles. Under normal conditions, swelling of these organelles is presumably prevented by opposing osmotic or matric forces. However, under saline conditions, organelles swell and cytoplasmic vacuolation occurs (e.g. Blumenthal-Goldschmidt and Poljakoff-Mayber 1968). It is suggested that the cell tends to take up extra salts in vacuoles and in organelles. Thus, chloroplasts of the salt marsh plant *Limonium vulgare* have high Na and Cl (Larkum 1968) and mitochondria from peas grown on saline media tend to accumulate Na and Cl (Livne and Levin 1967).

TABLE 3

Effect of salinity on ultrastructure of leaf cells of *Atriplex halimus*
(Blumenthal-Goldschmidt and Poljakoff-Mayber 1968)

Chloroplasts	Mitochondria	Nucleus	Other regions
At low NaCl and Na_2SO_4 concentration (-3 to -7 atm), slight swelling of grana	At -3 to -7 atm, cristae of mitochondria slightly swollen	Low salt concentrations, no effect on nucleus or nuclear membrane	Essentially no effect on plasmalemma and tonoplast membranes or on cytoplasm at low salt status
At intermediate concentrations (-11 to -17 atm), granal swelling much more pronounced appearance of lipid droplets	At -11 to -17 atm cristae very swollen, mitochrondria generally less electron dense. (Lipid droplets present in Na_2SO_4 treated plants)		At medium concentrations of Na_2SO_4, extensive vacuolation of cytoplasm and appearance of numerous myelin-like structures
At high concentrations (-19 to -23 atm) chloroplast structure completely disrupted, many appeared agranal. Lipid droplets present	Cristae more or less disappeared, mitochondria very swollen	High salt concentrations, double membrane of nucleus appeared swollen	At high salt concentrations, tonoplast membrane wavy and ill defined; plasmalemma less affected but often retreated from cell wall. Cytoplasm less dense and vacuolated

Salts not only have an effect on physical aspects but profoundly influence metabolism. Mitochondria *in vivo* swell in highly saline conditions. Packer *et al.* (1970) stated 'almost no research has been reported on direct measurements of ion transport in plant mitochondria'. Corn mitochondria in potassium acetate, with sucrose as an osmotic stabilizer, swell when NADH is added (Hanson and Miller 1969) whereas in KCl addition of substrate results in contraction of the mitochondria (Wilson *et al.* 1969). Lyons (1962) showed that addition of ATP and Mg to cauliflower mitochondria swollen in KCl resulted in their contraction. It therefore seems that ion uptake and swelling are intimately associated with the metabolic state of the mitochondria, but until further work is done in this area, their relations to salinity remain obscure.

Salts usually stimulate the respiration rate in tissues. Mitochondria isolated from pea seedlings grown under saline conditions have respiratory rates greater than those grown under low salt (Livne and Levin 1967). Rates of oxygen uptake were 6·12 and 11·4 μatom mg N^{-1} hr^{-1} respectively. It appears that two effects are operative here: (i) The effect of endogenous salt in the mitochondria over a period of time; and (ii) the effects of exogenous salt on isolated mitochondria. There is scope for further work to elucidate the situation.

State III respiration (i.e. all substrates non-limiting) of isolated soybean hypocotyl mitochondria is depressed more by increasing KCl concentrations than by sucrose (Flowers and Hanson 1969). This effect is shown in Figure 4.

Amongst the alkali metal salts, plant mitochondrial respiration is

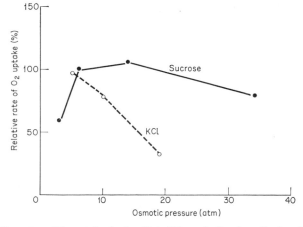

Fig. 4. Relative rates of O_2 uptake during State III respiration by mitochondria extracted from potato and in varied concentrations of KCl (O---O) or sucrose (●——●). KCl has a stronger effect relative to osmotic pressure than does sucrose. The 100% level corresponded to 162 nmoles O_2 mg^{-1} protein min^{-1}.

15

inhibited to a slightly greater extent by Na than K at equivalent concentrations; in addition, nitrates inhibit more than the corresponding chloride. As the inhibition by KCl does not alter the ADP/O ratio (Flowers and Hanson 1969) nor does 2,4-dinitrophenol relieve the inhibition, then it must be concluded that salinity does not inhibit the phosphorylating mechanism in the isolated mitochondrion, but has its primary effect on electron flow or a substrate dehydrogenase enzyme.

(d) Salt Effects on Chloroplasts and Photosynthesis

In chloroplasts isolated from salinized corn plants (at $-4 \cdot 2$ atm), the Hill reaction activity is depressed in those chloroplasts from NaCl treated plants, but the activity is considerably enhanced in chloroplasts isolated from plants treated in Na_2SO_4. Similarly, photosynthesis in whole leaves is depressed by chloride pretreatment and stimulated by sulphate pretreatment (Lapina and Bikmukhametova 1969), though this difference could be related to changed levels of organic acids resulting from excess cation uptake from sulphate solutions.

In vitro studies on isolated chloroplasts of spinach have shown that they behave as osmometers over a considerable concentration range: $0 \cdot 08$ to $0 \cdot 8$ M sucrose or salt ($NaCl$, $NaNO_3$, Na_2SO_4, KCl). As Dilley and Rothstein (1967) point out there is a larger osmotic compartment of the chloroplast responding to salts than to sucrose; the order of the salt effect is $NaNO_3 > NaCl > KCl > Na_2SO_4$. Increasing external salt or sucrose concentration to $1 \cdot 0$ M increased the buffering capacity of chloroplasts about four times (Dilley and Rothstein 1967).

At what concentration is salt needed for chloroplast function? Chloride is needed at about 5 mM for photosynthetic electron transport and acts in photosystem II (Hind et al. 1969); chloride (at about 200 mM) is reported to uncouple the photophosphorylation from the Hill reaction (Good 1962). Maximal Hill activity in Euglena chloroplasts is obtained with 100 mM chloride, with no specificity of the alkali metal cation (Satoh et al. 1970). However, the report of Harvey and Brown (1969) is at variance with these results, as their high salt chloroplasts showed high rates of photophosphorylation. Does this mean that there is further compartmentation of salts within the chloroplast?

Further evidence that cations themselves do not affect photophosphorylation but rather the anions exert the effect comes from data of Asada et al. (1968) where it was shown that sulphate (10^{-2} M) uncouples cyclic and noncyclic photophosphorylation but at 10^{-2} M NaCl or $NaNO_3$ the rate of photophosphorylation was stimulated.

At the present time it is difficult to correlate the in vivo and in vitro effects of salinity on chloroplasts; however, the evidence does point to an anion rather than cation effect on photosynthetic function, and that there may be localization of salts to compartments within the chloroplasts, e.g. the lamellar regions.

4. SALINITY AND ENZYME SYSTEMS

For certain enzyme systems there is a requirement for K for maximum enzyme activity and Na will not substitute for K in these situations. This subject has been reviewed very well by Evans and Sorger (1966). Perhaps the best known example of these enzymes is pyruvic kinase, but other enzymes involving steps in protein synthesis and nucleotide synthesis are known to have similar limitations. Examination of the K concentration required for maximum enzyme activity shows that the cell needs about 20 mM K. One way excessive salinity can reduce enzyme activity would be to reduce K in the cytoplasm to an ineffective level.

When pea plants were grown on a saline medium, Hason-Porath and Poljakoff-Mayber (1969) found that activity of malic dehydrogenase was affected, and there was a distinction between effects of NaCl and Na_2SO_4; on the NaCl medium a new isozyme was present. In bean plants grown on high NaCl there is a shift from glycolytic to pentose phosphate pathways, but assay of the enzymes present did not explain this shift (Porath and Poljakoff-Mayber 1968).

Salinity also has adverse effects on polynucleotide and protein synthesis, the ramifications of which spread to all areas of cellular metabolism. Sodium and potassium sulphates (50 mM) inhibited DNA synthesis markedly in soybean roots and Na was slightly more inhibitory than K. Both salts almost stopped protein synthesis, and retarded net RNA synthesis equally (Rauser and Hanson 1966). In a more detailed study, Kahane and Poljakoff-Mayber (1968) demonstrated a difference between chloride and sulphate salinities, and whether or not salts were added to the incorporation medium. Their results clearly show that protein synthesis is inhibited by salinity— with sulphate being more inhibitory than chloride.

Exposure to high NaCl appears to hasten leaf fall in *Atriplex* and it is attractive to think that senescence of leaves when NaCl levels are high would be a convenient way of excreting NaCl. Wade and Campbell (unpublished data) have found that ripening in banana tissue slices, a process similar to leaf senescence, is hastened by vacuum infiltration with 100 mM KCl or NaCl.

In general effects of salinity on metabolic processes are extremely diverse, yet there are considerable gaps in our knowledge. Even where studies have been made it has not always proved possible to separate effects of cations and anions, or of osmotic pressure.

5. SALINITY AND MEMBRANE PROPERTIES

Experiments such as that shown in Fig. 3 lead us to infer that Na ions have an action on membrane permeability, and that this effect is not brought about by K ions. In addition low [Ca] or high [H] reduce membrane selectivity and increase membrane permeability. The complementary action of Ca and H is analogous to their behaviour in relation to ion exchange in cell walls, and suggests that permeability is related to weak negative charges in or on the membrane. We will return to this point later.

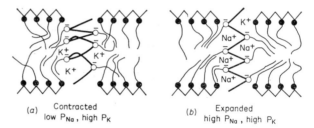

Fig. 5. Classical models for membrane structure show (*a*) a lipid bi-layer surrounded by protein. Physiological evidence leads to the requirement for polar pores (*b*).

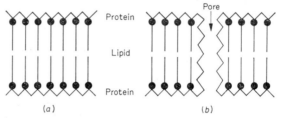

Fig. 6. The phospho-lipo-protein molecules can exist in forms between two extremes; (*a*) 'contracted' when only unhydrated K ions can enter the molecule and (*b*) 'expanded' when larger ions can penetrate (after Weiss 1969*b*).

Investigation of the structure of membranes in cells of many kinds has led to the classical view that the unit membrane has a double structure as shown in Fig. 5*a*. Essentially, a double layer of lipids, bound by H-bonding in the non-polar part of the molecule, is coated by outer layers of protein bonded to the polar part of the lipid. There is strong evidence for this organization both from electron microscopy and biochemical studies. More recent work suggests that lipid molecules need not be as highly ordered as in Fig. 5*a* but more randomly oriented as in Fig. 6*a*.

Physiological evidence for this lipid layer in the membrane comes from studies of permeability. Collander (1954) showed there was a strong correlation for a wide range of substances between a function ($P.MW^{3/2}$), combining permeability (P) with molecular weight (MW), and the olive-oil/water partition coefficient. More recently Wright and Diamond (1969) have measured the coefficient of reflection for a range of substances in gall-bladder membrane and find a regular distribution of this function against oil/water partition coefficients.

However, both Collander, and Wright and Diamond found that exceptions to the relation between permeability and lipid solubility were some small, polar molecules such as urea, methanol, water, that had higher permeability than expected from their lipid solubility. To account for these exceptions, and for some aspects of ion transport, the membrane is considered to have pores in it (Fig. 5*b*) which are permeable to ions and polar molecules.

This view has had some indirect support from the demonstration that certain cyclic compounds can act as pores in artificial lipo-protein membranes and have effects on ion transport (e.g. valinomycin). The pores need not be cyclic compounds though, for helical forms of short chain polypeptides such as poly-l-lysine can bind K preferentially to Na.

Recently Weiss (1969*a*, 1969*b*, 1969*c*, 1969*d*) has brought together relevant aspects of molecular theory of ion-exchange polymers and of rubbers and glasses to suggest a more definite model for pores in the membrane. His model also is used to explain energy-transduction and the coupled K/Na transport system but from the point of view of the present paper the most relevant part is the effect of these polymers on membrane permeability.

He suggests that phospho-lipo-protein molecules could form polar 'pores' in the membrane. The particular compound he takes as an example is a phospho-polyseryl molecule that has lipids attached to the phosphate groups. He suggests this might be

$$(-CO-NH-CH-)_n$$
$$|$$
$$CH_2$$
$$|$$
$$O$$
$$|$$
$$O=P-O-$$
$$|$$
$$O$$
$$|$$
$$CH_2-CH-CH_2$$
$$|\qquad\ |$$
$$O\qquad O$$
$$|\qquad\ |$$
$$CO\qquad CO$$
$$|\qquad\ |$$
$$R_1\qquad R_2$$

where n is between 4 and 6 and R_1 and R_2 are lipid hydrocarbons.

This polyseryl molecule is suggested to be in the form of a short helix with the lipid molecules extending laterally into the lipid layer (Fig. 6). The charged phosphate groups repel each other and tend to expand the spiral, while attraction between the lipid part of the molecule and lipid in the membrane resists this expansion. By analogy with molecular properties of rubbers, tension on the lipid molecules (due to repulsion of the phosphate groups) increases the degree of order of the lipid molecules which become held more tightly by H-bonding. The degree of expansion will be affected by the cations present, which can hold the phosphate groups together and contract the spiral.

The contracted spiral (Fig. 6a) can be stabilized by unhydrated K ions in the spiral or by Ca ions at the membrane surface. Hydrated Na ions are too large to penetrate the contracted spiral and have too large an energy of hydration for unhydrated ions to form readily. Lack of Ca or K will lead to expansion of the spiral (Fig. 6b). In this state the spiral would be able to accommodate the hydrated Na ion and so would be permeable both to K and Na.

From the point of view of plant studies two states are particularly relevant to salinity effects on the cell membrane. In the contracted state the permeability to Na would be low, but that to K could be high. In the expanded state the pores would be permeable to both K and Na. We can explain changes in membrane permeability as transition of the pores from one of these states to the other.

We suggest that in the plant membrane one effect of Na would be to hold open expanded pores. 'Expanded' and 'contracted' are not the only possible configurations and intermediate forms are likely, with say K at one end and Na at the other. Pores may be expected to change configuration depending on local ion concentrations. If K or Ca were present there would be a tendency for pores to be in the contracted state. It is suggested that higher numbers of Na ions on the outside and in the pores would reduce the chance of an expanded pore reverting to the contracted pore. The effect of H ions would be similar, as they would lead to reduction of charge density and so to reduction in the binding effect of K ions.

This reasonable extension of Weiss' model would explain the effect of Na in increasing membrane permeability, its reversal by Ca ions, and the complementary action of H and Ca ions. The relative effects of Ca, H and Na would depend on the surface charge on the membrane. For example, the strong Donnan system in the cell walls would favour divalent over univalent ions at the cell membrane surface, and the concentration of fixed charges would be reduced by local high concentrations of H ions. Differences in surface charge or in the pore density from one plant to another could explain different responses of plant cells to saline conditions.

6. CONCLUSION

We have tried to show in this survey that the plant cell tends to regulate its internal environment and that absence of regulation can lead to disturbance of cellular processes. There seems to be two kinds of salinity effect on the cell. *High levels of Na* have an action on membrane integrity, possible by displacing Ca or K from operative sites in the membrane. High Na levels can also interfere with enzyme processes which require K, such as pyruvic kinase, but there are few examples in plant cells of obligatory K + Na enzyme systems. On the other hand, *high levels of Cl* appear to have an action on organelle structure and so on respiration, photosynthesis and protein synthesis.

One unfortunate conclusion of reviewing this field is that too little work has been done on effects of salinity on cellular activity in plants.

REFERENCES

Asada, K., Deura, R., and Kasai, Z. (1968). *Plant and Cell Physiol.* **9**, 143.

Atkinson, M. R., Findlay, G. P., Hope, A. B., Pitman, M. G., Saddler, H. D. W., and West, K. R. (1967). *Aust. J. biol. Sci.* **20**, 589.

Blumenthal-Goldschmidt, S., and Poljakoff-Mayber, A. (1968). *Aust. J. Bot.* **16**, 469.

Carter, O. G., and Lathwell, D. J. (1967). *Agron. J.* **59**, 250.

Collander, R. (1954). *Physiologia Pl.* **7**, 420.

Coster, H. G. L. (1966). *Aust. J. biol. Sci.* **19**, 545.

Dilley, R. A., and Rothstein, P. (1967). *Biochim. biophys. Acta.* **135**, 427.

Dodd, W. A., Pitman, M. G., and West, K. R. (1966). *Aust. J. biol. Sci.* **19**, 341.

Evans, H. J., and Sorger, G. J. (1966). *Ann. Rev. Plant Physiol.* **17**, 47.

Findlay, G. P., Hope, A. B., and Williams, E. J. (1969). *Aust. J. biol. Sci.* **22**, 1163.

Flowers, T. J., and Hanson, J. B. (1969). *Plant Physiol.* **44**, 939.

Gale, J., and Poljakoff-Mayber, A. (1970). *Aust. J. biol. Sci.* **23**, 937.

Gale, J., Kohl, H. C., and Hagan, R. M. (1967). *Physiologia Pl.* **20**, 408.

Good, N. E. (1962). *Arch. Biochem. Biophys.* **96**, 653.

Greenway, H. (1963) *Aust. J. biol. Sci.* **16**, 616.

Hanson, J. B., and Miller, R. J. (1969). *Plant and Cell Physiol.* **10**, 491.

Harvey, M. J., and Brown, A. P. (1969). *Biochim. biophys. Acta.* **180**, 520.

Hason-Porath, E., and Poljakoff-Mayber, A. (1969). *Plant Physiol.* **44**, 1031.

Hind, G., Nakatini, H. Y., and Izawa, S. (1969). *Biochim. biophys. Acta,* **172**, 277.

Hyder, S. Z., and Greenway, H. (1965). *Plant and Soil.* **23**, 258.

Kahane, I., and Poljakoff-Mayber, A., (1968) *Plant Physiol.* **43**, 1115.

Lapina, L. P., and Bikmukhametova, S. A. (1969). *Soviet Plant Physiol.* **16**, (4), 532.

Lapina, L. P., Popov, B. A., and Strogonov, B. P. (1968). *Soviet Plant Physiol.* **15** (6), 890.

Larkum, A. W. D. (1968). *Nature* (Lond.) **218**, 447.

Larkum, A. W. D., and Hill, A. E. (1970). *Biochim. biophys. Acta.* **203**, 133.

Livne, A., and Levin, N. (1967). *Plant Physiol.* **42**, 407.

Lyons, J. M. (1962). Ph. D. Thesis. University of California.

MacRobbie, E. A. C. (1962). *J. gen. Physiol.* **45**, 861.

Packer, L., Murakami, S., and Mehard, C. W. (1970). *Ann. Rev. Plant Physiol.* **21**, 271.

Pitman, M. G. (1965*a*). *Aust. J. biol. Sci.* **18**, 10.

Pitman, M. G. (1965*b*). *Aust. J. biol. Sci.* **18**, 987.

Pitman, M. G. (1966). *Aust. J. biol. Sci.* **19**, 257.

Pitman, M. G. (1969). *Plant Physiol.* **44**, 1233.

Pitman, M. G., and Saddler, H. D. W. (1967). *Proc. Natl. Acad. Sci.* **57**, 44.

Porath, E., and Poljakoff-Mayber, A. (1968). *Plant and Cell Physiol.* **9**, 195.

Rauser, W. E., and Hanson, J. B. (1966). *Can. J. Bot.* **44**, 759.

Raven, J. A. (1967). *J. gen. Physiol.* **50**, 1607.

Satoh, K., Katoh, S., and Takamiya, A. (1970). *Plant and Cell Physiol.* **11**, 453.

Spanswick, R. M., and Williams, E. J. (1964). *J. expt. Bot.* **15**, 193.

Weiss, D. E. (1969*a*). *Aust. J. biol. Sci.* **22**, 1337.

Weiss, D. E. (1969*b*). *Aust. J. biol. Sci.* **22**, 1355.

Weiss, D. E. (1969*c*). *Aust. J. biol. Sci.* **22**, 1373.

Weiss, D. E. (1969*d*). *Aust. J. biol. Sci.* **22**, 1389.

Wilson, R. H., Hanson, J. B., and Mollenhauer, H. H. (1969). *Biochem.* **8** (3), 1203.

Wright, E. M., and Diamond, J. H. (1969). *Proc. Roy. Soc. B.* **127**, 227.

PART V   Social Considerations

Economic and Social Aspects of Saline Water Use and Management

B. J. CALLINAN and R. G. WEBSTER

Respectively Gutteridge, Haskins and Davey,
and
Victorian Pipelines Commission, Melbourne, Victoria

SUMMARY

Salinity problems resulting from high salinities in streams and in shallow watertables arise frequently from the clearing of forests and from irrigation. The major areas affected are the River Murray Valley and the south-western parts of Western Australia and Victoria.

The evaluation of the consequences of salinity problems must commence with clear knowledge and understanding of the economic and social bases upon which the region functions. The evaluations are difficult due to:

(i) The absence of bases upon which to commence.
(ii) Losses being frequently caused more to those downstream than to those whose lands create the problems.
(iii) The wide areas of adaptabilities of processes to conditions and salinities.

Salinity control measures are essentially long-term and their economic evaluation is best made with discount rates which are reduced for long-term costs and benefits. The social consequences, whilst difficult to evaluate, must be given due weight in the light of deteriorating conditions in the metropolises.

The effects of high salinities can be lessened in areas already affected, and avoided in areas about to be developed, by the application of lessons now available to proposed investigations, planning and control. Planning legislation can be used to exercise essential controls.

1. INTRODUCTION

Salinity has significant social and economic consequences because it affects the life and health of plants, animals and humans. In small quantities, salt is essential for life, but in greater concentrations, frequently exceeded

227

in nature it kills animals and plants. Excess amounts are difficult to combat because of the large volumes to be removed from the water or soil.

As much of the Australian continent is geologically old, flat, poorly drained and has low rainfall, much of the salt derived from the decomposition of rocks has accumulated in alluvial deposits in the plains. In some areas this has been influenced by the presence of former coastlines which have determined the position of terminal lakes for the rivers.

The River Murray Valley is the largest area in Australia affected by salinity; significant areas also occur in Western Australia and in south-western Victoria.

2. AFFECTED AREAS

(a) *River Murray Valley*

A large area with appreciable amounts of salt in the subsoils extends around the middle and lower parts of the River Murray Valley (Anon 1970, Fig. 1). In some of this area salt was deposited in terminal lakes, formed behind an arm of the sea which extended from the existing coastline approximately to Swan Hill. These deposits were buried later by further sediments from the high lands. The affected area can be divided into two zones differing in their soil and drainage characteristics and in the sources of the salinity problems.

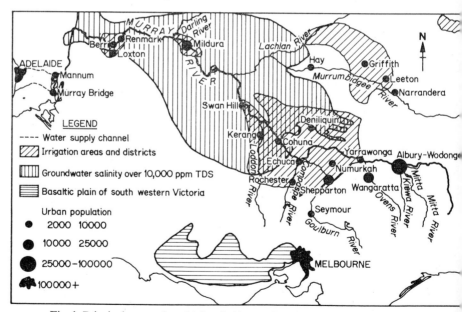

Fig. 1. Principal areas where high salinities are found in south-eastern Australia.

1.   The Riverine Plains Zone, in the eastern section (Fig. 2), has fine textured soils and poor natural drainage. Irrigation has been practised in parts of these plains since before the turn of the century and volumes of applied water gradually increased over the years. Cattle and sheep raising are the chief industries. Groundwater levels which were well below the surface before irrigation have now risen to within 60–120 cm of the surface over extensive areas, and an equilibrium position has been almost achieved by means of open drains and evaporation from the land surface.

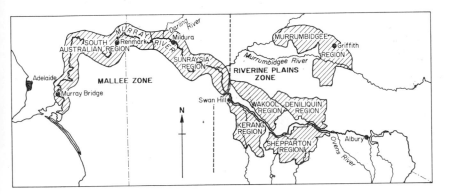

Fig. 2. Murray Valley Zones and Regions.

Because of the salt contained in the lower sediments the groundwater is highly saline, more than 20,000 parts per million (ppm) of total dissolved salts (TDS) in some areas. Unirrigated areas are the most obviously affected and patches of bare soil and white salt are not uncommon. There are less obvious effects on irrigated land, because of the leaching action of the applied water, but the economic losses are greater here since the salt still reaches into the root zone.

The Kerang Region is the worst affected and surveys have indicated that about two-thirds of the region, or 525,000 acres, has shallow, saline, ground-water creating major economic problems. Drainage water from the region is highly saline, and is discharged into the Murray, with consequent increases in salinity of the water available to towns and irrigators downstream. Salt concentrations up to about 600 ppm have been recorded downstream in the Mallee Zone; about two-thirds of this amount being sodium chloride. Although these are not high levels by world standards, a combination of these salinities with other adverse factors have caused production losses.

2.   The Mallee Zone (Fig. 2) soils are generally coarser-textured and more easily drained than those in the Riverine Plains Zone. The economy of this zone is based almost entirely on high value crops of grapes, deciduous and citrus fruits, and, to a lesser extent, dairying.

It is necessary for the well-being of the people of this zone that salinity be kept controlled and millions of dollars have been spent already on control measures of various kinds. The present situation is not so serious that existing developments are threatened but any significant changes in water use in the valley, in new irrigation areas, in drainage outlets or diversions of water will affect river salinity. Should these changes significantly increase river salinity, production in the zone could be depressed seriously. Thus, in considering the benefits and costs of new irrigation or drainage projects anywhere in the Murray catchment, the effects on river salinities should be assessed.

(b) Western Australian Streams

The history of water supply catchments in Western Australia demonstrates the effects of land policies on salinities (Collet 1968). Clearing of the virgin forest has increased the volume of runoff and also the salinity. This trend may be controlled by re-afforestation, although the use of pine plantations for this purpose reduces runoff to a level lower than virgin forest. Of the total of 2 million acre feet per annum which could be obtained by regulation of rivers in the south-west of the State, about one-third is brackish or saline.

(c) South-western Victoria

Another area with salinity problems is the south-western part of Victoria (Webster 1965). This is mostly a gently undulating basaltic plain with an average annual rainfall of 22 to 30 inches. Decomposition of the basaltic rock has produced considerable quantities of salts, mostly NaCl, in the soils and the rainfall over the ages has not been sufficient to leach them from the top soil. Some smaller adjacent areas have lateritic soils, with large amounts of salt in the subsoils.

Before settlement in the nineteenth century, most of western Victoria was lightly timbered by deep-rooted eucalyptus. Native grasses were also deep-rooted. Transpiration from this vegetation kept groundwaters at low levels. During settlement trees were mostly cleared and the natural grasses replaced with planted pastures having shallower roots. As a result groundwater levels rose, saline seepage came to the surface in depressions and along water courses and reached the rivers. Stream salinities in summer are now measured in thousands of ppm, and are too high for town water supplies or for irrigation, except under special conditions.

3. STANDARDS FOR WATER SUPPLIES

(a) Domestic

The World Health Organization has adopted standards for the maximum concentrations of substances affecting the potability of water generally acceptable to consumers, and also the maximum allowable concentrations beyond which potability is seriously impaired. For instance generally acceptable water may contain 500 ppm total salt, with up to 200 ppm as chloride; limiting values being 1500 ppm and 600 ppm respectively.

For domestic water, 80 ppm of total hardness as $CaCO_3$ is usually adopted as the optimal maximum value. Waters containing more than about 100 ppm usually require some degree of softening; this becomes essential when the hardness reaches 150 ppm.

(b) Industrial

There are no general standards for industrial water supply as each industry requires its own conditions to be met. In outline, the following are the requirements of some major groups of industries for water supply:

1.   *Pulp and Paper Manufacture*. General requirements are low turbidity, low colour water, free from all but very small amounts of Fe and Mn and total salts usually less than 200 ppm. Concentrations up to 1000 ppm in re-cycled water can be used for lower quality papers.

2.   *Steel Production*. The desirable water quality depends on the type of final product. Salt water and reclaimed sewerage water have been used overseas for some functions. In higher grade products water containing less than 250 ppm TDS is desirable.

3.   *Textiles*. In general, water qualities required are similar to the pulp and paper industry, but in dye house work much more stringent control standards pertain, particularly in some cases of fine fabrics where completely demineralized water is required.

4.   *Automotive and Electrical Industries*. TDS concentrations of less than 250 ppm are usually desirable to stop corrosion and deposition of dried salts on wetted parts. For some washing purposes, such as plating and washing electron tubes, demineralized water is used.

5.   *Chemical Industry*. Water is used in a wide variety of functions, from cooling, where corrosiveness is the criterion, to process water where a soft or demineralized water is required.

(c) Stock

Little research has been carried out on desirable limits of salt in drinking water for stock. Upper limits for salt concentrations which can be tolerated by animals have been set out in Table 1. These data are mainly based on field observations.

(d) Irrigation

Limits of salinity depend upon a number of factors such as drainage, soil salinity and rainfall, and also on farm management practices. However, by

TABLE 1

Upper limits used by State Authorities in Australia for total salts in water for livestock,
in ppm TDS
(Source: Anon 1969.)

Class of livestock	Qld.	N.S.W.	N.T.	S.A.	W.A.	Vic.
Poultry	3500	4000	—	3000[a]	3000	3500
Pigs	5500	4000	—	3000[a]	4500	4500
Horses	5500[b]	7000	6000	7000	6500	6000
Cattle						
Dairy	5500[b]	10,000	6000	7000	7000	6000
Beef	8500[c]	10,000	10,000	10,000	10,000	7000
Sheep						
Lambs, Weaners	—	—	—	—	10,000	4500
Ewes in Milk	—	—	—	—	10,000	6000
Adult, on dry feed	14,500	14,000	12,000	13,000	13,000	7000[e] to
Adult, on green grass	18,500	—	15,000	18,000	18,500[d]	15,000

[a] 4000 ppm if on salt free rations; 1500 if on high salt diet
[b] 7000 ppm if on green feed
[c] 10,000 ppm if on green feed
[d] for short periods
[e] if unaccustomed to saline water; if accustomed up to 15,000 ppm

The upper limit figures are conditioned by the maximum temperature, the type of feed and the time the animal has been exposed to the water.

assuming some conditions which are generally encountered and also certain standards of farm management, values can be derived as guides in assessing water quality. These values will allow production of 80–90 % of the optimum, obtainable with good quality water and high standards of farm management.

Farm management practices assumed in deriving the tolerable levels are; for horticulture, a water application method that does not wet the leaves, good drainage and the application of a leaching fraction of 0·25. For pastures the application of a leaching fraction of 0·15 has been assumed.

Then, limiting values of salinity which may be exceeded for short periods but not over a growing period are:

	Stone fruit	*Citrus*	*Vines*	*Clover*
TDS ppm	600	600	1050	450
Cl ppm	175	365	350	—

4. COST AND DESIRABILITY OF WATER TREATMENT

In the main groups of uses, there are no clear relationships between salinity levels and the desirability of treatment; because there are wide areas of adaptation of processes and procedures.

(a) Domestic

In Australia, a wide range of salinities is still accepted; probably caused by the scarcity of perennial sources of good quality water and the short histories of settlements. So long as there is a source of water, not noticeably polluted and usable for cooking and washing, it is acceptable. With treatment costs for usual turbidities and hardnesses at about 10 cents per 1000 gallons there are still few demands for quality improvements, although at this charge the annual cost per person would be about $5.00, or less than 50 cents per household per week.

(b) Industrial

Salinity levels that will be accepted before treatment is required range widely from industry to industry and often with the uses within 'an industry'.

(c) Stock

Salinity levels acceptable to most livestock are so high that availability of water is usually the critical factor.

(d) Irrigation

A recent study on salinity in the Murray Valley (Anon 1970) where economic effects are quite serious, has indicated that the effects of salinity on various forms of production are as set out in Table 2. These figures must clearly be broad in their application since they take no account of soil or climatic variations. The coefficients give an average effect; in some parts the soils or topography may be such that saline groundwater has virtually no effect, but in others, particularly low areas and depressions, conditions will encourage salinization. Without further relief works it is predicted that the areas of shallow watertables in the Riverine Zone will increase as shown in Table 3.

The direct economic loss in terms of production lost is estimated to be $4·2 million per annum in 1970, rising to $16·7 million in 50 years from now.

The gross value of the annual losses within each region, that would occur if no action is taken in the zone have been estimated and are given in Table 4. Studies have also shown that it would be possible to save about a third to

16

one half of these losses by providing drainage schemes and improving management.

TABLE 2

Production adjustment coefficients for the Murray Valley

| | | No surface drainage | | With surface drainage | |
Land use	Unaffected production	Saline shallow watertables	Non-saline shallow watertables	Saline shallow watertables	Non-saline shallow watertables
Horticulture	1·00	—*	0·70	—*	0·85
Rice	1·00	0·90	1·00	0·95	1·00
Other grains	1·00	0·85	0·90	0·90	0·95
Fodder crops	1·00	0·80	0·85	0·90	0·90
Perennial pastures	1·00	0·80	0·90	0·90	0·95
Annual pastures	1·00	0·60	0·85	0·80	0·90
Volunteer pastures and miscellaneous	1·00	0·50	0·80	0·75	0·90
Unirrigated land	1·00	0·30	0·75	0·50	0·85

* Horticulture is not practicable under these conditions.

TABLE 3

Predicted extent of shallow watertable areas in the Riverine Plains Zone
(× 1000 acres)

Year	Kerang Region (saline)	Wakool Region (saline)	Deniliquin (saline)	Region (non-saline)	Shepparton Region (non-saline)	Total (saline)	(non-saline)	Grand total
1970	520	40	0	0	80	560	80	640
1975	560	50	0	0	140	610	140	750
1980	620	80	10	190	210	710	400	1110
2020	730	160	250	250	550	1140	800	1940
Area of Region	790	860	950		1300			3900

TABLE 4

Gross value of the potential annual losses, in the Riverine Plains Zone, due to shallow watertables
($ million/annum)

Year	Kerang	Shepparton	Deniliquin	Wakool	Total
1970	3·8	0·2	0	0·2	4·2
1980	4·6	1·9	0·8	0·5	7·8
2020	6·2	6·6	2·9	1·0	16·7

5. AN ECONOMIC APPROACH TO SALINITY CONTROL

It is generally true that, for low and even moderate salinities, users adapt to water available and in fact, may be unaware that the water quality is worse than elsewhere. For example, in Adelaide, the salinity of the city water supply has risen to 600 ppm TDS, a situation which would be viewed with horror by manufacturers in Melbourne where the water supply normally contains about 60 ppm TDS. Also, in the towns of Coleraine and Casterton in western Victoria, salinities of 1000 to 1300 ppm TDS are normal, but do not cause undue concern. It is accepted there that rainwater is used for drinking and that only salt tolerant flowers will thrive in urban gardens. Some irrigators have managed to survive in this area. Households, industries and farms tend to adjust themselves to the environment in which they find themselves, making it difficult to put a value on the cost of poor quality water supplies.

In general terms the adverse effects of salinity increase rapidly after a certain level is reached (see Fig. 3). Figure 3 suggests that the cost of treatment or dilution becomes relatively less as salinity rises; while the willingness of the consumer to pay for relief rises with salinity. Assuming that the economic value is represented by the 'willingness to pay', which is reasonable, it would be economically desirable to reduce the salinity level to the point where the slope of the two curves is the same. For salinities below this point the estimated costs of a small reduction in salinity exceed the benefits and amelioration is not desirable.

It is suggested that, when a certain level of salinity (or of any other sort of pollution) is reached, the 'willingness to pay' increases quite steeply as illustrated by Fig. 3.

(a) Salinity and Economic Analyses

Benefit-cost analyses have been used to assess the economic desirability of water supply and drainage schemes which often affect river salinities, and they could be applied also to schemes designed mainly for salinity-control.

Almost every water supply or drainage scheme in Australia has an effect on water salinity. In south-eastern Australia the upstream parts of catchments usually have the highest rainfalls and produce the best quality runoffs, whilst in the south-west of Western Australia, it is generally the lower or downstream parts of catchments which have the higher rainfalls and lower salinities.

Water storages for city supplies will normally be built to conserve the better quality waters and the flows remaining in the rivers below the storages will be lower in quality, to the disadvantage of downstream users. Likewise, the use for irrigation in upstream areas of better-than-average quality water will result in some cost to the users of lower quality residual flows. Water schemes can of course, have a beneficial effect on salinities in the regions where regulated flows are provided. Many rivers which carry good quality

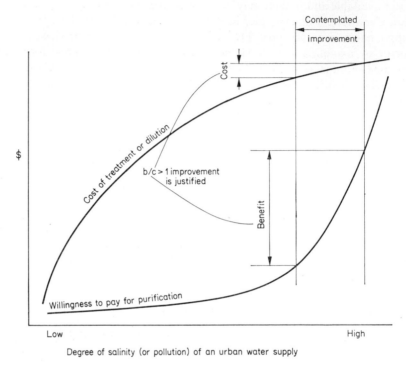

Fig. 3. Economics of user's attitude to water treatment.

regulated flows for irrigation downstream are also used for town supplies or minor irrigation diversions en route—to the benefit of all users. These effects should be included as costs or benefits in any benefit-cost analysis, even if they cannot be accurately quantified. Such considerations apply, for example, to future water schemes proposed in the Murray River Basin.

Deterioration of stream quality due to drainage and runoff is an inevitable effect of any new land settlement—whether dry farming or irrigation—and should always be recognized when examining proposals for changes in land use. Where there is a major change in salinity, or where salinity control is the main objective, it is necessary to ascertain first how the area functions economically and socially. Since the economies of areas differ, there can be no general procedures for estimating costs and benefits attributable to substantial salinity changes.

In the Kerang Region drainage schemes leading to large evaporating lakes have been constructed and may be expanded. Some relevant economic facts for this region are:

(i) Irrigation is almost entirely for pastures supporting dairy cows, beef and sheep. A substantial proportion of Australia's production of these items is exported.

(ii) Dairy production is subsidized.

(iii) Some farm equipment and supplies are manufactured in Australia behind tariff barriers so that farmers are paying more than world prices for them.

(iv) The region contains about 4000 farms which are almost entirely 'one family' units of about 200 acres each. Generally farm incomes are adequate by Australian standards.

(v) The total urban population of the region is about 25,000 and they are probably as prosperous as those in most similar Australian country areas. The towns exist almost solely as centres for the farming community.

Recent studies suggest that the shallow high salinity watertables cause a regional production loss of 10%. Without further drainage the situation will deteriorate in about 20 years to reduce production by about 30%. If farms are abandoned this would, in turn, react on the prosperity of the towns and reduce their populations.

The economic effects from schemes to improve drainage in the Kerang Region would:

(i) Avoid a production loss that would reduce farm incomes and overseas currency earnings.

(ii) Require the continuation of some direct and indirect subsidy payments from the taxpayer to the farmer.

(iii) Avoid a reduction in employment and a corresponding increase in capital city populations.

(iv) Avoid a reduction in spending on manufactured items such as farm equipment.

(v) Increase the amount of salt in drainage waters. This must either be disposed of by evaporation schemes with an additional capital cost or discharged with consequent deterioration in quality downstream and possible economic losses there to farmers, industries and urban areas.

(b) Evaluation of Economic Effects

Items (i) and (ii) above can be estimated in terms of current prices and trends, but it is not entirely clear what attitude should be taken towards subsidies. Should production losses be assessed using prices received over-seas for marginal production or should the subsidized prices, received by farmers, be used? If farm subsidies are part of national policy, and are designed to promote rural production and preserve rural population, then maybe production should be valued at the higher value, including subsidies. The more acceptable view would probably be that subsidies are designed to safeguard incomes of farmers affected by changing world conditions and, therefore, only the overseas prices for production should be allowed.

The effect on country towns (iii) is difficult to evaluate. At present these Murray Valley town populations are growing slowly. Local businesses have expectations of steady, if unspectacular, growth as community living standards improve. If a steady decline in rural production became apparent with, possibly, a significant number of farmers leaving the district, the towns would enter a period of no growth and likely decline. Some housing and public facilities would become redundant—as has happened to other towns depending on declining industries.

The immediate resulting economic cost would be the cost of constructing houses and facilities elsewhere. However, there is also a psychological effect on the inhabitants of a town that is doomed, or blighted, as was quite evident in the 1940s in the town of Tallangatta before inundation by the raised level of Hume Reservoir. People lose the incentive to make construc-tive efforts to improve or even maintain their surroundings. This social effect applies to both private and public activities.

The economic cost of shifting people, whether from farms or towns, is the cost of re-establishing them with housing and occupations elsewhere. The historical cost of establishing the farms about to become redundant is irrelevant here.

In quantitative terms, if the decline in rural income and hence in rural population can be estimated, the drop in town population will probably be about equal to the rural one. Including families, about five people will be involved for each prime worker on the farms. The cost of re-establishment, complete with housing, public facilities and services, has been estimated at $7000 per head and for industrial capital costs a further $3500 per head (Lansdown 1966). The cost of constructing Tallangatta, in the period 1953–58 was about $5000 per head, which is comparable with the above figures, after allowing for changing money values.

The above figures are economic costs and have no allowance for the social cost of a compulsory transfer. The social costs of uprooting people and communities can only be qualitatively assessed. However, they are real costs and should be included. An allowance of one-quarter of the economic cost would not be unreasonable.

The economic and social costs incurred in towns would not occur if the towns continued to grow, despite the reduction in rural income. This leads to the suggestion that, if the decline of these towns could be arrested or reversed by some other means, then the loss due to salinity problems would be confined to the farm sector of the economy.

However, the problem of declining country towns occurs everywhere, as the work force engaged in agricuture declines, and no really satisfactory solutions have been found. In Victoria, industries are encouraged to establish in country towns by such measures as uniform electricity tariffs, Government assistance for roads, water supply and sewerage schemes. In addition, concessions on rail freights and various forms of direct grants and subsidies cost $5·5 million in Victoria in 1969–70. Recent experience has shown that it is extremely difficult to attract industry to small country towns by such means. The growth of country towns can been couraged only by dealing also with the reasons that draw people away, which are mostly social. High speed rail and telephone communications, subsidized to suburban levels, and greatly improved secondary and tertiary education facilities would help to offset social disadvantages.

The future alternatives for the Kerang Region are:

1. Carry out no further major drainage—allow salinity to gradually increase and rural production and towns to decline. A rural industries stabilization programme could be instituted to purchase some farms— maybe 1 in 5—and their 'water right' removed. The holdings would then be re-arranged to provide evaporating areas.

2. As for 1, but prevent decline in towns by heavily subsidizing new industries, communications and education facilities. The first part of such a policy has precedents in the U.S.A. where funds for capital works were made available at special low interest rates in areas where unemployment exceeded certain limits. The second part would require an imaginative approach at Commonwealth and State levels to the social problems of country areas.

3. Maintain rural production and the growth of towns by the construction of drainage schemes with evaporation basins to avoid increases in saline drainage which would adversely affect production elsewhere.

(c) Discount Rates

The results of any economic assessment of works to reduce the effects of salinity will depend largely upon the discount rates adopted to calculate the present worths of future costs and benefits. The discount rate adopted is purely a reflection of social values, a basic definition being the 'social rate of time discount' or 'the premium which the community places on consumption this year instead of consumption in one year from now'.

It is usually assumed that the same social discount rate is applicable to consumption or benefits received in the next generation as to those received in the immediate future. For example, for a discount rate of 5 %, the present worth of consumption 5 years hence would be 78 % of its nominal value and the 'present worth' at year 20 of consumption 25 years from now would also be 78 % of its nominal value. This sort of procedure leads to a scaling down of really long-term benefits, mitigating against long-term projects such as the reduction of pollution.

It would probably be more rational to assume that, for benefits received many years ahead, the particular year in which the benefits are received is not of great concern. This could be expressed mathematically by the use of different discount rates for fixed periods during the period being considered, of, say 7 % for years 0–5, 4 % for years 5–25 and 1 % after 25 years. This would preserve the community's preference for immediate returns rather than short-term delays, and at the same time give due importance to really long-term benefits. This is indicated in Fig. 4.

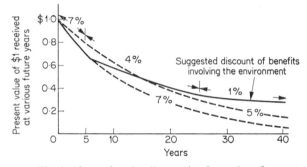

Fig. 4. Alternatives for discounting future benefits.

The benefits received at 40 years would then have their present value assessed at 27 % of their nominal value, compared with 14 % for a constant discount rate of 5 %, or 7 % for a discount rate of 7 %. For benefits received from measures to control salinity, such a procedure is more logical than the use of a fixed discount rate for all periods of time.

6. SALINITY CONTROL BY PLANNING

There are two basically different approaches to planning, to control the effects of high salinities in water and soil. High salinities can be regarded as being not of immediate major significance, and ignored as long as possible. Then, as salinity levels rise and it becomes socially and economically desirable to take ameliorative action, the best available solutions are obtained from engineering and economic studies. This approach has been followed so far here. Alternatively, salt can be regarded as a major determining factor in our environment and land use planned accordingly.

This alternative can be considered by contemplating the way in which land would be used if the subject were approached *ab initio*, without established towns, farms or communications. Then, in a country like Australia, with large areas of low rainfall and where water availability is an ultimate limitation on its development, it would be reasonable to lay down basic requirements for land development such as:

(i) Natural forests and grasses would not be cleared from areas where they prevent saline groundwater from coming to the surface.

(ii) Irrigation should preferably not be carried out in regions underlain by highly saline sediments.

(iii) Where groundwater is saline, irrigation would be limited to small discontinuous areas of high value crops.

(iv) Irrigation should be chiefly on land which can be used for a variety of purposes, both pasture and horticulture, to avoid reduction in versatility created by salinity problems.

These limitations should be applied to the development of new irrigation areas such as those based on the Ord and other rivers in northern Australia. In south-eastern Australia there is no *ab initio* position; towns and farms with communications and other facilities already exist and involve large investments. It has been reported that existing salinity levels can be stabilized by ameliorative action at a total capital cost of about $55 million over the next 20 years.

At present there is overproduction of some rural commodities. Changing economic conditions are already forcing some farmers to take up other occupations, and some land to go out of production. The effects of salinity in certain areas is superimposed on the existing general economic problems of farmers. If a reduction in the farm work force is desirable in the national interest, the salinity problem offers an added incentive to consider a reduction of irrigation in salt affected areas such as the Kerang Region.

7. LEGISLATION

The control of land use by planning legislation is accepted now as an essential part of government and local government activities, but is directed usually to establish acceptable relations between the industrial, commercial, residential, recreational, services and rural uses. However, planning legislation has been used to minimize the effects of floods by controlling developments on floodplains in the U.S.A. It has been used here to prevent urban development in areas that cannot be economically or desirably protected from periodical inundation, and could be used similarly to lessen the effects of salinity, by preventing close development of some areas, and by limiting development in others.

Planning control is exercised usually through local governing bodies but a hierarchy of 'controlling bodies' is developing ranging through government departments, commissions and boards; to regional authorities; to local councils, trusts and authorities. The controls that could be exercised by such planning schemes would include:

(i) Prohibition of irrigation in areas where shallow high salinity watertables will occur.

(ii) Determination of minimum sizes of holdings, annual maximum quantities of water per holding, and the proportion of a holding that can be irrigated.

(iii) Reservation of lands for drainage collection and disposal on each holding and/or in certain areas.

Some of these controls are already exercised by irrigation and water supply authorities, but they could well be supplemented to meet the wider range of requirements now being recognized. It is agreed now by most that, to avoid the development of large areas with shallow high salinity watertables and drainage problems that now beset the Kerang Region, it should not have been so intensely irrigated. With present knowledge, planning controls could be used to prevent salinity problems elsewhere or to lessen their effects.

REFERENCES

Anon (1969). *Quality Aspects of Farm Water Supplies.* Dept. of National Development, Canberra.

Anon (1970). *Murray Valley Salinity Investigation.* Report for the River Murray Commission by Gutteridge, Haskins and Davey.

Collett, D. B. (1968). Int. Rept. Dept. Publ. Works, W.A.

Lansdown, R. B. (1966). *Aust. Planning Inst. J.* **4**, 174.

Webster, R. G. (1965). Proc. 2nd Australasian Conf. Hydraulics and Fluid Mechanics, B7.

Administrative and Legal Aspects of Saline Water Use and Management

S. D. CLARK* and I. MEACHAM

*Respectively, University of Melbourne and
State Rivers and Water Supply Commission, Melbourne, Victoria*

SUMMARY

The Senate Select Committee on Water Pollution reporting in 1970, pointed to the lack of effective control, at that time, over the dangers of water pollution throughout Australia. One possible form of administrative structure at the State level, to combat these dangers, is exemplified by the central administration set up by the Environment Protection Act, passed by the Victorian Parliament late in 1970, to cover all aspects of environmental pollution. At the inter-State and Commonwealth-State levels there are special legal and administrative problems to be faced. Control of salinity on the River Murray will depend on a practicable solution to these problems being found. A satisfactory administrative structure to operate at these levels could be built on the experience and advice of central pollution-control administrations, established within the separate States.

1. INTRODUCTION

Within limits set by technological and socio-economic criteria, there are certain things that ought to be done to control salinity in certain waters that have, or could have, a beneficial use. To ensure that what ought to be done will be done requires the intervention of law and administration. In the long run, the control of salinity will be dealt with largely under a legal and administrative structure embracing all aspects of water quality, perhaps of environmental quality generally. This paper discusses some basic principles involved and relates them to the Australian scene, with particular reference to the River Murray.

* Research for this paper was supported in part by the Australian Research Grants Committee and the Australian Water Resources Council.

2. THE SITUATION IN AUSTRALIA—1970

The recent (1970) report of the Senate Select Committee on Water Pollution lists 132 Statutes in force in the various States of the Commonwealth containing provisions relating to water pollution. It lists also 92 separate bodies involved in the administration of those Statutes. The Commonwealth itself accounts for another 5 Statutes and 25 Ordinances, administered by 13 separate bodies.

Despite this plethora of laws and administrations, or rather because of it, there was very little effective control over water pollution. The Committee stated: 'There is nothing in the present piecemeal and parochial administration of water to prevent the insidious growth of pollution excesses'.

In Victoria alone, at the time of the Committee's Inquiry, there were 27 Statutes containing reference to water pollution, largely repetitive and prohibitive in nature. Policing powers were conferred on no less than 22 specific bodies, as well as on all waterworks trusts, sewerage authorities and river improvement trusts. Regulatory powers, as distinct from statutory prohibitions, were provided in at least 6 Statutes but had been used to promulgate only one set of regulations of State-wide application and two by-laws of local application—none of which could be claimed to be completely successful, even in the limited fields concerned.

This sorry picture was fairly typical of all States. The many administrations could be likened to the legs of a headless centipede, a few scratching at the ground within reach, the rest inert for lack of any coherent plan or purpose. The problem could be solved either by adding a head, or by scrapping the whole thing and starting again. At the end of 1970, Victoria chose the former solution as will be described later in this paper.

Salinity, as a distinct aspect of water pollution, has only in recent years received special mention in the Victorian Statutes. In 1967, provision was inserted in the Water Act (Sec. 379 AA) empowering the State Rivers and Water Supply Commission to make by-laws for the control of saline discharges to sources of supply. This provision was prompted by the increasingly common practice of pumping groundwater to surface drainage lines so as to control water tables in the northern irrigation districts.

The Commission has also begun to exercise indirect control over saline drainage discharges to the Murray from riverside lands irrigated under licence. New diversion licences are not being issued below Nyah unless the Commission is satisfied that the applicant has taken measures to dispose of drainage away from the river.

Other measures taken by Victoria to mitigate the salinity problem on the Murray have included drainage disposal schemes in the Kerang area and the Sunraysia area, serving comprehensive irrigation systems. In both cases, saline drainage water that would flow naturally to the Murray is diverted to evaporation basins away from the river. These works were financed by the Commonwealth out of funds set aside for a National Water Programme, concerned primarily with water conservation. It is easy to see that the objective of water conservation is aided by works such as these which reduce the requirement for dilution flows.

The control of salinity in the River Murray poses a specially difficult problem because of the involvement of four Governments—the Commonwealth and the States of New South Wales, Victoria and South Australia. More will be said later of the legal aspects of the relationship between the four parties, and of possible approaches to future action on the problem of salinity.

The present Agreement between the four parties (the River Murray Waters Agreement) provides for the construction of certain storages and diversion weirs, and provides also for the allocation of costs and the allocation of water. It makes little mention of water quality, the only relevant provision being that during a period of restriction the River Murray Commission may set aside a quantity of water 'for dilution in South Australia' prior to the sharing of remaining resources. The quantity to be set aside is left to the discretion of the Commission.

A more definite reference to salinity is made in the amending Agreement still awaiting (December, 1970) ratification by the South Australian Parliament. Provision there is made for dilution flows, up to specified maxima, to prevent salinity at Swan Hill and Merbein exceeding 300 parts per million of total dissolved solids.

3. REVIEW OF BASIC PRINCIPLES

We will now consider some of the basic principles that should be considered in formulating a legal and administrative structure to control salinity in sources of water supply.

Law and administration are obviously complementary. Law is futile without an administration to implement it. Conversely, an administration cannot have any real power except that conferred on it by law. In this context, law means statutory law.

The activities that will need to be controlled by the administration are of two kinds. First, there must be control over the dispersal of wastes into waters that have a beneficial use. Secondly, there must be control over the consumptive use of waters that are required for dilution of permitted waste disposal.

Whatever new administration may be set up for these purposes, it cannot entirely supersede existing bodies already involved in the administration of drainage and water supply. Nor could it rationally limit its concern to problems of salinity. The new administration must be concerned with all aspects of water pollution control, and must act largely through existing hierarchies of bodies directly concerned in the field with the acceptance, collection and disposal of wastes, and with regulating the use of water.

The central administration should be representative of, or at least highly sensitive to, various interests affected by water quality control, of which the most obvious are public health, water supply, agriculture, wild life, sewerage and drainage authorities, and industry. Some of these interests will appear in the dual role of both water users and water polluters.

The central administration should aim to gain co-operation by persuasion rather than coercion and to do this it must have considerable discretion in negotiating arrangements that will serve its objectives.

The term 'central administration' has been used above to indicate some focus of power that will co-ordinate the formulation and enforcement of standards and procedures which may, however, still largely be applied by existing local authorities. The question arises as to the proper geographical scope of such a central administration.

From the point of view of jurisdiction, such administrations could certainly be set up on a State-wide basis in Australia. The possible role of the Commonwealth is discussed later with particular reference to the River Murray.

From the technical point of view, any central administration should have jurisdiction on at least a catchment-wide basis. This, however, is not as simple a proposition as it may sound. Artificial transfers of water between catchments by engineering works are becoming more and more common, and the number of completely independent catchments is decreasing. Some catchments, notably those of the Murray and the Snowy, extend into more than one State. Groundwater 'catchments' do not necessarily coincide with surface water catchments.

These overlaps could be accommodated by a central administration with jurisdiction over the whole continent, that is a Commonwealth administration. Perhaps this will be the long-term solution, but it is hardly practicable at present. The more immediate role of the Commonwealth could be based on the following considerations:

   (i) Research and dissemination of information on common problems could be centralized on a Commonwealth-wide basis.
  (ii) Adoption of a system of classification of waters and quality standards on a Commonwealth-wide basis could prevent inter-State competition for new industries being pursued by imprudent lowering of standards.
 (iii) Finance required for anti-pollution works may be beyond the scale that could be borne by individuals, industries or States.

Whatever the scope of a central administration, the question will arise as to what position it should occupy in overall government structure. Frequently such bodies are absorbed within a health administration, but there a school of thought that strongly favours an entirely new agency.

4. VICTORIAN ENVIRONMENT PROTECTION ACT, 1970

The Victorian Parliament, late in 1970, passed legislation to set up a State-wide administration to control not only water pollution, but environmental pollution generally. It deals with water, air, soil, noise and litter.

The most notable feature of this legislation is the underlying concept of administrative evolution. It does not scrap any existing law or administration. It provides primarily for rationalization and leadership of administrative resources already available.

Three new bodies are created which could be described respectively as executive, advisory and appellate.

The executive body, the Environment Protection Authority will consist of three full-time members. Its main function will be to recommend to the Government appropriate environment protection policies, to administer licensing under the Act in accordance with adopted policies and, to establish and maintain liaison and co-operation with other States and the Commonwealth. Control over pollution will be exercised largely by delegation of powers to 'protection agencies' which are defined as including 'any person or body, whether corporate or unincorporate, having powers or duties under any other Act with respect to the environment or any sequent of the environment in any part or parts of Victoria'.

The Authority will be advised by an Environment Protection Council consisting of seventeen part-time members representing various State departments and instrumentalities and other interested bodies including the Victorian Chamber of Manufacturers, the Victorian Trades Hall Council, the Municipal Association of Victoria and the CSIRO. There will also be Ministerial nominees in the disciplines of town and country planning, and ecology, and one to represent the 'general public'.

Appeals against decisions of the Authority or of protection agencies will be dealt with by the Environment Protection Appeal Board, consisting of a barrister and solicitor and two persons experienced in environmental control or management. The Board will operate with a minimum of legal formalities. Its decisions will be final, except that questions of law may be referred to the Supreme Court.

It is considered that this legislation will overcome the main legal and administrative problems plaguing water pollution control in Victoria, and could well serve as a model for other States. It combines broad representation of interests in the Council, with a small and therefore workable decision-making membership of three in the Authority.

5. THE RIVER MURRAY PROBLEM

Some reference has already been made to the problem of salinity control on the River Murray. It is of interest to examine some of the historical background because its implications extend generally to questions of Commonwealth-State relations in regard to environmental protection.

The wrangles of the 1840s over which of the two Colonies, New South Wales or Victoria, would eventually possess the Riverina led to a clarifying Imperial Act in 1855 which declared that:

> 'The whole watercourse of the said River Murray from its source . . .
> to the Eastern Boundary of the Colony of South Australia; is and shall
> be within the Territory of New South Wales.'

The formula aptly permitted the mother Colony to regulate navigation, smuggling and customs which then caused significant problems. Yet it was soon found to contain hidden traps. There was doubt whether ordinary common law rights to use water adhered to riparian land on the southern bank and, when agreements were made with the Chaffeys to develop Mildura, the problem was whether Victoria had power to grant them a right to divert Murray waters. For South Australia the issue was whether the other colonies could be restrained from diverting water from the river or its tributaries. South Australia had already established profitable river trade which extended to navigable tributaries such as the Darling and the Murrumbidgee. In an effort to secure permanent navigation, she even asserted a right to the uninterrupted flow of non-navigable tributaries like the Goulburn and Loddon.

These conflicting interests led to a feud which reflected three inconsistent contentions:

(*a*) South Australia's claim to maintain permanent navigability in the Murray and major tributaries;

(*b*) Victoria's claim as the first colony to exploit the advantages of irrigation, to a right to divert from the Upper Murray and all tributaries in its territory;

(*c*) New South Wales' claim, based on territorial rights, to the exclusive use of waters in the Upper Murray and territorial tributaries, regardless of the claims of her neighbours.

In 1845, pastoral licences were taken over Pental Island in the Murray, then described as being in Port Phillip District. After separation, rents were paid to Victoria until, in 1859, New South Wales demanded all revenues received and pompously informed the licensees where their fiscal allegiance lay. The occupiers were content to render unto Caesar, and sought to ride out the wrangle by paying rent to both Colonies. New South Wales wanted satisfaction, however, and finally provoked Victoria by nabbing the occupiers, who had isolated some sheep on the island, for importing diseased stock into New South Wales. To whom could Victoria turn? There was no local inter-colonial forum to resolve the difference, and the Privy Council, which could hear disputes between residents of the one Colony, did not regard itself as having judicial powers over disputes between autonomous Colonies. It would only hear the dispute if each Colony agreed to abide by its decision. They did, and the island was awarded to Victoria.

This first flurry was of enduring importance. It showed that the Imperial Government accorded certain independence to the Colonies and doubted its power to intervene without their consent or to enforce its decision. This lent a certain hollowness to South Australia's consistent threats to appeal to England for redress of its grievances. Secondly, because the Privy Council apparently invoked the Queen's Prerogative rather than its own inherent judicial power to make its award, it cast doubt on whether the dispute was really a 'judicial' dispute and whether there was any law to apply to the case. These are problems which plague us still.

From this time on, the Murray proved a constant source of irritation. The archives abound with querulous letters from South Australia, bland rebuffs from New South Wales and acerbic editorial comment from news-papers of every hue. There were countless suggestions and counter-suggestions for inter-Colonial meetings. Royal Commissions were as abundant as they are today, but no substantial agreement was reached. By 1886, several important developments rendered the dispute even more acrimonious. Deakin had influenced Victoria to pass important irrigation laws to hasten exploitation of the tributaries and the Mildura scheme was about to draw water from the Murray. New South Wales sought to follow suit, and made an agreement with Victoria, through their respective Royal Commissioners, that all the water in the Upper Murray belonged jointly to those two Colonies. South Australia was outraged, not only by these developments which threatened to decrease the annual flow, but also because the river trade was imperilled as railways snaked out from Melbourne and Sydney and siphoned off the trade with generous preferential tariffs. This was the background against which statesmen gathered for the Federal Convention Debates.

Our Commonwealth Constitution is firmly based on the American model. When the founding fathers gave the Commonwealth power over

17

trade and commerce, they had before them important decisions on the analogous power in the American Constitution. There, the Federal Government had been accorded plenary power to legislate for the control of any river and its tributaries which was, for any part of its length, potentially navigable, There is little doubt that the Commonwealth was intended to have similar power. South Australia, in fact, saw her salvation in the American decisions. Her flagging river trade might be revived if the Commonwealth, as benevolent protector, were given power to control the Murray and the plundering railways. To make assurance doubly sure, she successfully pressed for the inclusion of section 98:

> 'The power of the Parliament to make laws with respect to trade and commerce extends to navigation and shipping, and to railways the property of any State.'

The other States were agreeable, provided the Commonwealth exercised its plenary powers in a way which protected irrigation. Thus we obtained section 100:

> 'The Commonwealth shall not, by any law or regulation of trade or commerce, abridge the right of a State or of the residents therein to the reasonable use of the waters of rivers for conservation or irrigation.'

Mr Higgins objected to these qualifications of the broad trade and commerce power, for he foresaw that they might limit the potential flexibility of Commonwealth action. It is doubtful whether even he could have foreseen that, within seventy years, the common opinion would be that the Commonwealth would be powerless to invoke the trade and commerce power to impose controls on the Murray.

Probably the key factor in this unexpected result was the Commonwealth's reticence to take the initiative and use its power to settle the Murray question in the early years of Federation. After 1901, the upstream States maintained that they could divert as much water as they wished, provided they put it to 'reasonable' use. South Australia argued that section 100 allowed only a 'reasonable' amount to be diverted, and any interference with navigation was necessarily unreasonable. The River Murray Leagues at Corowa in 1902 finally coerced their unwilling statesmen to convene an Inter-state Royal Commission. Its members were, however, politically intransigent and South Australia dissociated itself from the majority emphasis on irrigation. The debate raged for the next ten years. Agreements were made and repudiated, yet the Commonwealth remained aloof.

The Inter-State Commission set up in 1912 had specific investigatory and arbitrative powers to solve river disputes. Potentially it could have imposed a settlement on the warring States but, before it could act, most of the powers of the Commission were declared unconstitutional by the High Court. It was not until 1914 that the States finally got together with the Commonwealth and signed the first River Murray Waters Agreement. South Australia got her locks to support a navigation trade long since dead, the other States were guaranteed water for irrigation and the issue apparently subsided.

Perhaps it was wisdom which led the Commonwealth not to intervene and restrained South Australia from carrying out her threats to force a showdown in the Courts. Yet with settlement by compact several legal issues remained unanswered. Some of the problems which remain to vex politicians and lawyers are:

(*a*) Could the Commonwealth, if it chose, legislate unilaterally to control the Murray and, inferentially, problems of salinity?

At least one witness before the recent Senate Committee thought that a confluence of constitutional powers would permit the Commonwealth to impose broad national controls over pollution. Another view is that the early failure of the Commonwealth to flex its legislative muscles has meant that the trade and commerce power has atrophied. In fact, when the validity of the Commonwealth action in undertaking the Snowy Mountains Scheme was mooted in 1948, advocates relied not on the trade and commerce power but on the defence power and the fact that electricity would be supplied to Canberra. Analogies with the plenary Federal trade and commerce power in America are probably no longer apt.

(*b*) Could a dispute between the States over the use or pollution of the Murray be heard by the High Court?

The River Murray Waters Agreement effectively avoided judicial scrutiny. We have developed a tradition in Australia of inter-governmental agreement and parallel legislation in situations where there is legal doubt as to which Parliament really has power to deal with the matter. The Snowy Mountains Hydro-electric Agreement of 1957 was such a case. More recently the Off-Shore Oil Agreement of 1967 adopted the same tack. The question of legislative power is thus withdrawn from the Courts and, at the same time, the High Court has rarely had the opportunity to declare whether it would accept any dispute for hearing. Sometimes, agreements, like the Off-Shore Oil Agreement, specifically provide that the compact is not to be justiciable by the Courts.

The only analogous case to reach the High Court was a dispute over the drawing of the South Australia–Victoria boundary. The Court, although it found itself able to decide that particular matter, indicated that it might refuse to decide a dispute which required political rather than strictly judicial techniques to be applied for its resolution. The Court could take the same view of certain disputes about the Murray, particularly in the light of the Privy Council's actions over Pental Island. In most situations it would probably accept jurisdiction, but the alacrity with which the United States Supreme Court intervenes in such disputes cannot be relied upon as accurate precedent.

(c) If the Court agreed to hear a dispute, what law would it apply?

Where there is no compact or statutory law, the High Court must apply the common law. But it is uncertain whether there is such a thing as common law between sovereign States joined in a Federation.

Before 1914, South Australia argued that the common law riparian doctrine applicable to private persons applied by analogy to the States. She had much to gain from a doctrine which subjects irrigation by an upstream owner to the overriding proviso that the water must be allowed to flow substantially undiminished in quantity or quality. Such a rule has been virtually abolished by all States but Tasmania as manifestly inapplicable to our circumstances. Yet it is the common law and it would solve South Australia's grievances about water quality, although it would be ironic for the Court to apply a rule which the States themselves have tried to abolish.

Perhaps some special common law has grown up to govern State relations. The Court has never squarely faced the issue whether there is a Federal common law. Probably it would hold that there is, and may possibly adapt the 'doctrine of equitable apportionment', which grew up to solve State conflicts in the United States and is in current vogue with Public International Lawyers.

The future possibilities of salinity control on the River Murray must be considered against this background of legal uncertainty.

Salinity control will require action on both saline inflows and on the management of dilution flows. The latter aspect already receives some mention in the River Murray Waters Agreement, but the former aspect is altogether outside the control of the River Murray Commission which administers the Agreement. Saline inflows to the Murray come from land drainage, including artificially constructed or improved drainage systems, and from seepage. Both land drainage and seepage are influenced to a high degree by wide-spread irrigation development. Physical works or operational rules to control these inflows are matters for the individual States. If there is to be a co-ordinated approach to the salinity problem on the Murray, what should be the make-up and powers of the co-ordinating administration?

One possibility would be to enlarge the functions of the River Murray Commission, to give it some prescriptive control over saline inflows. This would mean a revolutionary change in the Commission's role, and would require an equally revolutionary change in its constitution. Decisions would require a complex assessment of agricultural and economic factors, affecting the prerogatives of the States within their own territories. Even if this were acceptable to the States, which seems most unlikely, it would leave unsolved the longer-term problem of pollution of other kinds than salinity.

Another possibility would be to set up a separate Advisory Council endowed by the States with power to classify waters throughout the Murray catchment for the purposes of water pollution control, and to issue permits for disposal of wastes (including saline drainage). Such a Council would have representatives from the Commonwealth and the four States of Queensland, New South Wales, Victoria and South Australia, and possibly also from the Border Rivers Commission and the River Murray Commission. If the States had each set up their own central water pollution control administration, those administrations would supply the representatives. Otherwise the matter of appropriate representation might be difficult to resolve.

Yet another possibility would be for the Commonwealth and the States to come to some mutually satisfactory arrangement for the setting up of a Committee or Bureau to co-ordinate the exercise of State powers of control over water pollution. From the legal point of view this would be more simple and direct than attempting to confer appropriate powers on a supra-State body. However, such a Bureau could be effective only if powers within each State were clearly established and this could depend on the prior existence of a central administration in each of the States. Another prerequisite to successful operation might well be the willingness of the Commonwealth to provide financial assistance.

6. CONCLUSIONS

To summarize the main points that emerge from discussion of legal and administrative aspects of salinity control:

> *First*, salinity control can best be dealt with under wider measures for water pollution control, which in turn may be incorporated in even wider measures for environmental control.

> *Secondly*, co-ordination of law and administration should be tackled initially on a State-wide basis, and for this purpose the Victorian Environment Protection Act, 1970, could well serve as a model.

Thirdly, co-ordination on the inter-State or Commonwealth-State level would be facilitated by the prior creation of central administrations in each State, which could also best advise Governments on the form that higher-level co-ordination should take.

PART VI Perspectives

Implications of the Present State of Scientific Knowledge for Technical Management

H. N. ENGLAND

Formerly of Water Conservation and Irrigation Commission, Sydney, N.S.W.

SUMMARY

Salinity, from a management viewpoint, is discussed under the headings of hydrology, use of saline waters and control of soil and stream salinity, with incidental reference to other Symposium papers.

The main theme is the conflict between control of soil salinity under irrigation and downstream river salinity, with the conclusion that the high quality of Australian surface waters should be preserved at the expense of minor loss of land to salt in the semi-arid floodplain environment, where most irrigation development and potential are situated.

1. INTRODUCTION

This is necessarily a personal account. With the subject matter of this Symposium ranging over so wide a field it is inevitable that this presentation will reflect the author's experiences, prejudices and enthusiasms, and from the viewpoint of the specialists—especially those whose eruditions were baffling—will lack balance and depth.

The author is handicapped by the lack of a hydrological theme and of the presentation of salinity, except in tidal situations, as a feature of aridity. Further, the author is particularly handicapped by the lack of a review of Australian hydrology, and the links between our recent geological history and the quantity and quality of our water resources.

Australia is a country of low relief with no perennial snow. Its catchments are not actively eroding, indeed secular decay has left a mantle of material from which soluble constituents, either original or weathering products, have been leached.

Because of its low relief and latitudinal position it is also an arid country. In spite of its aridity its rivers, even those which traverse extensive arid or semi-arid plains without further tributary inflow, are, in general, low in natural salinity, except during periods of very low flow.

One notable exception is the River Murray, in which a substantial increase in natural salinity in its lower reaches is now compounded by salinity deriving from irrigation.

The virtual absence of Pleistocene orogeny also means an absence of extensive river terraces and of extensive alluvial fans at debouchment onto the plains, and thus only a minor groundwater component in river flow. Indeed, the groundwater systems associated with many Australian rivers derive largely from the rivers by way of influent seepage or periodic flooding. Thus, salinity increases with distance from the river, and groundwaters, except where they occur in close association with rivers, are seldom present in adequate quantity and quality for large-scale irrigation.

The absence of extensive river terraces and alluvial fans also means that Australia has little land that, by overseas standards, is ideally suited to irrigation—immature unleached soils underlain by coarse sediments with free under-drainage back to the river. Our extensive irrigation schemes, existing and potential, lie on extensive floodplains comprising senescent and mostly infertile non-arable soils underlain by fine textured sediments with little under-drainage capacity—conditions which demand high quality irrigation water.

At present concern and controversy on salinity is virtually confined to the quality of water for irrigation, especially in the Lower Murray—the irrigation settlements in South Australia, and the Sunraysia Districts of Victoria and New South Wales.

The major theme of this paper is that, by taking advantage of its unique environment, Australia has the opportunity of preserving both its irrigation and the quality of its water resources.

2. HYDROLOGY AND SALINITY

(a) Under Natural Conditions

Swaine and Schneider (this volume) have shown that, in addition to the broad climatic control over both the composition and concentration of soluble salts in surface waters and groundwaters, by which bicarbonates are the main salts in humid climates but at low concentrations, whilst chlorides and sulphates predominate in arid climates with concentration generally increasing with increasing aridity, the composition of the salts also reflects the character of the rocks in the catchment (and in the case of groundwaters the characteristics of the host rocks also).

As salinity determinations are so much more accurate than hydrometrics, the different characteristics of surface waters from different parts of a river catchment afford opportunity for very great refinements in hydrographic and hydrometric techniques and in operational control of regulated streams. As illustrations: the relation between time of travel between points and river stage can be determined with greater accuracy; at a confluence the larger component flow can be calculated with an accuracy little short of that in measurement of the smaller component.

Geochemistry is such a powerful tool and modern analytical techniques are so simple that systematic analysis, even if only for conductivity, should go hand in hand with all routine hydrographic operations and with operational control of regulated streams.

(b) Urban and Industrial Development

There is a great volume of literature dealing with the effects of urban and industrial development on the quality of river waters and analyses usually show a general rise in salinity levels. However, pollution, rather than hydrology, is the main consideration in these studies, and there is no evidence to show to what extent the higher levels are due to additions of soluble salts to the system, or to concentration of salts in the various biological and industrial processes in which water is a vehicle. Generally, increases in salinity, directly or indirectly due to urban and industrial activities, are slight in relation to water pollution.

(c) Rural Land Development

As Holmes (this volume) points out, soil and stream salinity have developed in parts of south-west Western Australia and western Victoria from land 'development'—removal or partial removal of the timber cover and its replacement by native or introduced pasture, with or without arable farming. This results from a reduction in transpiration, including the effects of a shallower root zone, and thus increased groundwater accessions and a rise in the watertable level.

Probably most of the land susceptible to such changes has already been developed and, with the exception of some catchments in Western Australia referred to by Callinan and Webster (this volume), would probably have been developed even if the results could have been foreseen.

(d) Water Conservation

It follows that water conservation by damming a river will tend to increase the average salinity of the downstream flows in accordance with evaporation from the storage, although this is complicated by the effect of rain on the storage. This effect may be negligible in humid regions, and indeed the overall effect may be beneficial, in that regulated flows may reduce the salinity downstream of tributary flows—which, since salinity is largely a function of aridity, will generally be more saline because of orographic factors—and reduce tidal encroachment in estuaries.

Such benefit, in addition to suppression of salinity 'slugs' is claimed for operation of the proposed Chowilla Dam (Anon 1970a). However, such statements as '. . . Chowilla will have the effect of lowering the average long-term salinity conditions' (p. 285) can be misleading, as average is not used in the ordinary sense of being weighted for flow but as the average on a regular time sampling basis. The weighted-for-flow average salinity of the discharge must be increased since a substantial proportion, about 25%, of the water detained in the dam is lost by evaporation. Since neither diversion nor actual use of water is regular either in time or rate, it does not follow that the improvement will be general; neither does it follow that the salinity of Lake Alexandrina will necessarily be improved.

The Menindee Lakes Storages have disadvantages in common with Chowilla—a very shallow storage designed for long-term drought mitigation under conditions of high evaporation—but they have the additional disadvantage of being largely off-river storages. Of the four major component lakes: one is an on-river storage, two can be flushed but only to a limited extent (using outlets designed only for river regulation), and the fourth cannot be flushed at all. Further, under conditions of operation for maximum volumetric yield, the downstream storages in prolonged dry periods will be topped up from time to time with resultant high salinity build up from concentration to the extent of several times the depth of storage. The means of operating the Menindee Lakes Storages, to ensure acceptable salinity levels in prolonged dry periods, have not been worked out, but it is clear that this objective is incompatible with maximum volumetric yield.

It follows that shallow storages in arid regions should be short-term storages (ideally they should be only adjuncts to upstream storages and depleted before mid-summer); carry-over storages should be a last resort and should then be on-river storages; and any off-river storage should have capacious provision for flushing. However, flushing of an on-river or off-river storage may be at the expense of the quality of a downstream storage. Under arid saline conditions there may be 'room' only for one major storage, and—as Pels (1967) proposes for the Murray—only one diversion.

(e) Under Irrigation

Holmes (this volume) gives instances of loss of land and of loss of water quality from salinity, but quotes examples like the Nile Valley and the east China alluvial plains, where both have been preserved. He does not advance any reasons for the difference.

In the Nile Valley irrigation has produced very little change in its hydrology. Until modern engineering permitted diversion of the Lower Nile and thus perennial irrigation in the Delta—which has been attended by some watertable and salinity troubles—Egyptian irrigation consisted merely of control of the annual flood, and the only land irrigated was land which was naturally flooded, if not annually, then frequently, and presumably was non-saline. Like the Lower Murray the narrow floodplain of the (Egyptian) Nile is incised into terrain which has no relationship to the river but unlike the Lower Murray has not cut into a groundwater system which now feeds it with saline water.

On the other hand such rivers as the Tigris-Euphrates and the Indus and its tributaries, where irrigation has been or is accompanied by widespread soil salinization, run in extensive old alluvial plains in which salt had accumulated since the flood frequency waned.

Now Pakistan is faced with the problem of reclaiming salted land and preventing further losses by tube-well drainage without raising the salinity of the Indus to unusable levels. The proposed means of dealing with the saline water, largely by diverting it out of the valley, are most elaborate and expensive and probably are justified only by national prestige and population pressure.

Similarly California is faced with staggering costs in getting rid of saline drainage and groundwaters in the San Joaquin Valley. Other rivers such as the Colorado and Rio Grande have become virtually saline drains because they flow through what is usually regarded as 'ideal' irrigation land—high level terraces with free under-drainage back to the river.

The Rio Grande between Elephant Butte Dam in New Mexico and the Mexican border presents a classic case of salinity from over-regulation and over-exploitation of river waters. When the author was there in 1957 the dam had spilled once in its life of over 40 years. The waterway in the downstream gravelly reaches had been lost, and was being canalized at great expense so as to lower the watertable and reduce the enormous losses from phreatophytes, (with consequent increase in salinity). The alluvial terraces downstream of the gravelly section were fully developed to irrigation. As a result of recycling of drainage water the river water was almost too saline for use before it reached the Mexican border, (cotton could not be planted on the tops of the ridges), and all that reached the Mexican border in normal years was a trickle of brine. The United States certainly would not have endured peacefully what Mexico has had to put up with in the valleys of the Colorado and the Rio Grande.

Australia presents an entirely contrasting picture. Instead of valleys filled with the coarse detritus from Pleistocene orogeny and capped by immature soils from present day erosion, our rivers meander in vast floodplains slowly built up of fine grained materials and capped by fine textured senescent soils. For the same reasons, the salinity of our rivers is very much lower than in other parts of the world.

We are indeed fortunate that by conventional standards we have very little good irrigation land: land comprising freely draining soils underlain by materials which permit free natural underdrainage or economic artificial subsoil drainage. Generally, except for more or less unique cases like the Nile Valley, such land gains its freedom from salinity troubles at the expense of salting of downstream land or water or both.

(f) The River Murray Salinity Problem

The recent report on the River Murray Salinity Investigations (Anon 1970a) is a comprehensive one covering the physical environment, and the history and causes of salinity of soil and water with recommendations for control of both. The author finds himself in strong disagreement with practically all the major items in the hydrology of the riverine plain, which bear on assessment of the salinity hazard and means of dealing with it, but space will permit only an indication of the areas of disagreement.

In the first instance, there is disagreement as to the source of increased groundwater accessions which the consultants ascribe directly to irrigation and the author substantially to indirect causes—the cumulative effect of irrigation and winter rains. The argument is not academic, as in the former case the accessions are related to the volume of the importations of water, and in the latter to the area irrigated, and they could be reduced by intensifying the use of available supplies. For the same reason, the author advocates provision of surface drainage from the outset instead of waiting until high watertables develop. Further, the author believes that the volumes of accessions necessary to bring about the observed rate of watertable rise are exaggerated about tenfold.

The author also disagrees with the rationalization that in a generally saline environment the phreatic water is necessarily saline, and there will be measurable reduction in yields wherever the watertable reaches 6 feet (180 cm) from the surface, and all this land will require drainage. Apart from the fact that most riverine plain soils have a shallower critical watertable depth (Talsma 1963), there is evidence, from Tullakool (Stannard personal communication) and from unpublished work on the Murrumbidgee region, which suggests that much of the cover floodplain is not salt-liable even with the minimum of irrigation. Further experience has shown that under these conditions high watertables do not respond to (tube-well) drainage.

In discussing the concept of an equilibrium in the riverine plain without drainage, the consultants suggest a loss of 20 to 25 % of land to salt. This is on the basis of a 20 % loss of land to salt in part of West Pakistan where 80 % of the land is intensively irrigated for rice production and overlooks the partial irrigation basis of the riverine plains schemes and their fairly rigidly limited water supplies. At the minimum viable farm size, water supplies are sufficient for intensive irrigation of only 20 to 25 % of the farm area, intensive irrigation in this case would be of perennial pasture. On this basis the loss of land would be 5 to 8%, perhaps rather more if amalgamation of smaller farms yields more liberal water supplies.

The first land affected would be road and channel verges, and low-lying land; the latter might include some irrigated land, but with few exceptions farmers should be able to make full use of all available water supplies and with only a slight loss in production.

Disregarding these contentious issues, we might put the report (Anon 1970*a*) in perspective by comparing the present salinity position in the Murray with the potential position, assuming that the consultants' premises regarding the riverine plain are sound and that their recommendations are put into effect.

The normal year's salt inflow to the Murray is about 1·3 million tons, and the largest discrete source is Barr Creek with a normal year's salt load of less than 0·3 million tons. In both cases, drought years' salt loads are less although concentrations are higher. About 40% of the normal year's salt load is from upstream tributaries at extremely high dilution. The annual importations of salt into the irrigation schemes served by the Murray/Goulburn is about 0·35 million tons. If extreme control measures were now taken the maximum salt load that could be prevented from entering the river would be little more than 0·3 million tons.

The report recommends general subsoil drainage for areas with high watertables, now or as they develop, and storage of drainage waters that are too saline for use, diluted or undiluted with diverted waters, i.e. storage of all drainage discharges from Wakool and Kerang regions, and part from Deniliquin and Shepparton regions.

These discharges, together with surface drainage discharges, are to be prevented from gaining direct access to the river by impounding them in constructed or natural evaporation basins. Of the natural basins, Lake Tyrrell is totally enclosed, but the others, natural or artificial, lie on the floodplains of the Murray, its tributaries or ana-branches.

The annual volumes of subsoil drainage waters to be dealt with are:

Wakool and Kerang regions	136,000 ac. ft
Deniliquin and Shepparton regions	97,000 ac. ft

Assuming concentrations of 20,000 ppm for Wakool and Kerang and 5000 ppm for Deniliquin and Shepparton, the eventual annual salt load from subsoil drainage is 3·8 million tons. In addition there is the surface drainage salt load, say a total of 4 million tons as compared with importations of 0·35 million tons.

It is clear that there will be uncontrollable flushing to the river of the saline waters in the drainage system, whenever there is substantial local stormwater run-off, and that the problem of salinity slugs from these sources will be intensified. It appears also that uncontrolled flushing of the evaporation basins in the flood plain during floods, which may be only minor floods, could entail Lake Victoria diversions or preclude provision of a downstream on-river storage. On the other hand, if the basins are not periodically flushed, they will require replacement from time to time, as capacity is lost through crystallization of chlorides, and ultimately more land will be lost from drainage than without it.

Clearly implementation of the drainage recommendations, far from solving the Murray salinity problem, would create a much more serious one, and another solution must be found. There seems to be little room to manoeuvre between the two extremes of banning subsoil drainage, or permitting it and eventually implementing the channel diversion scheme.

The choice should be made now. Although it is desirable that further knowledge should be acquired on the salinity hazard, the decision will rest less on technical considerations than on moral, social and political values: whether it is better to destroy, or at least seriously impair, 1000 miles of river in the name of conservation, and to sacrifice (many of) those who have the greater moral right to the water, the riparian holders; or to maintain the comfort and convenience of the close-knit politically active irrigation communities.

To the author the choice is clear: the irrigation communities in the riverine plain (except the horticulturists) should learn to live with the salt hazard, even though it may be an uncomfortable and, in some situations, a precarious existence.

There is only one possible way of dealing with salinity 'slugs' in the river before they reach the Sunraysia district and that is by employing an *en route* storage for dilution, but as previously pointed out any off-river storage in such a climate should have provision for flushing which could demand a diversion weir.

It is clear that control of salinity 'slugs' by dilution would require close monitoring of upstream salinity and flows, presumably not merely continuous recording but telemetering to the dilution control station.

3. USE OF SALINE WATERS

(a) Industrial Aspects

The quality of water for industry is idiosyncratic to the particular industry and there is no point in discussing the various standards. However, there are two general disabilities of saline water in industry: the electrolytes enhance corrosion of metals and may call for resistant metals or alloys or sacrificial anodes; and portland cement is corroded by waters containing sulphates.

It is understood that an Australian standard for sulphate resistant cement will soon be erected. This will be similar to the American standard— potential tri-calcic aluminate will be limited to 5%. Presumably this heralds its availability, which may result in the use of concrete agricultural pipes instead of clay pipes for drainage in irrigation areas.

Generally, industry should be expected to site itself in accordance with site advantages, and water quality is one of the obvious factors in site selection. Disregarding the possibility of a change in water standards with new processes and techniques, the main concern of industry is with preservation of water quality.

There has been some deterioration of quality of Adelaide metropolitan waters with the exploitation of more arid local catchments and groundwaters. However, the problem has not been so much due to total salinity as to hardness, which can be overcome by base-exchange treatment. This is now being widely used for domestic purposes. The quality of River Murray waters, which are being increasingly used to supplement local supplies, is superior in both respects, hardness and total salinity.

Salinity of natural waters is not always a disadvantage. Advantage has been taken in Queensland of the detergent properties of (bicarbonate) waters of the Great Artesian Basin, and probably of the temperature also, for wool scouring.

(b) Salinity Effects on Animals

Macfarlane (this volume) points out that land mammals can selectively absorb or reject electrolytes to maintain, within narrow limits, the composition and concentration of their body fluids, sodium being the main ion. These animals can adapt within wide limits to the salinity of feed and water, and it is only sudden changes at either end of the scale that are important to domestic animals. Salt supplements may be necessary upon change to drought feeding, particularly scrub feed with its low Na and high K content (Denton *et al.* 1961). The deficiency would be greater where there is loss of salt through sweating or lactation.

At the other end of the scale tolerable salt intake depends on whether the feed or the water is saline. Salt in the feed can be eliminated by increased intake of water but with saline water the effect would be cumulative.

There is more knowledge of the salt tolerance of sheep than of other domestic animals. Whilst they can tolerate quite saline water, 1% to 2% NaCl, and indeed can rapidly adapt to higher concentrations, this is at the expense of food intake, i.e. they do not thrive on salt water. However, there is a limit to salt intake and sheep on saline feed such as salt bush demand

18

fresher water and for salt excretion more of it, and indeed may need to water twice daily. Full exploitation of salt bush requires ample and narrowly spaced supplies of fresh water (Wilson 1966), but in salt bush country groundwaters are frequently saline.

Channelled stock supplies of drainage from the Murrumbidgee Irrigation Areas to the salt bush plains in the Wah Wah District of the riverine plain have been a great boon, and it is fortunate that the proposal to use Coleambally drainage waters on adjoining grass country with good quality groundwaters, instead of on the salt bush plains with frequent low quality groundwaters further west, has been abandoned.

(c) Salinity Effects on Plants

Campbell and Pitman (this volume) and Robinson (this volume) show how complex are the salinity effects on plant cells and whole plants, and that the problem is not explained either by osmotic effects or specific ion toxicity, both complex in themselves.

Whilst it appears that in some cases damage is due to high sodium build up in the plant and others to high chloride, it is noteworthy that some types of citrus rootstocks and some barley varieties are more effective than others in excluding both Na and Cl. It is clear that there are quite wide differences in the tolerances of cultivated plants to salts in the soil solution and that salt tolerant crops and varieties should be selected for saline waters or situations.

Western U.S.A. experience on the tolerance of crops is summarized by Richards (1954) who states that the relative salt tolerances are comparable with those established in Holland, despite differences in climate and cultural practices.

The same *relative* salt tolerances should apply in Australia, but there is little experience here in the use of saline waters and there are no systematic studies. Experience, more or less casual, seems to be limited to: early attempts to use waters of the Coonamble Embayment of the Great Artesian Basin; occasional tidal encroachment in estuaries where irrigation is practised, chiefly for vegetables; and occasional damage to citrus and stone fruit trees in the Lower Murray Valley.

However, in the latter half of the 1960s, especially in N.S.W., there was substantial exploitation of groundwaters with varying levels of salinity stimulated by: drought and water restrictions; introduction of the water allotment scheme in the N.S.W. Irrigation Districts supplied from the Murray; high prices for some crops; and introduction into Australia of new techniques of well (bore) construction. It now seems likely that with the generally depressed state of agriculture this interest in exploitation of groundwaters will wane.

Some general principles emerge from the papers before us:

1. Reproductive growth may be affected before there is any sensible effect on vegetative growth—which implies that pasture or forage crops may be preferable to seed crops, and in the vegetable line, leaf and root crops to fruit crops.
2. Some crops, notably citrus and stone fruits, are not only sensitive to Cl in their leaves but absorb Cl through them—which implies that water with any substantial chloride content should not be used for overhead sprinkling of these crops but should be applied directly to the land or by under-tree sprinklers.
3. Under high transpiration it becomes increasingly difficult for the plant to exclude Na and Cl—which implies a double salinity jeopardy in drought years.

Questions unanswered are: the extent to which salinity absorption is cumulative within the season and, for perennial crops, from season to season; and the effect of variation in the salinity level. The latter includes the influence of rain, since virtually all Australian irrigation is in semi-arid climates, including leaching of salt from foliage.

Answers to these questions are needed to decide the best manner of integrating the use of saline groundwaters with good quality surface waters and for control of salinity in the Lower Murray.

Richards (1954, pp. 67 and 81) also lists comparative tolerances of crops to boron. Although small quantities of this ion are necessary for plant growth the tolerable limits for crops are very low ranging from 4 ppm in the irrigation water down to 0·3 ppm. Australian surface waters are generally low in boron but it may be a problem in the use of groundwaters especially in the re-use of drainage waters in the Mallee region, where boron concentrations should be monitored. As with chlorides, citrus and stone-fruits are most sensitive to boron. The sensitivity of tobacco leaf quality to chloride is well known.

(d) Some Aspects of Quality of Water for Irrigation

There is a very voluminous literature on this wide subject. Toxic effects of specific ions have been touched on and here some comment is made on the hazards of total salinity in which the immediate concern is effect on the crop, and of sodium and bicarbonate, in which the primary concern is the effect on the soil with the crop as the ultimate concern.

Salinity Hazard. The variation in accepted standards from country to country is striking. This is a reflection of the salinity of their water resources and the adoption of techniques to combat high salinity, but it might also indicate an association of natural conditions. Certainly in Australia the environmental factors responsible for the low salinity of surface waters also dictate the need for low salinity water in the situations where conditions are otherwise suitable for widespread irrigation—river floodplains.

The salinity standards most familiar to Australian workers are those of the U.S. Salinity Laboratory (Richards 1954). They are conservative by the standards of many countries and, it is understood, are now so regarded by most U.S. workers; but as they are erected for U.S. conditions it does not follow that they will be conservative for Australian conditions.

The upper limit set by the consultants to the River Murray Commission for pasture water in the riverine plain is 750 μmhos cm^{-1}, requiring a leaching factor of 0·15. This is the upper limit of the U.S. standard for water of moderate salinity requiring a moderate amount of leaching and in most instances no special practices for salinity. A leaching factor of 0·15 regarded as moderate by U.S. standards appears to be extraordinarily high for the general run of riverine plain soils. The difficulty there, even with the red-brown earth soils, is to obtain adequate penetration of irrigation water and on all appearances effective leaching except in special situations—the combination of permeable soils overlying coarse sediments in the beds of ancestral rivers or prior streams—would occur only from heavy winter rains.

This effect of rainfall on all aspects of the quality of water for irrigation is sadly neglected, indeed one might gather from the literature that irrigation invariably takes place in an absolute desert environment. As an illustration: at a salinity symposium held in Teheran a paper was presented (Bottini 1961) showing that long term, indeed traditional, use of brackish waters for irrigation in Italy had not been attended by any harmful effects on soils, but it took a question to elicit that the localities enjoyed an annual rainfall of between 400 and 600 mm (which presumably had a predominant winter incidence).

Sodium Hazard. The harmful effect of high sodium waters on soils was recognized before the base-exchange phenomenon was discovered and since then has had a voluminous literature.

Laboratory workers, particularly in U.S.A., have established a relationship between the exchangeable sodium percentage (ESP) that disintegrated soil material will assume when in equilibrium with water of a particular sodium adsorption ratio (SAR). Again this assumes that irrigation takes place under absolute desert conditions, but the relationship seems to apply in the field in south-western U.S.A.

Quirk and Schofield (1955), as Quirk (this volume) points out, worked on the converse problem: on the effect of the SAR value of the water in reclaiming sodic soils. They showed, in the laboratory on pads of disintegrated soil material, that there is a threshold electrolyte level of the leaching water, varying positively with the ESP of the soil, below which the soil particles are structurally disrupted. Again there is some support from field experience in south-western U.S.A.

However, there is a wide experience in Australia of reclamation with and without subsoil drainage, using high quality water (and rainfall) on soils that have been salinized for many years. This experience is with the red-brown earths and the grey and brown clays of the riverine plain, and with brown solonized soils of the mallee zone. During the years that these salted soils have been exposed to irrigation and rainfall they would have suffered innumerable cycles of salt accumulation and leaching, a regime which in theory, and in the laboratory, would lead to sodium adsorption. Yet, as far as the author is aware, there has never been any suggestion from field workers of any change at any time in soil structure except at the surface, or in any soil moisture relationships and behaviour including hydraulic conductivity and response to drainage.

This strongly suggests that sodium adsorption has not occurred and this is why reclamation can be effected by water with a low electrolyte content.

It also raises other questions:

1. Whether these and other mature Australian soils would be affected by irrigation waters containing neutral salts, especially in *semi*-arid environments.
2. Whether the (short-term) effect on the crop should not be the sole criterion of water quality (again assuming only neutral salts).
3. Whether it is worthwhile diluting saline waters solely for the purpose of reducing the SAR value.

Bicarbonate Hazard. Experience of bicarbonate waters in Australia seems to be limited to unsuccessful early attempts to use the waters of the Great Artesian Basin, particularly in the Coonamble Embayment. Another factor of significance is that bore drains usually seal themselves by very pronounced deflocculation. There is no apparent reason to question overseas standards, in particular the definitive standards quoted by Richards (1954, p. 81).

4. CONTROL OF SALINITY

(a) Groundwaters

The most common sources of deterioration of groundwaters are salt water intrusion in coastal situations and irrigation, although over-exploitation can increase salinity by inducing flow from more sluggish and more saline parts of an aquifer.

Where intrusion of saline water is from the top, as under irrigation, the whole body of the water in the aquifer deteriorates because of the density factor, as shown by Wooding (this volume). However, this factor permits maintenance of phreatic waters in a fresh sate.

(b) In Estuaries

In dealing with estuarine conditions, Wood (this volume) seems more concerned with dispersion of discrete or continuous introductions of saline or polluted water rather than with the more common salinity problem in estuaries, that of tidal encroachment. In most situations tidal encroachment must be endured: control by means of barrages is too expensive, and by operation of storages constructed for this purpose is both too expensive and too wasteful of water.

(c) Water Conservation, Irrigation, Drainage and Reclamation

Here there is almost invariably some conflict between control of soil salinity and control of river salinity so that integration of control measures is necessary.

The special situations in which no conflict is evident are those such as the Nile Valley where there is little disturbance of the hydrologic equilibrium, and a combination of conditions which seems to occur widely in the riverine and other floodplains in Australia—a combination of clay soils, especially selfmulching clay soils, underlain by a considerable thickness of massive clays apparently becoming more impermeable with depth. Here, for reasons not fully understood, soil salinity does not develop despite high watertables, high salinity of subsoils and underlying sediments. High quality water is of course essential.

Otherwise, there is immediate conflict where there is free natural under-drainage back to the river or delayed conflict where saline watertables develop gradually. With good quality water the phreatic water can be maintained in a fresh state, for which a perennial cover may be necessary, but at the expense of salting some low-lying land or dry land. Alternatively, salting can be prevented, or salted land reclaimed, by drainage, a course which is essential for saline waters.

The two systems of drainage (besides deep arterial drains) in modern use are tile drainage and pumping from bores and wells—in (Anglo-) Indian terminology tube-well drainage.

All aspects of tile drainage, technical and economic, are pretty well understood and it has the advantages that drainage can be restricted to the land that really needs it. The salinity of the effluent is often low enough for re-use, especially with dilution, and usually there are prospects of freshening within a few decades

On the other hand tube-well drainage is not well understood and conditions for its efficient operation are rare. It is frequently used under watertable conditions but here tile drainage is preferable. It should be used only where aquifers are semi-confined. Even under the best conditions its disadvantages are numerous: investigation of well sites and well fields is experimental with little chance of forecasting the order of costs; operation and maintenance costs are high; more land than is necessary is drained; the discharge derives from deep levels and is usually saline with no prospects of short-term freshening (on indications in the riverine plain, not within the 100 year term). Thus tube-well drainage on any substantial scale can create salinity disposal problems more serious than those it attempts to solve.

Whatever control measures are adopted the downstream salinity of the river is likely to suffer—from effluent seepage direct into the river or into surface drains discharging thereto, and from drainage discharges or run-off from salted land reaching the river by design or not. Fortunately in the Murray Valley much of the drainage discharges in the highly saline environment of the mallee zone can be prevented from reaching the river, as its wind-sculptured relief with frequent land-locked basins is in no way related to the river. Clearly control of salinity in a river basin requires integration of policy on regulation, irrigation and especially drainage.

(d) Desalination

Although Lane and Mansfield's paper (this volume) bears on some of the fundamentals of desalination, this Symposium is not directly concerned with it. However, there is one aspect of desalination, whatever the process, with which we are concerned and that is the disposal of the brine. This may be only a minor problem where small quantities of inland waters are treated, but with massive treatment of seawater even the discharge of brine into the ocean requires careful siting in relation to currents, whilst discharge into estuaries should be out of the question.

(e) Socio-Economic Aspects

Callinan and Webster (this volume) present an economic approach to salinity control based largely on the Kerang region, and conclude with a plea for planning and land-use controls to avoid or minimize salinity losses in future irrigation schemes. Their estimates of the present losses and the projected scale of losses in the Murray–Goulburn irrigation scheme (which are not all due to salinity) are, naturally enough in view of some common authorship, those of the consultants to the River Murray Commission.

As previously indicated, the author disagrees profoundly on the physical basis on which these estimates were erected, and sees no reason why these partial irrigation schemes, and with few exceptions the individual holdings of which they are comprised, should not be able to make productive use, with little disturbance of the present pattern, of all the water that is or is likely to become available to them, without subsoil drainage except for horticulture.

This will involve some minor loss of land, mostly dry land, to salt and some farm reconstruction may be necessary. But the economic loss will be slight and any farm reconstruction involved will be minor compared with that necessary to amalgamate farms of sub-standard size.

The author could not agree more on the desirability of planning, but believes that attempts at planning would fail because in many quarters there is continued doctrinaire belief that high watertables result only directly from irrigation, and that all land with a high watertable in a saline environment must become salted.

In any case, there will be unforeseeable watertable and salinity developments, as well as cultural and economic ones, and however well an irrigation scheme is planned at the outset, periodic re-planning will be necessary.

(f) *Administrative and Legal Aspects of Water Salinity*

Clark and Meacham (this volume) start with the proposition that salinity is a form of pollution with the implications that they have similar origins and call for similar control measures. In doing so they may be in distinguished company—the Senate Select Committee on Water Pollution—and may have tacitly accepted that committee's definition of salinity (Anon 1970b): 'Water pollution is an impairment of water function, which has, or may have, an effect on subsequent water use'. The author cannot accept the implications that over 97% of the earth's waters, being saline, are polluted and that Nature is the great polluter.

On the other hand the report asserts, in conflict with its definition, that pollution is almost invariably man-made. By contrast salinity, even of river waters, is largely a natural phenomenon. The waters of the Darling (Barwon) when first discovered by white explorers were too saline to drink, and the worst and most disastrous occurrence of salinity in the Murray was in 1914 and must have been almost entirely natural in origin. Moreover other manmade stream salinity of any consequence is from irrigation, but here it is not the individual irrigator or drainer who is responsible so much as the Crown which, with a few exceptions, planned the irrigation schemes and has accepted saline discharges into drainage systems under its control.

All the significant sources of salinity and all the weapons to fight it are under the control of the various State irrigation authorities, individually for intra-state waters and jointly for inter-state waters: operation of storages, drainage policy in irrigation schemes, diversion of natural or artificial drainage flows from the river; banning of drainage discharges from riparian holdings either directly or under the terms of the irrigation licence.

Clark and Meacham imply that control of salinity in Victorian waters will come under the new environmental pollution legislation. If this is the case it seems to derive from a lack of understanding of the occurrence of salinity, and to be an emotional, rather than a rational, response. They also make much of the division of control over the Murray waters, but in posing the question of Commonwealth control over salinity (and pollution) they overlook a weakness in much centralist argument on complex issues—that it may be less difficult to achieve agreement amongst States than among, or even between, Commonwealth departments.

Although all the bodies constituting the River Murray Commission could, by acting in concert, exercise all the necessary powers for control of salinity in the Murray, the Commission itself possesses only the limited power of providing dilution flows in periods of restriction. Some widening of these powers awaits ratification by South Australia, but it seems desirable that, in addition, the Commission be fortified with power to provide works, wholly or partly, for the purpose of salinity control.

REFERENCES

Anon (1970*a*). *Murray Valley Salinity Investigation*. Report for the River Murray Commission by Gutteridge, Haskins and Davey.

Anon (1970*b*). Report from the Senate Select Committee on Water Pollution in Australia, Commonwealth Government Printing Office, Canberra.

Bottini, O. (1961). UNESCO Arid Zone Res. **14**, 251.

Denton, D. A., Goding, J. R., McDonald, I.R., Sabine, R., and Wright, R. D. (1961). UNESCO Arid Zone Res. **14**, 193.

Pels, S. (1967). The Winston Churchill Memorial Trust Fellowship Report No. 2, Part A. (Canberra).

Quirk, J. P., and Schofield, R. K. (1955). *J. Soil Sci.* **6**, 163.

Richards, L. A. (Ed.) (1954). *Diagnosis and Improvement of Saline and Alkaline Soils*. USDA Handbook No. 60.

Talsma, T. (1963). *Meded. Landb. Hoogesch., Wageningen* **63** (10), 1.

Wilson, A. D. (1966). *Aust. J. agric. Res.* **17**, 155.

Salinity and Water Use: Future Research Directions

A. E. MARTIN

Division of Soils, CSIRO, Cunningham Laboratory, St Lucia, Queensland

SUMMARY

Future research directions in salinity at the molecular level are already predetermined, and will probably concern the details of ion pumping in cell membranes, the development of new antibiotics, the emergence of salt-tolerant plants and the like. The real problems lie in the catchments and will need the application of terrestrial field research for their solution. A brief analysis of the status of field research is presented and some reasons for its unpopularity are suggested. It is concluded that new research should concentrate on the location of saline soils, sediments and groundwaters more intensively than hitherto, on the origin of terrestrial salt, on the factors responsible for secondary salinity in soils, water supplies and irrigation areas, and on the criteria for evaluating salt-affected soils and techniques for their reclamation. There is acute need for research on the social consequences of a contracting population in irrigation enterprises that suffer partial failure.

1. CURRENT RESEARCH TRENDS

The composition of the earth's crust is such that a significant fraction of it is an aqueous electrolyte solution, mostly Na^+ and Cl^- but containing smaller amounts of Mg^{++}, Ca^{++} and K^+ and the anions $SO_4^=$ and HCO_3^-. It is not strictly true to say that seawater contains sodium chloride since chloride ions (535 meq l^{-1}) exceed sodium ions (459 meq l^{-1}) and solid NaCl will precipitate only on evaporation of seawater to low bulk. Nonetheless seawater sequestered either in dilute form in coastal or subcoastal rainfall, or as connate water (trapped in sediments from a previous marine cycle), preserves its identity largely in the chloride ion, the cation suite being more or less altered by ion exchange. Solar distillation ensures that much of the land surface is relatively free of salts, and we have seen that salinity in surface horizons of soils and sediments is related to the hydrologic cycle.

275

It is accepted that life originated in the sea. Two essential features for the maintenance of organic life are auto-replication and the provision of barriers to cope with environmental extremes. Presumably the successful development of selective salinity barriers was one of the first essentials in the origin of life in the marine environment. Biological material characteristically tends to exclude Na^+ and Cl^- and to accumulate K^+, $H_2PO_4^-$ and the alkaline earth cations. We have learnt that this is accomplished by selective ion pumps using ATP as their energy source. So the development of protective cell membranes which incorporate specific ion pumps must have been an early prerequisite.

As discussed by McFarlane in this Symposium, the presence of moderate amounts of electrolyte inside living organisms is quite important (see also Williams 1970), so that while Na^+ and Cl^- are sensibly excluded, the uptake of K^+ is required to stabilize the tertiary conformation of certain enzymes. No doubt K^+ is eligible as it is the next most abundant alkali metal to Na^+. It is known that pyruvic kinase from rabbit muscle (Sorger et al. 1965) and acetaldehyde dehydrogenase from yeast (Sorger and Evans 1966) require K^+ for maximum specificity. Sodium-potassium pumping is involved in neural transmission and muscle contraction, while Ca^{++} and Mg^{++} are structure-formers (in skeletal tissue or enzymes).

For plants, salt tolerance is subject to adaptation and may be controlled by only a few genes. Within species, wide differences in tolerance are found and can probably be manipulated. Tolerance of wheat varieties to Al^{+++}, and soya beans to Cl^- are known to be controlled in each case by a single gene pair. Although more detailed experimentation has yet to be done, in principle it should be possible to breed salt-tolerance in most economic plants to a point where this feature is no longer a limiting factor. This is important for irrigated production, which is undertaken mostly in semi-arid regions which are potentially saline.

For animals, the distribution of salt-tolerance is bimodal (Potts and Parry 1964, p. 120) but continuous; not only do different kinds of animals find satisfactory ecological niches in salinities ranging from zero to that of seawater, but some species can tolerate both. For example, the migratory fishes and many crustaceans live in fresh and salt water and have developed special mechanisms to cope with each.

Most of these briefly summarized salinity relationships depend on the properties of biological membranes, whose structure and function has received considerable attention, resulting in a vast literature. According to Weiss (1969a) there is, however, little understanding at the molecular level of the processes concerned with ion transport in cells, with the transmission of nerve impulses or with the details of ion pump operation. Clearly this will continue to be an active research field; the seminal papers of Weiss (1969a–d) on energy transduction in membranes are likely to lead to a rich harvest of new data. Campbell and Pitman have briefly discussed some aspects of Weiss' theory in this Symposium.

The effects of excess salinity on biological material are partly osmotic; this effect can be measured in soils, sediments or water by using the colligative properties of electrolytic solutions, of which the most convenient is electrical conductivity. Excess salinity may also include specific ion toxicity, e.g. from Cl^-, $B_4O_7^=$ or even Li^+, and for these cases it is often necessary to measure the concentrations of particular ions. The development of ion-selective electrodes is one practical outcome of membrane theory, developed in particular by Eisenman (1967) and co-workers for the hydrogen- and alkali metal-sensitive glass electrodes. This is also an active area of research. It has clear implications in research on salinity in soils and sediments, the details of salt relationships in plants and animals and in pollution control. This is, therefore, a research direction that is already predetermined, but two areas of study that can be regarded as 'spin-off' from the central problem can be defined. One is the development of ion electrodes that approach the specificity of biomembranes. Already an electrode using the antibiotic valinomycin is now commercially available (Frant and Ross 1970) which shows a K^+/H^+ and K^+/Na^+ selectivity of $> 10^4$. Obviously others will follow, and the practical stability of these devices over extended periods of time will need to be studied especially if they are to be used in semi-permanent installations in catchments. The second area of study, related to the normal salt relationships of organisms, concerns the development of new antibiotics. It is known that many of these substances, particularly the macrocyclic antibiotics valinomycin, nonactin, and dinactin, act by modifying or reversing the action of ion pumps in cell membranes (see Mueller and Rudin 1967); some synthetic polyethers (Pedersen 1968; Durst 1969, p. 8) have been prepared that have similar properties, so it is possible that synthetic antibiotics, tailored to control specific pumping mechanisms in the cell membranes of bacteria, may be a practical reality.

To summarize, the salt relationships of plants and animals are generally understood in outline, and the nature of research is such that we can expect further developments in the detail of these relationships. There is therefore, little point in stressing the direction of research at this level because it will continue, particularly under the stimulus of increasing concern with pollution control.

Likewise the problems of water desalination for industrial and domestic use will receive increased attention as our rivers and streams become progressively more saline, or as demands for processing saline waters increase in desert regions. Active research is continuing on this aspect and the Sirotherm process (in which ion exchange resins can be regenerated by heating) is worth mention as an example of the practical application of basic research. In this connection the properties of the ice sandwich (Miller

1970) as a semipermeable membrane deserves further study and practical development.

It can be appreciated that, with respect to the management of quality in Australian soils and waters, these kinds of investigation are corrective, rather than effecting a cure at the source of the problem. The real issues lie in the catchments and rivers, not in the laboratory; in the recognition of saline sediments and groundwaters and in the changes imposed on them by agriculture, mining, urbanization or reforestation. These issues have been comparatively neglected in the past, and this neglect is partly responsible for the growing problems not only in salinity but in the field of pollution generally. The rest of this paper is therefore devoted to the possible reasons for this neglect, and to the directions in which future study should be channelled.

2. THE NEGLECT OF FIELD STUDIES

It is worth digressing briefly on some characteristics of scientific research. What is sought is a generalization that reduces complexity to a simple statement or a few simple measurements. What is usually found, however, is proliferation of descriptive data from which it is difficult or impossible to extract a generalization. Thus most research tends to be explanatory, rather than predictive, because it tends to explore successively lower levels of integration from the observable down to the molecular. It so happens that prediction from the molecular level to the observable is rarely satisfactory or complete. Seminal theories like the Krebs cycle or the structure of DNA, based on biochemistry or molecular biology, are the exception, especially in natural systems or in living organisms. Such predictions are more common in physics than in biology; and reach their peak of usefulness in engineering, obviously because engineering systems are man-made and their component functions can be accurately described.

So my first point is that we tend to make the components of our system too small. Agricultural science is full of such examples, particularly in soil fertility, where it is now realized that yields of economic crops are only partly controlled by adding fertilizers, and that many unidentified factors can cause more yield variation than the manipulation of plant nutrients. Naturally I am not suggesting that modern fertilizer practices be abandoned; in many parts of Australia soils are so poor that additions of N, P, K, S and micronutrients are essential; but our search for the soil factors controlling crop yield has only just begun because of our preoccupation with chemical sub-systems.

Ecologists know the problems in defining an ecosystem and in establishing relationships between its various components. Occasionally they find it possible to construct a model system from their data without going into the detailed reasons for the observed interactions between components. So my second point is an extension of the first, and is a restatement of the principle of Occam's razor: to understand a system it is necessary to reduce the number of its components to a minimum. If we accept the proposition that salinity control resides in the headwaters of catchments, we can make various choices as to which components can be measured, and how.

Before elaborating this further, there is a third point that needs comment and which concerns scientists themselves. Any study of a system, such as a large catchment or any other similar land unit, requires a long time and considerable field work. Although the report of the Murray Valley Salinity Investigation (Anon 1970) contains a remarkable amount of data, it is clear that there is still a paucity of vital information, in spite of decades of study by scores of workers. Comparatively few such field studies on large systems have been made. The reasons are simple and related to each other:

(1) The amount of field work (as mentioned) is large, and has to be backed up by a massive volume of laboratory analyses.
(2) Most scientists tend to concentrate on successively smaller areas of research because the chance of finding something new is greater as the degree of fragmentation increases.
(3) The number of scientists engaged on such work is low and decreasing, because the rewards (publications and resulting professional advancement) are meagre.

The first reason for lack of data could be partly dealt with by using semi-automated procedures. Reasons (2) and (3) concern respectively the philosophy of research, and research management and planning. They reach back to questions of research training and to the recognition of research skills by management, and are complicated by social factors. One result is that promising field workers retreat to the laboratory, usually irreversibly. I doubt if these topics are considered relevant in the present Symposium; but unless they are recognized and solved our knowledge of processes in the surface mantle of the earth will be perpetually frustrated. I think these shortcomings in the philosophy of field research and in the training of scientists are responsible for the lack of suitable data, not only in the control of salinity and pollution, but also in pedology and agronomy, and for the absence of a better-organized structure of knowledge in these sciences.

It should be stressed at this stage that the term 'field studies' means 'terrestrial field studies' in the context of this paper. Animal and plant physiologists will insist (rightly) that whole animals or whole plants can legitimately be studied as field units; the point is that soils, catchments and rivers are undefined by boundaries such as skin, membranes or cuticles and that the process occurring in terrestrial units are open-ended (rather than truly cyclic) and more difficult to measure than in whole organisms. With these restrictions and impediments to the development of field studies in mind, we can now turn to some research problems.

3. FUTURE RESEARCH

Important problems concern the recognition of saline areas, and the criteria employed to establish them. Northcote and Skene (unpublished) using empirical criteria, conducted a survey of saline and sodic soils in Australia which is a useful basis for more detailed research. It is worth noting that free salt (determined by electrical conductivity) occurs in different kinds of soil profiles and is not restricted to the classical sequence—solonchak, solonetz, solodized solonetz, soloth—established in Russian pedology. Free salt occurs at depth in cracking clays and in gradational profiles such as the solonized brown (Mallee) soils. Thus, salinity is not related ubiquitously to soil morphology in Australia, and is found in various topographic situations and in circumstances which must often be described as post-genetic—the salt arrived after the soil profile features developed.

The origin of this salt is an important research problem. It is often assumed to be cyclic (i.e. precipitated in rain contaminated by ocean spray); there is evidence (Hutton and Leslie 1958) of a decrease in the salt content of rainwater, and of a change in composition, with distance from the coast, at least in Victoria. More gauging stations are needed, especially in northern Australia (preliminary results from Katherine, N. T., are given by Wetselaar and Hutton 1963), to establish the importance of cyclic salt as a permanent annual accession which leads to soil and sediment salinity. The large areas of saline soils noted in south-western Queensland and northern South Australia by Northcote and Skene suggest that salt accession may not only result directly from oceanic sources. The distinction between cyclic and connate salt is probably academic; rather the observations of Northcote and Skene should be extended into more detail in the settled areas. If it is accepted that 85% of Australians will, within the next 25 years, be living on the eastern littoral between Cooktown and Melbourne, then the necessity for detailed studies of the salinity of the important catchments and rivers in this region becomes apparent.

So far we have discussed primary salinity. Secondary salinity in soils results from disturbance of the hydrologic cycle, either from irrigation or from clearing of native forest in catchments. It is more insidious, and creates greater problems than primary salinity because it usually appears (as in the Murray system or some Western Australian watersheds) long after settlement has been established. The task of defining the conditions under which secondary salinization may occur in finite time is one of the most difficult problems in field research now facing us. In principle, as discussed by Holmes in this Symposium, the kinds of measurement required are known. In practice, the work load of sampling, analysis and data reduction is high and the need for rapid assessment of future salinity problems in any developing area is urgent. Collis-George and Davey (1960) published an iconoclastic article (which has been largely ignored) on the need for instrumented soil fertility experiments. This proposal could be adapted to the monitoring of salinity changes. Because the minimum period of observation should not be less than five years, and since comparisons between treatments and replications are important features of the design of any meaningful experiment, it is now opportune to see how 6–10 catchments can be monitored simultaneously. Although semi-automatic laboratory analyses can reduce the work load, field sampling at the desirable intensity demands heavy labour; so the possibility of establishing *in situ* sensors, with telemetering and data-logging facilities, can now be considered a practical possibility.

Another possibility for future research is the use of small-scale simulation models. Cope (1958) reported an excellent field study of salinity in Victoria. Quoting the definitive observations of Hutton and Leslie (1958) the occurrence of salt is related to the water budget equation referred to by Holmes and by Peck in this Symposium. Over geological time, the annual net accession of salt from the sea is unimportant compared with its residence time in a sediment. Equation (3) of Holmes' paper in this Symposium provides a model that is susceptible to experimental studies on a small scale. If the crucial environmental parameters such as sediment permeability, evapotranspiration and salt influx can be varied in such experiments we might eliminate some unimportant parameters and identify new ones.

The total area of salt-affected soils in Australia is calculated by Northcote and Skene to be nearly $2 \cdot 5 \times 10^6$ km^2, of which only one-sixth is truly saline. The remainder are sodic soils (either alkaline or with pH less than 8·0), defined as containing more than a small proportion of their total exchange capacity as Na$^+$. Thus strongly sodic soils contain more than 15% of their exchange capacity as exchangeable Na$^+$. This grouping is arbitrary and refers obliquely to soil permeability. It is known (see Quirk's paper in this Symposium) that organic matter and sesquioxides greatly modify the adverse effect of exchangeable Na$^+$ on permeability, so that the use of exchangeable sodium percentage as a diagnostic in reclamation potential is probably misleading. Is it possible to devise a more rapid and reliable method of measuring permeability directly?

The criterion used for defining saline soils is based on their effect on salt-sensitive plants. The electrical conductivity of the saturation extract of soils (Richards 1954) is the most acceptable criterion because it allows for differ-

19

ences in water-holding capacity between soils of different texture, as well as measuring a property closely related to osmotic pressure. However, this measurement is not practically convenient and is usually replaced by the more rapid determination of conductivity at constant soil : water ratio, for which the direct correlation with plant behaviour is poor. It would seem more useful to characterize soil salinity without any assumptions about plants. Thus, assuming that 'NaCl' is the limiting factor (and by an accident of nature this compound contributes mostly to conductivity) the measurement of the ion product $[Na^+].[Cl^-]$ in a soil suspension may characterize its salinity rapidly and reproducibly. This ion product could be determined directly by an electrode train containing elements sensitive to Na^+ and Cl^- in series, both of which are available commercially. Having thus established a salinity criterion for soils, it is then the task of the agronomist to apply more specific tests, having regard to the salt tolerance of the crops adaptable to a particular homoclime, and to determine the safety limits of particular soils.

If we adopt the proposals recommended in this paper, that more field data is needed, the question of sampling and analysis of the field units needs considering. It is likely that we tend to be too precise in some of our laboratory measurements. Quite good models can often be constructed with very approximate data. There is the further problem of choosing the right measurements. A compulsive attitude still exists towards the collection of field and laboratory data, which seems to result from a system of established reflexes. Colour, texture, concretions, and a host of laboratory determinations are faithfully and, it seems, perpetually recorded, in the hope that something useful may eventually be found. The more adventurous process their results with a computer, producing attractive dendrograms which, by a cyclic argument, are justified on the grounds that they reproduce the author's original intuition. While a computer can be programmed to establish relationships, and while this technique is a powerful sorter of information, it often fails because the scope of the data fed in is too restricted. So we require less (but more discriminative) data, if the understanding of field events in salinity is to progress towards more efficient management practices, and in a sufficiently short period of time.

The reclamation of saline and sodic soils needs more research under Australian conditions. Gypsum appears to be the cure-all, yet one result of its application may be to release more Na^+ and Cl^- into the rivers, thus increasing salinity downstream. The surface management of soils has received little attention in Australia, and new research is needed into the factors affecting rainfall acceptance and on the basic conformation of the surface structure of soils. Reclamation is still largely rule-of-thumb, with a background of overseas theory.

Finally, there is urgent need for research into the social consequences of the failure of large-scale irrigation systems, and into methods of avoiding such failures, or of providing alternatives for the dispossessed as increasing salinity forces a community to contract in size and cut its losses.

This paper stresses the agricultural aspects of salinity. This is not only because salinity is a potential agricultural hazard; in the logistic chain rainfall-catchment-reservoir-use-effluent, it clearly holds a strategic position. So the management of our agricultural systems at the headwaters are of crucial importance to industry and our urban communities; ultimately they may influence our survival.

ACKNOWLEDGMENTS

I am grateful to Dr W. T. Williams for valuable discussions, and to Dr T. J. Marshall, K. H. Northcote and G. Blackburn for criticism of earlier drafts of this paper.

REFERENCES

Anon (1970) *Murray Valley Salinity Investigation*. Report for the River Murray Commission by Gutteridge, Haskins and Davey.

Collis-George, N., and Davey, B. M. (1960). *Soils and Ferts*. **23**, 307.

Cope, F. (1958). *Catchment Salting in Victoria*. Soil Conservation Authority, Victoria.

Durst, R. A. (1969). *Ion-selective Electrodes*. National Bureau of Standards Publication No. 314, Washington.

Eisenman, G. (Ed.) (1967). *Glass Electrodes for Hydrogen and Other Cations*. Marcel Dekker, New York.

Frant, M., and Ross, J. W., Jr. (1970). *Science, N.Y.* **167**, 987.

Hutton, J. T., and Leslie, T. I. (1958). *Aust. J. agric. Res.* **9**, 492.

Mueller, P., and Rudin, D. O. (1967). *Biochem. biophys. Res. Comm.* **26**, 398.

Miller, R. D. (1970). *Science, N.Y.* **169**, 584.

Pedersen, C. J. (1968). *Fed. Proc.* **27**, 1305.

Potts, W. T. W., and Parry, G. (1964). *Osmotic Regulation in Animals*. Pergamon Press, London.

Richards, L. A. (Ed.) (1954). *Diagnosis and Improvement of Saline and Alkali Soils*. USDA Handbook No. 60.

Sorger, G. J., Ford, R. E., and Evans, H. J. (1965). *Proc. Natl. Acad. Sci.* **54**, 1614.

Sorger, G. J., and Evans, H. J. (1966). *Biochim. biophys. Acta* **118**, 1.

Weiss, D. E. (1969*a*). *Aust. J. biol. Sci.* **22**, 1337.

Weiss, D. E. (1969*b*). *Aust. J. biol. Sci.* **22**, 1355.

Weiss, D. E. (1969*c*) *Aust. J. biol. Sci.* **22**, 1373.
Weiss, D. E. (1969*d*). *Aust. J. biol. Sci.* **22**, 1389.
Wetselaar, R., and Hutton, J. T. (1963). *Aust. J. agric. Res.* **14**, 319.
Williams, R. J. P. (1970). *Quart. Rev. chem. Soc.* **24**, 331.

APPENDIX

Conversion to S.I. Units

Most papers in this volume employ the *Système International d'Unités*, or units derived therefrom. Exceptions occur in economic, engineering and some biological papers.

The following table lists the needed conversions to S.I. units.

1 inch	$=2{\cdot}45 \times 10^{-2}$	m
1 foot	$=0{\cdot}3048$	m
1 mile	$=1609$	m
1 acre	$=4046{\cdot}86$	m^2
1 gallon (Imp.)	$=4{\cdot}546 \times 10^{-3}$	m^3
1 ton	$=1016$	kg
1 atm	$=101\ 325$	$N\ m^{-2}$

AUTHOR INDEX

GENERAL INDEX